D0265531

You read it first in

GRANTA 25

MARTIN AMIS
LONDON FIELDS

Now read the
rest of it—
before
everyone else does.

JONATHAN CAPE £12·95 ISBN 0224 02609 7

NEW WRITING AT THE RSC

LONDON, AUTUMN 1989

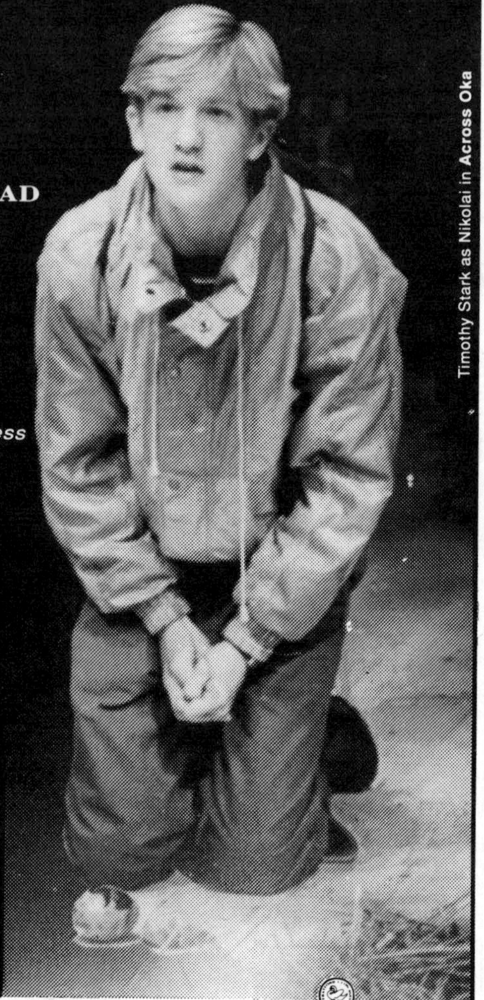

Timothy Stark as Nikolai in Across Oka

THE PIT

BARBICAN
BOX OFFICE 01. 638 8891

SOME AMERICANS ABROAD
World Premiere *by Richard Nelson*
Until 12 September

ACROSS OKA
by Robert Holman
Until 28 October

MARY AND LIZZIE
World Premiere *by Frank McGuinness*
20 September- 2 November

THE LOVE OF THE NIGHTINGALE
by Timberlake Wertenbaker
Until 4 November

RSC/ALMEIDA SEASON 1989

ALMEIDA THEATRE
BOX OFFICE 01. 359 4404

KISSING THE POPE
World Premiere *by Nick Darke*
19 September - 26 October

H.I.D. (HESS IS DEAD)
World Premiere *by Howard Brenton*
26 September - 24 October

Our Mailing List Members

* enjoy priority booking for all RSC shows
* receive special offers for Stratford and London

You can join the mailing list by telephone using Access/Visa
Call **0789 205301** or write to
The Mailing List Department, Royal Shakespeare Theatre, Freepost, Stratford -upon -Avon CV37 6BR

RSC
Royal Shakespeare Company

Sponsored by
Royal Insurance

Arts Council Funded

GRANTA

BIRTHDAY SPECIAL

28

Editor: Bill Buford
Commissioning Editor: Lucretia Stewart
Assistant Editor: Tim Adams
Managing Editor: Angus MacKinnon
Editorial Assistant: Judith Martin

Publisher/Consultant: Alice Rose George
Associate Publisher: Piers Spence
Financial Manager: Monica McStay
Subscriptions: Gillian Kemp
Advertising and Circulation: Alison Ormerod

Picture Research: David Brownridge
Design: Chris Hyde
Executive Editor: Pete de Bolla
US Associate Publisher: Anne Kinard, Granta, 250 West 57th Street, Suite 1316, New York, NY 10107.

Editorial and Subscription Correspondence: Granta, 44a Hobson Street, Cambridge CB1 1NL. Telephone: (0223) 315290.
All manuscripts are welcome but must be accompanied by a stamped, self-addressed envelope or they cannot be returned.

Granta is photoset by Cambridge Photosetting Services, Cambridge, England, and printed by Hazell Watson and Viney Ltd, Aylesbury, Bucks.

Granta is published by Granta Publications Ltd and distributed by Penguin Books Ltd, Harmondsworth, Middlesex, England; Viking Penguin Inc., 40 West 23rd St, New York, New York, USA; Penguin Books Australia Ltd, Ringwood, Victoria, Australia; Penguin Books Canada Ltd, 2801 John Street, Markham, Ontario, Canada L3R 1B4; Penguin Books (NZ) Ltd, 182–90 Wairau Road, Auckland 10, New Zealand. This selection copyright © 1989 by Granta Publications Ltd.

Cover by the Senate.

Granta 28, Autumn 1989

ISBN 014-01-2359-8

SUPPORTED BY THE EASTERN Arts

MINERVA PAPERBACKS

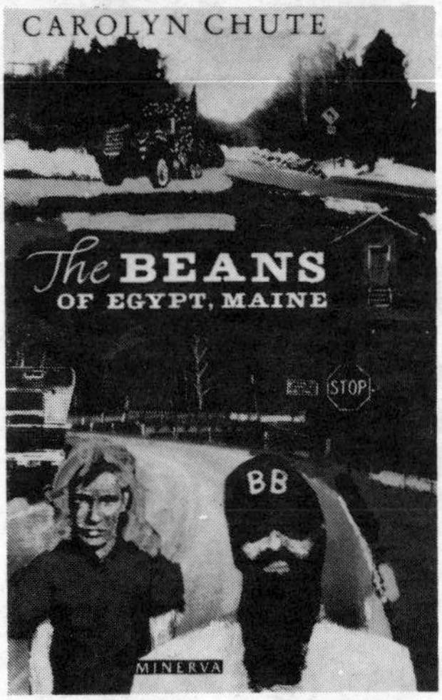

BLOOMSBURY

DOUBLE FEATURE
TERENCE STAMP
"A born writer" *Sunday Times*
The third, and final part of the film star's bestselling autobiography
June £14.95 0 7475 0393 1

A VILLAGE AFFAIR
JOANNA TROLLOPE
"Sensitivity is peppered with humour in a highly readable book." *Daily Mail*
June £12.95 0 7475 0365 6

MRS FRAMPTON
PAM GEMS
"A first novel of great cunning and enormous charm." *The Times*
May £12.95 0 7475 0358 3

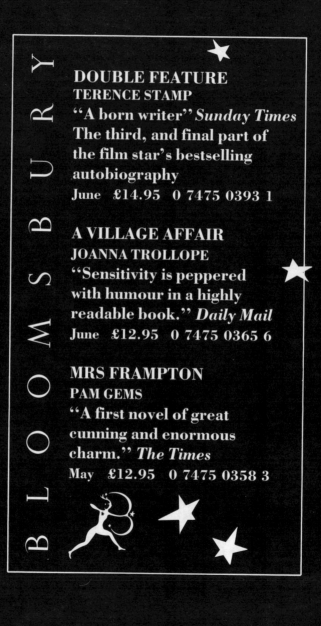

CONTENTS

PRiMO LEVi

OTHER PEOPLE'S *trades*

Elegant, provocative and often witty essays from "one of the most important and gifted writers of our time" *(Italo Calvino).*

Published on 16 October
£12.95

STAN BARSTOW

Give Us This Day

His new novel – a poignant, closely observed recreation of civilian life in a small Yorkshire community during the Second World War.
£11.95

MICHAEL JOSEPH

GRANTA

JOHN SIMPSON

TIANANMEN SQUARE

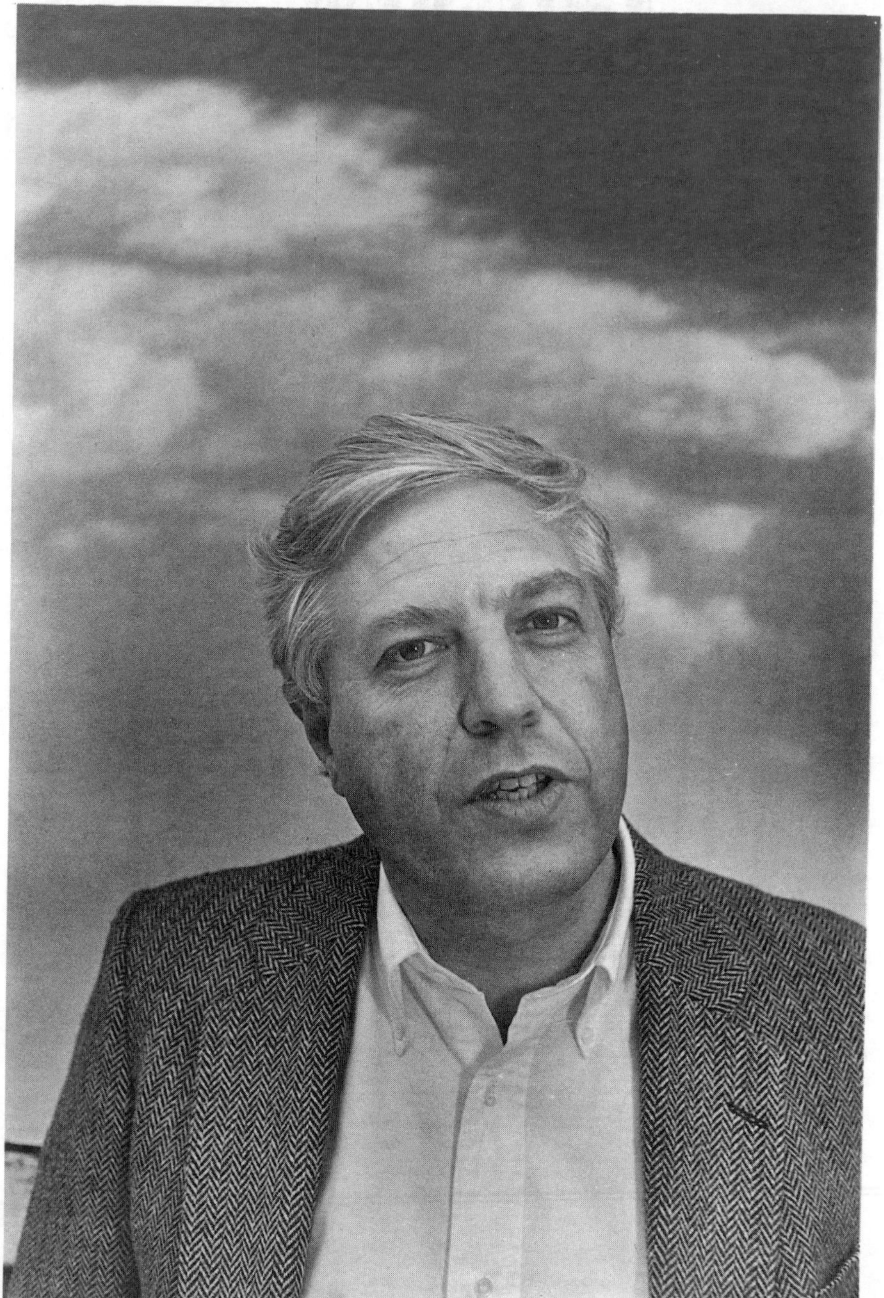

It was humid and airless, and the streets around our hotel were empty. We had set out for Tiananmen Square: a big, conspicuous European television team—reporter, producer, cameraman, sound-recordist, translator, lighting man, complete with gear. A cyclist rode past, shouting and pointing. What it meant we couldn't tell. Then we came upon a line of soldiers. Some of them had bleeding faces; one cradled a broken arm. They were walking slowly, limping. There had been a battle somewhere, but we couldn't tell where.

When we reached Changan Avenue, the main east-west thoroughfare, it was as full of people as in the days of the great demonstrations—a human river. We followed the flow of it to the Gate of Heavenly Peace, under the bland, moonlike portrait of Chairman Mao. There were hundreds of small groups, each concentrated around someone who was haranguing or lecturing the others, using the familiar, heavy public gestures of the Chinese. Other groups had formed around radios tuned to foreign stations. People were moving from group to group, pushing in, crushing round a speaker, arguing, moving on, passing along any new information.

For the most part these were not students. They were from the factories, and the red cloths tied around their heads made them look aggressive, even piratical. Trucks started arriving from the outskirts of the city, full of more young workers, waving the banners of their factories, singing, chanting, looking forward to trouble.

People were shouting: there was a battle going on between tanks and the crowd, somewhere to the east of the city centre. Details differed, and I had trouble finding out what was being said: I watched the animated faces, everyone pushing closer to each new source of information, pulling at each other's sleeves or shoulders. Tanks and armoured personnel carriers, they were saying, were heading towards the Square. They were coming from two directions, east and west. The crowds that gathered couldn't stop them.

'It's a different army. It's not the Thirty-eighth!' The man who said this was screaming it, clutching at our translator, holding on to him, trying to make him understand the significance of it. 'It is *not* the Thirty-eighth!' It had been the Thirty-eighth Army that had

Photo: Barry Lewis (Network)

tried to recapture the city twice before. The soldiers had been unarmed: the commander, the father of a student in the Square, had ordered that operations be carried out peacefully.

We pushed our way towards the Square where, despite the rumours and the panic, we saw something very different: several thousand people standing in silence, motionless, listening to a large loudspeaker, bolted to a street lamp:

> Go home and save your life. You will fail. You are not behaving in the correct Chinese manner. This is not the West, it is China. You should behave like a good Chinese. Go home and save your life. Go home and save your life.

The voice was expressionless, epicene, metallic, like that of a hypnotist. I looked at these silent, serious faces, illuminated by the orange light of the street lamps, studying the loudspeaker. Even the small children, brought there with the rest of the family, stared intently. The order was repeated again and again. It was a voice the people of China had been listening to for forty years, and continued listening to even now. But now no one did what the hypnotist said. No one moved.

And then, suddenly, everything changed: the loudspeaker's spell was broken by shouts that the army was coming. There was the sound of a violent scraping, and across the Avenue I saw people pulling at the railings that ran along the roadway and dragging them across the pavement to build a barricade. Everyone moved quickly, a crowd suddenly animated, its actions fast and decisive, sometimes brutal. They blocked off Changan Avenue and the Square itself, and we began filming—flooding the sweating enthusiasts with our camera-light. People danced around us, flaunting their weaponry: coshes, knives, crude spears, bricks. A boy rushed up to our camera and opened his shabby green windcheater like a black marketeer to reveal a row of Coca-Cola bottles strapped to his waist, filled with petrol and plugged with rags. He laughed, and mimed the action of pulling out each bottle and throwing it. I asked him his age. He was sixteen. Why was he against the government? He couldn't answer. He gripped another of his Molotov cocktails, laughing all the time.

That the army was coming was no longer rumour but fact and our translator heard that it would move in at one o'clock. It was half-past midnight. In the distance, above the noise of the crowd, I thought I could hear the sound of guns. I wanted to find a vantage point from which we could film, without being spotted by the army. But the tension that was bonding members of the crowd together did not have the same effect on the members of our small team. It was hot and noisy. We argued. We started shouting, and I headed off on my own.

I pushed through the crowds, immediately feeling better for being on my own. There were very few foreign journalists left in the Square by now, and I felt especially conspicuous. But I also felt good. People grabbed my hand, thanking me for being with them. I gave them a V for Victory sign and was applauded by everyone around me. It was hard to define the mood. There was still a spirit of celebration, that they were out on the streets, defying the government, but the spirit was also giving way to a terrible foreboding. There was also something else. Something I hadn't seen before: a reckless ferocity of purpose.

I crossed back into the main part of Tiananmen Square, the village of student tents. There were sticks and cardboard and broken glass underfoot. The smells were familiar and strong—wood-smoke, urine and heavy disinfectant. A couple clung to each other, her head on his shoulder. I passed in front of them, but they didn't raise their eyes. A student asked me to sign his T-shirt, a craze from earlier days. He had thick glasses and a bad complexion, and he spoke English. 'It will be dangerous tonight,' he said. 'We are all very afraid here.'

I finished signing his shirt, at the back below the collar. He grabbed my hand and shook it excitedly. His grip was bony and clammy. I asked him what he thought would happen.

'We will all die.'

He straightened up and shook my hand again, and slipped away between the tents.

The camp was dark. There were a few students left; most of them had gathered in the centre of the Square, around the Monument to the People's Heroes. I could hear their speeches and the occasional burst of singing—the Internationale, as always. Here, though, it was quiet. This was where the students had

Photo (following pages): Zong Hoi Yi (Vu)

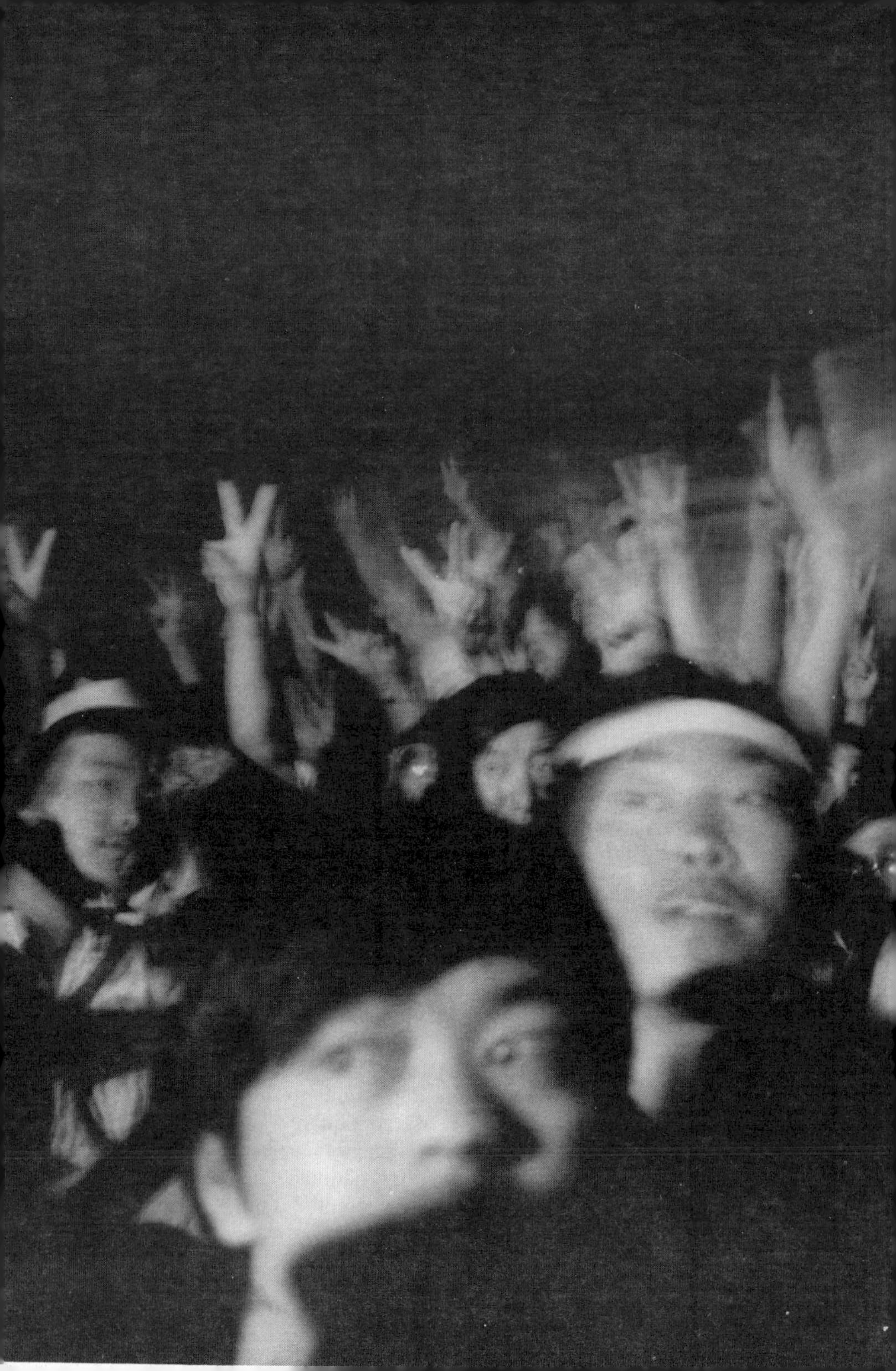

Photos (these pages): Zong Hoi Yi (Vu); (following pages): Dario Mitidieri (Select)

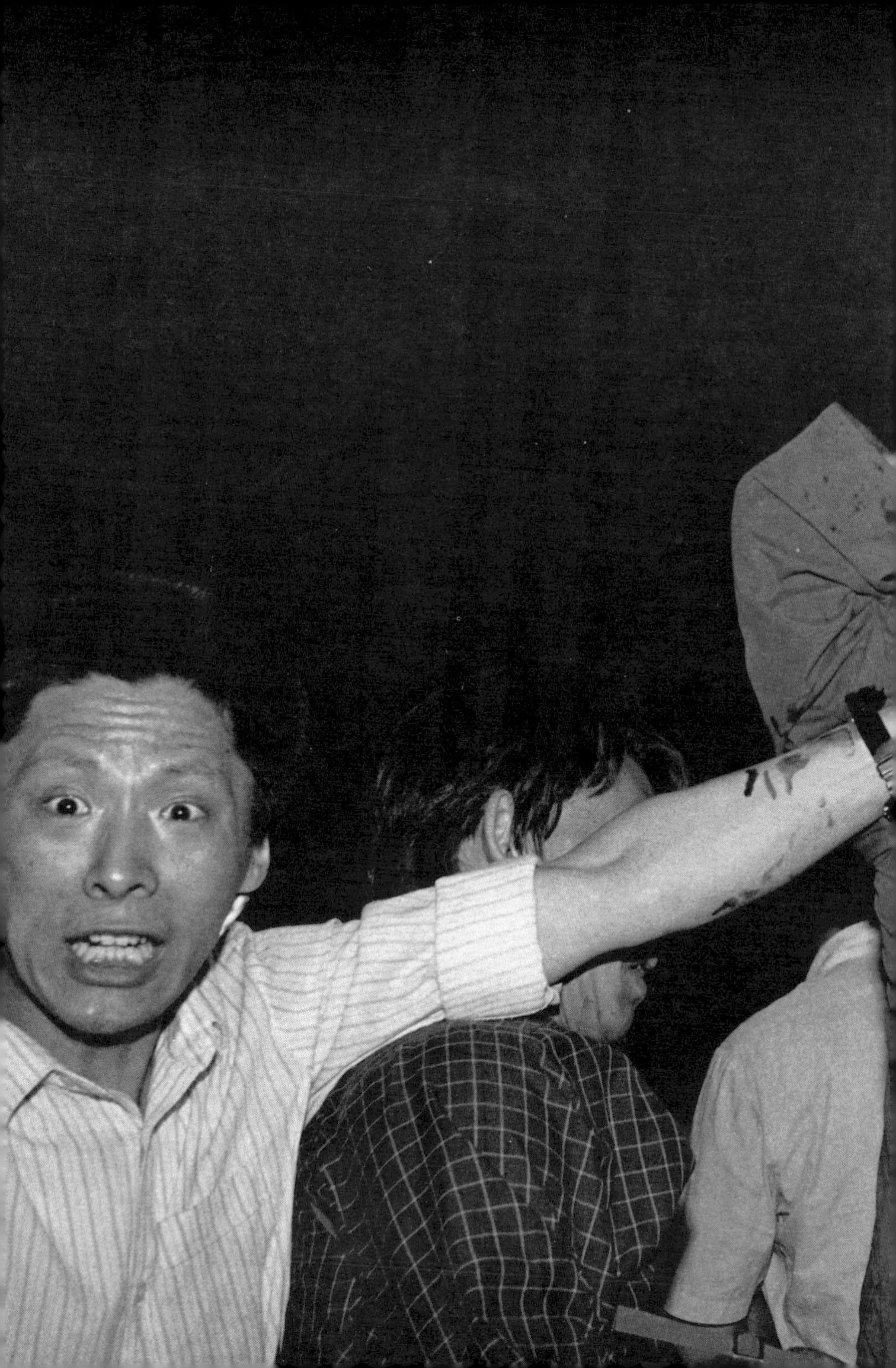

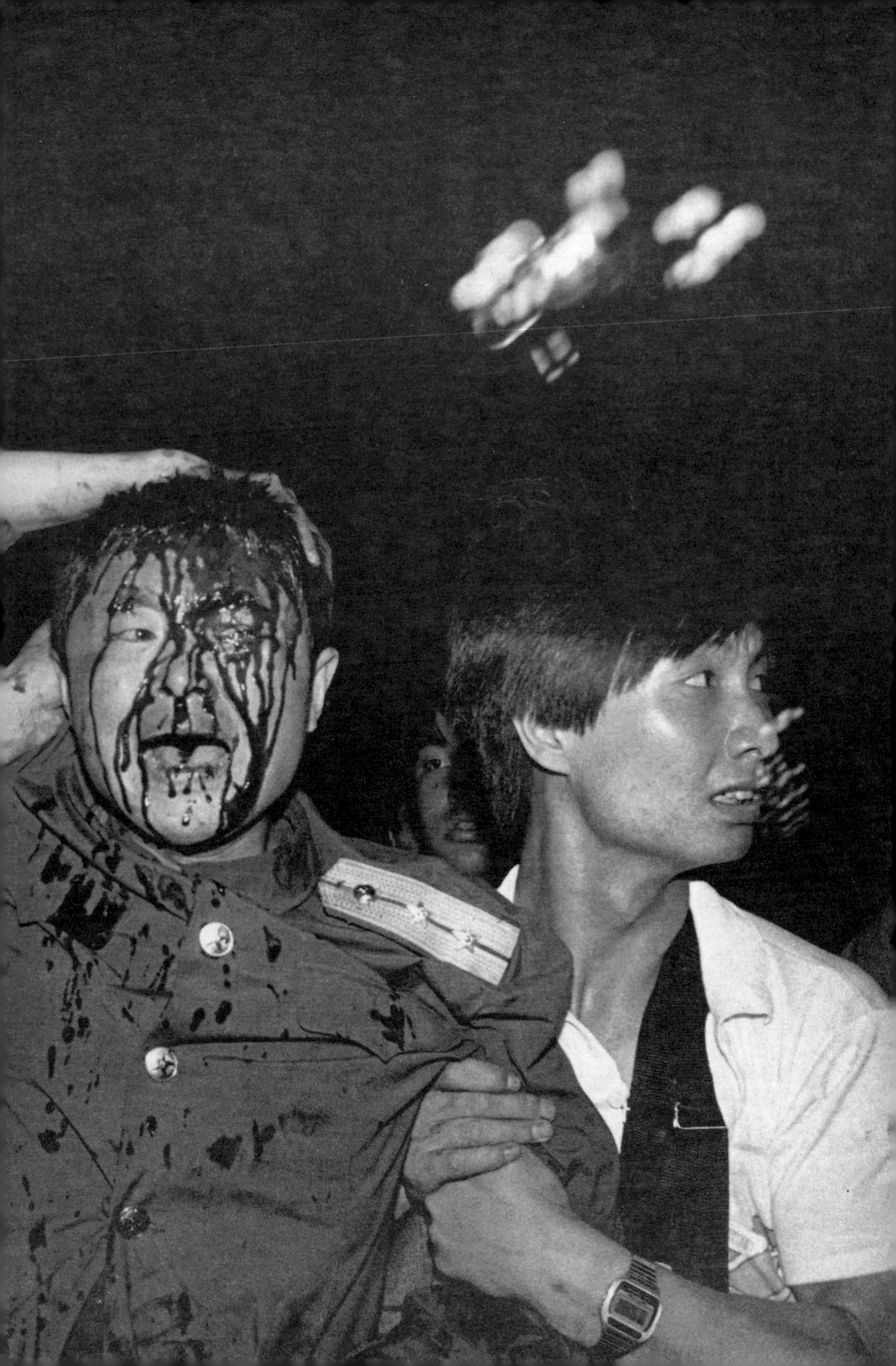

chosen to build their statue of the Goddess of Democracy, with her sightless eyes, her torch held in both hands. The symbol of all our aspirations, one of the student leaders called her: the fruit of our struggle. To me, she looked very fragile.

The speeches and the songs continued in the distance. Then suddenly they stopped. There was a violent grinding and a squealing sound—the familiar sound of an armoured personnel carrier. I heard screaming, and behind me, in the Avenue, everyone started running. When I finally spotted the vehicle, I could see that it was making its way with speed down the side of the Square. It seemed uncertain of its direction—one moment driving straight for the Square, and then stopping, turning, stopping again, as if looking for a way to escape. There was a sudden angry roar, and I know it was because the vehicle had crushed someone under its tracks. It then turned in my direction—it was pointed at me—and I felt a different kind of panic. The action was starting and I was separated from my colleagues: it is an article of faith to stay with your camera crew in times of danger.

The vehicle carried on, careering back and forth. It must have knocked down six or seven people. By now it was on fire, having been hit repeatedly by Molotov cocktails. Somehow, though, it escaped and headed off to the west.

Then a second armoured personnel carrier came along Changan Avenue, alone and unsupported like the first. This time everyone turned and ran hard towards the vehicle, knowing that they, with their numbers and their petrol bombs, had the power to knock it out. They screamed with anger and hate as the vehicle swung randomly in different directions, threatening to knock people down as it made its way through the Square. The Molotov cocktails arched above our heads, spinning over and over, exploding on the thin shell of armour that protected the men inside. Still the vehicle carried on, zigzagging, crossing the Avenue, trying to find a way through the barricade. A pause, and it charged, head-on, straight into a block of concrete—and then stuck, its engine whirring wildly. A terrible shout of triumph came from the crowd: primitive and dark, its prey finally caught. The smell of petrol and burning metal and sweat was in the air, intoxicating and violent. Everyone around me was pushing and fighting to get to the vehicle. At first I resisted; then, close beside it, I saw the light of a camera, just where the crowd was starting to swarm. There were only three cameramen still filming in the entire Square, and I knew that my colleague was the only one crazy enough to be that close. Now I was the one fighting, struggling to get through the crowd, pulling people back, pushing them out of my path, swearing, a big brutal Englishman stronger than any of them. I tore one man's shirt and punched another in the back. All around me the men seemed to be yelling at the sky, their faces lit up; the vehicle had caught fire. A man—his torso bare—climbed up the side of the vehicle and stood on top of it, his arms raised in victory, the noise of the mob welling up around him. They knew they had the vehicle's crew trapped inside. Someone started beating at the armoured glass with an iron bar.

I reached the cameraman and pulled hard at his arm to get his attention. He scarcely noticed me, amid the buffeting and the noise and the violence, and carried on filming. He and his sound recordist and the Chinese lighting man were a few feet from the vehicle: close enough to be killed if it exploded or if the soldiers came out shooting. But I couldn't make them step back, and so we stayed there, the four of us, the heat beating against our faces as people continued to pour petrol on the bonnet and roof and smashed at the doors and the armoured glass. What was it like inside? I imagined the soldiers half-crazed with the noise and the heat and the fear of being burned alive.

The screaming around me rose even louder: the handle of the door at the rear of the vehicle had turned a little, and the door began to open. A soldier pushed the barrel of a gun out, but it was snatched from his hands, and then everyone started grabbing his arms, pulling and wrenching until finally he came free, and then he was gone: I saw the arms of the mob, flailing, raised above their heads as they fought to get their blows in. He was dead within seconds, and his body was dragged away in triumph. A second soldier showed his head through the door and was then immediately pulled out by his hair and ears and the skin on his face. This soldier I could see: his eyes were rolling, and his mouth was open, and he was covered with blood where the skin had been ripped off. Only his eyes remained—white and clear—but then someone was trying to get them as well, and someone else began beating his skull until the skull came apart, and there was blood all over the ground, and his brains, and still they kept on beating and beating what was left.

Then the horrible sight passed away, and the ground was wet where he had been.

There was a third soldier inside. I could see his face in the light of the flames, and some of the crowd could too. They pulled him out, screaming, wild at having missed killing the other soldiers. It was his blood they wanted, I was certain, it was to feel the blood running over their hands. Their mouths were open and panting, like dogs, and their eyes were expressionless. They were shouting, the Chinese lighting man told me afterwards, that the soldier they were about to kill wasn't human, that he was just a thing, an object, which had to be destroyed. And all the time the noise and the heat and the stench of oil burning on hot metal beat at us, overwhelming our senses, deadening them.

Just as the third soldier was lifted out of the vehicle, almost fainting, an articulated bus rushed towards us stopping, with great skill, so that its rear door opened just beside the group with the soldier. The students had heard what was happening, and a group had raced the bus over to save whomever they could. The mob did not want to give up its prize. The students tried to drag the soldier on board, and the crowd held on to him, pulling him back. By some mischance the bus door started closing and it seemed that he must be killed.

I had seen people die in front of me before. But I had never seen three people die, one after the other, in this way. Once again the members of the crowd closed around the soldier, their arms raised over their heads to beat him to death. The bus and the safety it promised were so close. It seemed to me then that I couldn't look on any longer, a passive observer, watching another man's skin torn away or his head broken open, and do nothing. I saw the soldier's face, expressing only horror and pain as he sank under the blows of the people around him, and I started to move forward. The ferocity of the crowd had entered me, but I felt it was the crowd that was the animal, that it wasn't properly human. The soldier had sunk down to the ground, and a man was trying to break his skull with a half-brick, bringing it down with full force. I screamed obscenities at the man—stupid obscenities, as no one except my colleagues could have understood them—and threw myself at him, catching him with his arm up, poised for another blow. He looked at me blankly, and his thin arm went limp in my grasp. I stopped shouting. He relaxed his grip on the brick, and I threw it under the bus. It felt wet. A little room had been created around the soldier, and the student who had tried to rescue him before could now get to him. The rest of the mob hadn't given up, but the students were able to pull the soldier away and get him on to the bus by the other door. He was safe.

The vehicle burned for a long time, its driver and the man beside him burning with it. The flames lit up the Square and and reflected on the face of the Monument where the students had taken their stand. The crowd in Changan Avenue had been sated. The loudspeakers had stopped telling people to save their lives. There was silence.

The students sang the Internationale. It would be for the last time, and it sounded weak and faint in the vastness of the Square. Many were crying. No doubt some students joined in the attacks on the army, but those in the Square kept to their principle of non-violence. Although the army suffered the first casualties, it was the students who would be the martyrs that night.

My colleagues and I wanted to save our pictures in case we were arrested, and I told the others that we should go back to the Beijing Hotel and come out again later. I now feel guilty about the decision; it was wrong: we ought to have stayed in the Square, even though the other camera crews had already left and it might have cost us our lives. Someone should have been there when the massacre took place, filming what happened, showing the courage of the students as they were surrounded by tanks and the army advancing, firing as it went.

Instead, we took up our position on the fourteenth floor of the Beijing Hotel. From there, everything seemed grey and distant. We saw most of what happened, but we were separated from the fear and the noise and the stench of it. We saw the troops pouring out of the Gate of Heavenly Peace, bayonets fixed, shooting first into the air and then straight ahead of them. They looked like automata, with their rounded dark helmets. We filmed them charging across and clearing the northern end of the Square, where I had signed the student's T-shirt. We filmed the tanks as they drove over the tents where some of the students had taken refuge, among them, perhaps, the young couple I had seen sitting silently, their arms around each other. Dozens of people seem to have died in that way, and those who saw it said they could hear the screams of the people inside the tents over the noise of the tanks. We filmed as the lights in the Square were switched off at four a.m. They were switched on again forty minutes later, when the troops and the tanks moved towards the Monument itself, shooting first in the air and then, again, directly at the students themselves, so that the steps of the Monument and the heroic reliefs which decorated it were smashed by bullets.

Once or twice, we were ourselves shot at, and during the night the security police sent men to our room to arrest us: but I shouted at them in English, and they went away, uncertain of the extent of their powers. Below us, people still gathered in the Avenue, shouting their defiance at the troops who were massed at the farther end. Every now and then the crack of a rifle would bring down another demonstrator, and the body would be rescued by a trishaw driver or the crew of an ambulance. Below us, the best and noblest political protest since Czechoslovakia in 1968 was being crushed as we watched. I knelt on the balcony, beside the cameraman and a Chinese woman, one of the student leaders.

She had taken refuge in our room because we were foreigners. I shouted at her to go back inside, but she refused, turning her head from me so that I wouldn't see she was crying, her hands clenched tight enough to hurt, intent on watching the rape of her country and the movement she and her friends had built up in the course of twenty-two days. I had seen the river of protest running along Changan Avenue in that time; I had seen a million people in the streets, demanding a way of life that was better than rule by corruption and secret police. I recalled the lines of the T'ang dynasty poet Li Po, that if you cut water with a sword you merely made it run faster. But the river of change had been dammed, and below me, in the Avenue where it had run, people were dying. Beside me, the cameraman spotted something and started filming. Down in the Square, in the early light, the soldiers were busy unrolling something and lifting it up. Soon a great curtain of black cloth covered the entrance to Tiananmen Square. What was happening there was hidden from us.

Photo: Zong Hoi Yi (Vu)

ff
faber and faber

THE BEST
INTERNATIONAL FICTION TODAY

Walter Abish
Paul Auster
Murray Bail
André Brink
Aldo Busi
Peter Carey
Anne Devlin
Michael Dibdin
Lawrence Durrell
Ellen Gilchrist
William Golding
Allan Gurganus
Rodney Hall
Wilson Harris
Desmond Hogan
G. Cabrera Infante
Rachel Ingalls
Kazuo Ishiguro
P. D. James
Denis Johnson
Garrison Keillor
Danilo Kiš
Tadeusz Konwicki
Milan Kundera
Hanif Kureishi
Mario Vargas Llosa
John McGahern
Deirdre Madden
Adam Mars-Jones
Lorrie Moore
Frank Moorhouse
Jayne Anne Phillips
Dennis Potter
Manuel Puig
Jane Rogers
Vikram Seth
Joseph Skvorecky
Emma Tennant
Amos Tutuola
Nigel Williams

GRANTA

Salman Rushdie
6 March 1989

Photo: Gilles Peress (Magnum)

Copyright © 1989 Salman Rushdie and Granta Publications Limited. All rights reserved. No part of this poem may be reproduced, stored in a retrieval system or transmitted, in any form or by any means, electronic, mechanical, photocopying or otherwise without the prior written permission of the copyright owners. No part of this poem may be reproduced, whether for private research, study, criticism, review or the reporting of current events, without the written permission of the publishers, Granta Publications Limited. Any unauthorized reproduction of any part of the poem may result in civil liability and criminal prosecution.

Boy, yaar, they sure called me some good names of late:
e.g. opportunist (dangerous). E.g. full-of-hate,
self-aggrandizing, Satan, self-loathing and shrill,
the type it would clean up the planet to kill.
I justjust remember my own goodname still.

Damn, brother. You saw what they did to my face?
Poked out my eyes. Knocked teeth out of place,
stuck a dog's body under, hung same from a hook,
wrote what-all on my forehead! Wrote 'bastard'! Wrote 'crook'!
I justjust recall how my face used to look.

Now, misters and sisters, they've come for my voice.
If the Cat got my tongue, look who-who would rejoice—
muftis, politicos, 'my own people', hacks.
Still, nameless-and-faceless or not, here's my choice:
not to shut up. To sing on, in spite of attacks,
to sing (while my dreams are being murdered by facts)
praises of butterflies broken on racks.

THE ACCLAIMED NEW MASTERPIECE BY ONE OF AMERICA'S GREATEST WRITERS

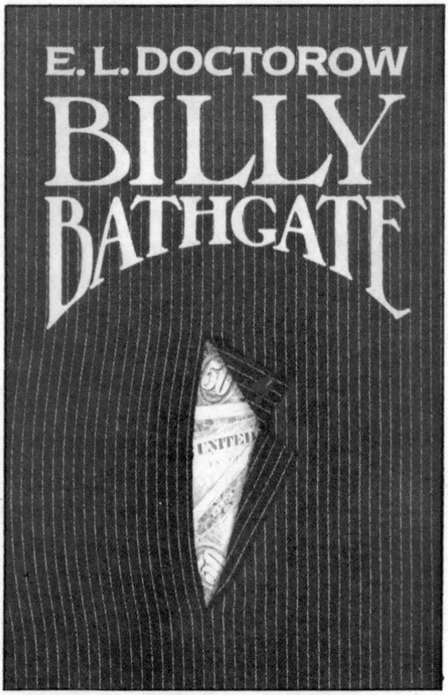

'*Billy Bathgate* is the kind of book you find yourself finishing at three in the morning after promising at midnight you'll stop after one more page... The star, of course, is Billy Bathgate himself. He's Huck Finn and Tom Sawyer with more poetry, Holden Caulfield with more zest and spirit.'
ANNE TYLER, *NEW YORK TIMES BOOK REVIEW*

'The result is that rarity: the grand entertainment that is also a triumphant work of art'
PETE HAMILL, *WASHINGTON POST BOOK WORLD*

'Mr Doctorow has created an American romance... Breath-taking... Stunning accomplishment'
CHRISTOPHER LEHMANN-HAUPT, *NEW YORK TIMES*

'Convincing, mesmerizing and finally unforgettable'
PAUL GRAY, *TIME*

Available 2 September 1989 Hardback, £12.95

Three of E.L. Doctorow's widely acclaimed novels, now reissued to coincide with the publication of *BILLY BATHGATE*

'Like ragtime, the jazz form made famous by Scott Joplin, Doctorow's book is a native American fugue, rhythmic, melodic and stately... He has seized the strands of actuality and transformed them into a fabulous tale'
TIME

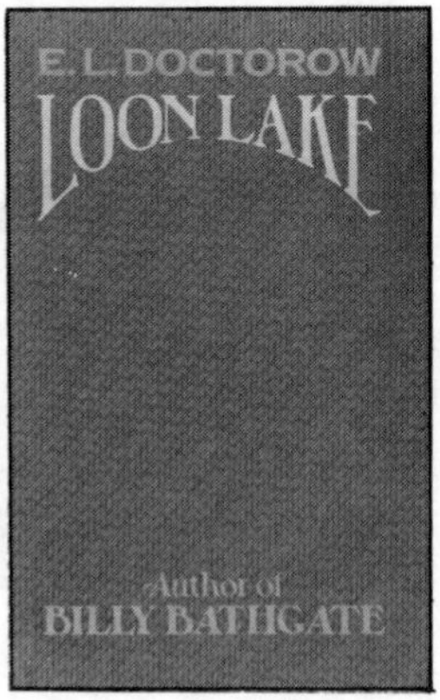

'*Loon Lake* concerns itself with capitalism in general and with the history of the union struggle in the early parts of this century... Doctorow's faith in his version of American history, and his willingness to run the large artistic risks involved in asserting it, make him one of the bravest and most interesting of modern novelists'
NEW YORK REVIEW OF BOOKS

'A masterpiece... I would place Mr Doctorow's achievement as a political novelist above that of any contemporary except Solzhenitsyn'
THE GUARDIAN

Available September 1989
Hardbacks, £11.95 each

M
MACMILLAN
LONDON

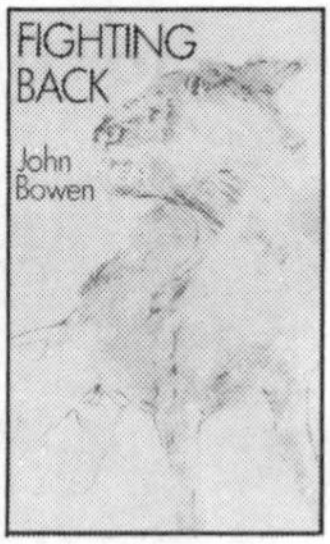

FIRST LIGHT
Peter Ackroyd

'. . . our most exciting and original writer . . . one of the few English writers of his generation who will be read in a hundred years time.'

The Sunday Times *£12.95*

EVA LUNA
Isabel Allende

'a finely woven tale . . . This novel confirms Isabel Allende's reputation as Latin America's foremost female writer.'

Financial Times *£11.95*

DICTIONARY OF THE KHAZARS
Milorad Pavić

'When you finish the novel you will be mesmerised and baffled. The best solution is to pick up the second copy and start again . . . it is a masterpiece.'

The Sunday Times *£11.95*

FIGHTING BACK
John Bowen

'Bowen weaves a splendid yarn, peopled by the grotesque, the dotty, the doughty and the austere.'

The Sunday Telegraph *£11.95*

Hamish Hamilton

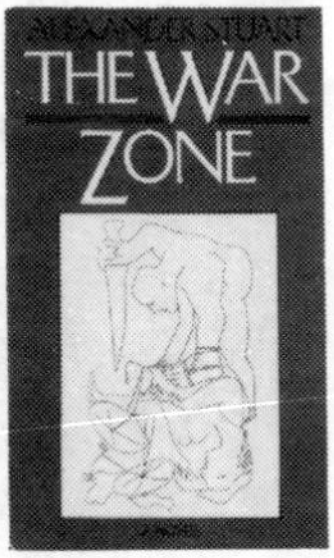

MY SECRET HISTORY

Paul Theroux

'Compulsively readable . . . beautifully structured and paced . . . Reading the superb *My Secret History* gives us privileged access to the secret self of Paul Theroux.

Literary Review *£12.95*

THE LOVER OF HORSES

Tess Gallagher

'lilting and powerful stories . . . These tales of uncelebrated people who live in small American towns and humdrum suburbs are superb.'

The Sunday Times *£11.95*

JIGSAW

Sybille Bedford

'Of all the women writers this century, Sybille Bedford is, to my mind, the finest . . . a book for reading and re-reading.'

London Evening Standard *£12.95*

THE WAR ZONE

Alexander Stuart

'A compelling novel that is as accomplished as it is shocking.'

Time Out *£11.95*

Hamish Hamilton

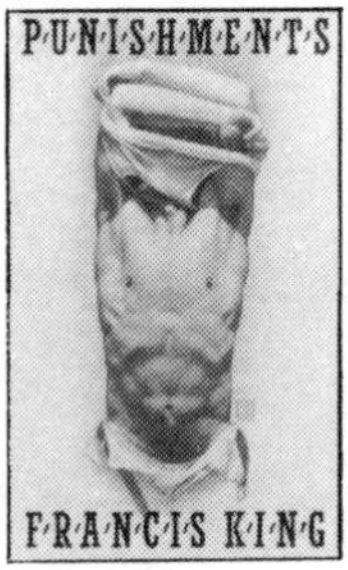

RESTORATION

Rose Tremain

Set in the 17th century at the Court of Charles II, *Restoration* is a fine work of great imagination, a rich, boisterous, brilliant novel with a dark and savage side. *£12.95*

THE MEMOIRS OF LORD BYRON

Robert Nye

In a cunning mix of truth and fiction, history and invention, Robert Nye supplies definitive answers to all the questions of the Byron 'mystery'. *£11.95*

PUNISHMENTS

Francis King

'a writer of masterly self control . . . He has written an admirable study of profound anguish . . . an emotionally powerful novel.'

The Sunday Telegraph *£12.95*

GEEK LOVE

Katherine Dunn

'Captivatingly original . . . this audaciously conceived, sometimes shocking tale of love and hubris in a carnival family exerts the same mesmeric fascination as the freaks it depicts.'

Kirkus Review *£12.95*

Hamish Hamilton

VERONICA, OR THE TWO NATIONS

David Caute

'steamily inventive' *Literary Review*. A brilliant novel about incest, politics and self-destruction.

£11.95

THE SCAPEWEED GOAT

Frank Schaefer

A primal, intense and unforgettable tale on the excesses of religion and the evils of fanaticism.

£11.95

THE TEETH OF ANGELS

Caitlin Levene

'very good indeed. I was very impressed by her writing and enjoyed the imaginative scope of these stories.'
Cosmopolitan *£11.95*

CHIMERA

Simon Mawer

A superb first novel set in Italy and moving between the war and the present day – gripping, atmospheric and unputdownable.

£12.95

Hamish Hamilton

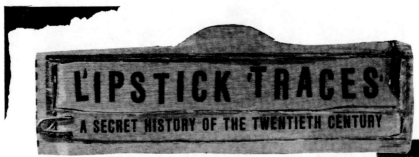

LIPSTICK TRACES
A SECRET HISTORY OF THE TWENTIETH CENTURY

Greil Marcus

"A book nobody interested in the period or in how we're preparing to leave the twentieth century can afford to ignore."
Gordon Burn, The Face

formules

"A highly personal book, a kind of quest by America's most acute citizen of pop culture to elucidate 'the secret the Sex Pistols didn't tell' ... (written in) clear and yet passionate prose."
Jerome McGann, London Review of Books

connexions

"Lipstick Traces brings... intellectual agility and critical enthusiasm to bear on European art movements and British punk... An exhilarating and impressive study."
Duncan Webster, Q Magazine

£14.95

Secker & Warburg

GRANTA

IAN JACK

UNSTEADY PEOPLE

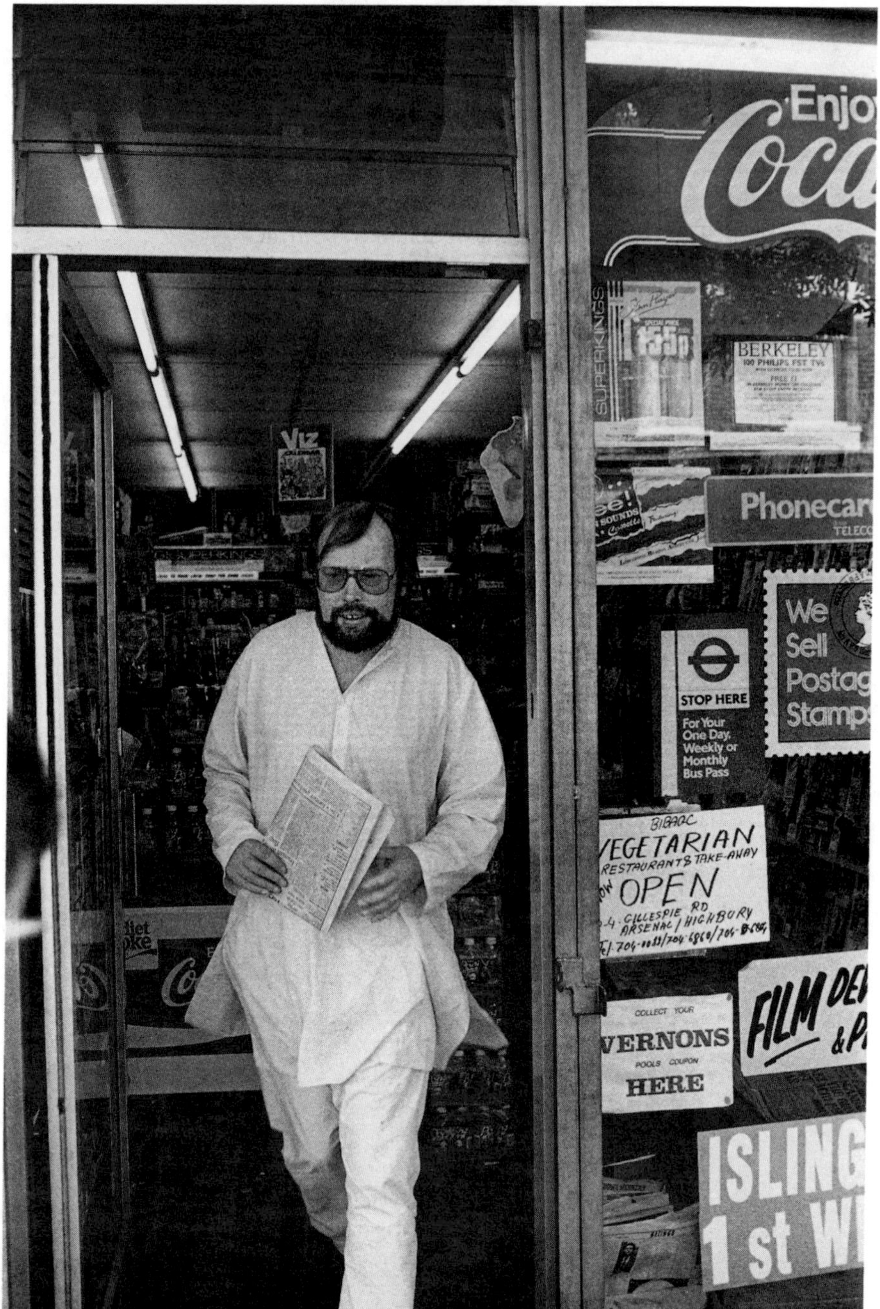

Enjo
Coca
SUPERKINGS
BERKELEY
100 PHILIPS FST TVs
Viz
Phoneca
STOP HERE
For Your
One Day,
Weekly or
Monthly
Bus Pass
We
Sell
Postag
Stamps
VEGETARIAN
RESTAURANTS TAKE-AWAY
OPEN
GILLESPIE RD
ARSENAL / HIGHBURY
COLLECT YOUR
VERNONS
POOLS COUPON
HERE
FILM
ISLING
1 st W
HALF

On 6 August last year a launch overturned in the River Ganges near Manihari Ghat, a remote ferry station in the Indian state of Bihar. Many people drowned, though precisely how many will never be known. The district magistrate estimated the number of dead at around 400, the launch-owner at fourteen. The first estimate was reached by subtraction: 529 tickets had been sold and only a hundred passengers had swum ashore. The second estimate came from the number of bodies the launch-owner said he had counted stretched out on the bank. But then the river was in flood; hundreds of bodies could have been swept far downstream; scores may still be entangled in the wreckage or buried in the silt. The launch-owner had good reason to lie.

It was, in its causes and consequences, an accident which typified the hazards of navigating the River Ganges. Monsoon rains had swollen the river and changed its hydrography, cutting new channels and raising new shoals. The launch was overcrowded. Licensed to carry 160, it seems to have set out with at least three times that number, nearly all of whom were fervent Hindu pilgrims travelling from their villages in north Bihar to a shrine which lies south of the river. Devotees of Lord Shiva, the destroyer, they wore saffron robes and carried pots of sacred Ganges water on their shoulders. Eyewitnesses said the launch left the north bank to the chanting of Shiva's name, the chorus *'bol bam'* rising from the massed saffron on the upper deck; until, hardly a hundred metres from the shore, the chants turned into screams.

According to a survivor quoted in the Calcutta newspapers, what happened was this. As the launch moved off, its stern got stuck in the shallows near the bank. The skipper decided to redistribute his vessel's weight, to lighten the stern by weighing down the bow. He asked his passengers to move forward; the stern bobbed up and the launch surged forward, head down and listing badly, to run a few hundred feet into a submerged sandbank and capsize.

In Bihar a revengeful clamour arose which sought to identify the guilty and exact punishment. The Bihar government and its servants blamed the launch-owner and charged him with murder. The opposition blamed government corruption and the conduct of the police. According to Ajit Kumar Sarkar, a Marxist member of the Bihar Legislative Assembly, the launch took six hours to sink,

Photo: Barry Lewis

and many victims could have been saved had not the police beaten back agitated crowds of would-be rescuers on the shore. According to the police, corruption had made their job impossible; almost every Ganges ferry flouted safety legislation because the ferry-owners organized 'gangs to protect their interest.' Bihar had a 'steamer mafia' whose profits had perverted the political administration. Chief among this mafia was Mr Bachcha Singh, the 'steamer tycoon of Bihar' and owner of the launch that had gone down at Manihari Ghat.

Some days after the accident another of Mr Singh's vessels approached the wreck, ostensibly with the task of dragging it off the sandbank and on to the shore. Watchers on the bank, however, saw something different. They saw the second vessel pressing down on the wreckage of the first. It seemed to them that the other ship had come to bury the launch and not to raise it, thus destroying the evidence and, in the words of the *Calcutta Telegraph*, 'obscuring the gravity of the tragedy.' In the face of public protest the second ship backed off.

Where, meanwhile, was the steamer tycoon, Mr Bachcha Singh? Nobody could say. The Chief Minister of Bihar promised 'stern action', charges of murder and negligence were registered in the courts and some of Mr Singh's property was seized. But the police said they could not find Singh himself. He was, in the English of official India, 'absconding' and so the courts declared him an 'absconder'.

Thereafter public interest evaporated with the monsoon rains. Manihari Ghat became just another Ganges launch disaster. The people who had died were poor. None had relatives influential enough to secure the lasting attention of the press or the government, both of which in any case were soon preoccupied with other problems.

What was the precise truth of the affair? Nobody could say. Truth in its least elevated and most humble sense, truth as detail, truth as times and numbers, truth arrived at by observation and deduction—this kind of truth left the scene early. Like Mr Singh, it absconded. Unlike Mr Singh, it did not reappear.

Six months later I met the steamer tycoon at his house in Patna, the state capital. To European eyes, the house looked like something a Nazi cineaste might have built. It had the smooth curves of a pre-war suburban Odeon and a large tower with two large swastikas etched high up in the concrete; they were visible from my cycle rickshaw long before the mansion itself swung into view. Mr Singh had called it 'Swastika House'—the name was on the gate—but only because he was a devout Hindu and the swastika is an ancient Hindu symbol of good fortune.

Fortune had been good to Mr Singh. It was manifest in his living arrangements, the dozens of domestic servants, his house's fifty bedrooms and thirty bathrooms, the superior quality of his tipped cigarettes. All of this (and a good deal else—apartments in Calcutta, real estate in the USA) derived from Mr Singh's role as the Ganges' principal ferryman. But his person as opposed to his surroundings seemed untouched by wealth. He was a small old man with heart trouble who wore loose Indian clothes and tapped ash from his Gold Flake King Size into an old spittoon.

We sat on his terrace and drank tea from mugs. I wondered about the murder charge. What had happened to it?

Nothing, said Singh, the case would never come to court. Did I understand the caste system? In Bihar caste was the key to everything. The murder charge had been instigated by the then Chief Minister, who was a Brahmin. Singh belonged to the Rajput caste, and Rajputs were the Brahmins' greatest political rivals. The charge had been politically inspired.

And now?

'Now the Chief Minister is a Rajput. He is known to me. Case finish.'

He apologized for his English and called for his son, who, he said, would be more intelligible to me. This proved to be only partly true. The younger Singh was reading Business Administration at Princeton University, ferry profits having dispatched him to the United States when he was an infant, and his English crackled with the abrasive nouns of the new capitalism. 'Cash-burn . . . acquisition and diversification . . . buy-out.' It was strange to hear these words in Bihar, still governed by ancestry and feudal law, but they completely matched the younger Singh's appearance. In

T-shirt, shorts and sneakers, he might have stepped out of a college tennis game. The sight of son next to father, crouched beside his spittoon, was a testament to the transforming power of money.

The father had recalled his son to Patna soon after what both referred to, opaquely, as 'the tragedy'. The son looked at his new surroundings with cold eyes. Corruption, poverty, ignorance, tradition—they ruled life here. It was sickening. Outside the family, nobody could be trusted. Did I know, for example, that after the tragedy peasants from adjacent villages had brought newly-dead relatives to the river, so that their bodies could be discreetly inserted among the launch's victims and compensation claimed?

I hadn't heard that, but maybe it was true; Bihar can sometimes be a desperate place. But what did he think had caused the accident?

'Panic and stupidity,' said the younger Singh. He thought for a moment. 'Basically these people weren't willing to make the smart move and analyse the situation.'

Of course these were ludicrous words; passengers packed on a tilting motor launch cannot be expected to plan their next five minutes like Wall Street commodity brokers. But the longer I travelled through Bihar, squashed on trains and river boats, the more I recognized the younger Singh's detachment as an indigenous sentiment rather than an American import.

Certain facts about Bihar were undeniable. The launch-owners were greedy and their craft decrepit and dangerous; the police were corrupt and tended to enforce the law of the highest bidder—the younger Singh said himself that his family had put off police inquiries with a few thousand rupees; and covert supplies of money moved through the system at every level—an honest police-officer could have his orders countermanded by a corrupt district administrator, an honest district administrator could be transferred or demoted by a corrupt politician. To behave dutifully and honestly in this amoral environment involved great courage and sacrifice. It was no surprise that the safety of the travelling public, especially a public so lacking in clout, did not figure highly in the minds of their appointed guardians.

My fellow-travellers would talk quite frankly about all this—humbug is not a Bihari vice—but then they also echoed the younger Singh: people in Bihar, they would say, did not know how to behave. They were 'uneducated' and 'ignorant' and, most of all, 'backward'. The populations of western democracies hesitate—still—to describe their fellow-citizens so bluntly, at least in public. But Biharis have no such inhibitions. The ancient social pyramid of caste enables those at the top to look down at those below with a dispassionate prejudice, at an inferior form of human life.

'I'm afraid we are not a *steady* people,' an old man said to me one day, and I could see exactly what he meant. Often the unsteadiness was frightening. The resources of transportation are scarce all over India; there is a continual press and scramble for tickets and seats wherever you go. But young Biharis travel on the roofs of trains even when the compartments below are empty and rush listing ferries like a piratical horde. Even the old and lame press forward as though fleeing some imminent disaster.

Towards the end of my journey in Bihar I met another Singh, a relative of the steamer tycoon, who operated a couple of old steamboats just upriver from Manihari Ghat. In an interval between crossings he took me up on to the bridge of his ferry, which was berthed at the foot of a steep bank, glistening and slippery with unseasonal rain. At the top of the slope men with staves, Singh's employees, were restraining a crowd of waiting passengers. Then the steamer's whistle gave two hoots; the men with staves relented; and the crowd, with its bicycles and milk-churns, came rushing down the bank towards us, slithering and whooping.

Singh looked down at his customers as they milled across the gangplank and then laughed like a man in a zoo. 'Crazy people. What can you do with them?'

On 15 April this year ninety-five people were crushed to death on the terraces of a football stadium in Sheffield, northern England. Most of the dead came from Liverpool, and all of them were supporters of Liverpool football club, who that day were to play Nottingham Forest in the semi-final of English football's premier knock-out competition, the Football Association

Cup. The deaths came six minutes after the kick-off. The match was then abandoned.

I read about the disaster in Delhi on my way back to London. Newspaper reports speculated on the possible causes and recalled that the behaviour of Liverpool fans had prompted the crush which killed thirty-nine people at the European Cup Final in Brussels in 1985, all of them Italian supporters of the other finalists, Juventus of Turin. It seemed something similar had happened in Sheffield. Liverpool fans had swept into the ground and pressed their fellow-supporters forward until they were squashed against the barriers and fences which had been erected some years before to prevent unruly spectators rushing on to the pitch and interfering with the game.

All that winter in India I'd heard about death in Britain. Planes fell to earth and trains left the rails, and Mrs Thatcher's face appeared on Indian television talking of her sympathy and concern. There were shots of disintegrated fuselages, body bags, shattered railway coaches. Indian friends tutted at the carnage, and I recognized in their reaction the momentary interest—the shake of the head, the small ripple of fascination—that passes through a British living-room when news of some distant tragedy flits before it; say, of the last typhoon to strike Bengal.

Meanwhile, the India I saw reported every day on the news—orderly, calm, soporific—looked more and more like the country I came from—or at least as I had once thought of it. Accidents such as Manihari Ghat were certainly reported, but rarely filmed. We watched the prime minister greeting foreign delegations at the airport, men in good suits addressing seminars and shaking hands, women cutting tapes and accepting bouquets. Indian news, or what India's government-controlled television judged to be news, took place indoors in an atmosphere notably free of dust, flies and mess. There was a lot of cricket. The mess—grief and ripped metal under arc lights—came from abroad, imported by satellite and shiny film-cans—they were like luxury items, a new spice trade going the other way—which the makers of Indian bulletins slotted in between the hand-shaking and the seminars as if to prove that disaster could overtake the foreign rich as well as the native poor, and that it was not confined to terrorism in the Punjab or the chemical catastrophe at Bhopal.

There were two train crashes in the southern suburbs of London (forty dead); a Pan Am Jumbo which exploded over Lockerbie (270 dead); a Boeing forced to crash-land on a motorway (forty-seven dead). All of them had specific and identifiable causes—a bomb, signal failure, faulty engines—though the roots (what caused the cause?) led to a vaguer territory: under-investment in public utilities, 'international terrorism', the collapse of civic feeling under a political leader who has said she cannot grasp the idea of community. This kind of worry—the cause of the cause—had bobbed to the surface of British life like old wreckage ever since the Channel ferry *Herald of Free Enterprise* turned over at Zeebrugge in 1987, the first in a series of large accidents which has marked Britain out as a literally disastrous country. But from the distance of India, Sheffield looked different. It seemed to turn on the behaviour of a fervent crowd; there was, in that sense, something very Indian about it.

When my landlord in Delhi said he thought football in England must have assumed 'a religious dimension', it was difficult to resist the parallel: saffron pilgrims struggling to board their launch at Manihari Ghat, the mass of Liverpudlian red and white which surged into the stadium at Sheffield. And the parallels did not end there. In fact the nearer I got to home the closer they became.

Changing planes in Paris, I bought a newspaper and read about M. Jacques Georges, the French president of the European Football Association. An interviewer on French radio had asked M. Georges if he thought Liverpool was peculiar in some way, given its football club's recent history of violent disaster. Well, said Georges, Liverpool certainly seemed to have 'a particularly aggressive mentality'. The crowd that had stormed into the ground at Sheffield had scorned all human feeling. 'I have the impression—I am distressed to use the expression—but it was like beasts who wanted to charge into an arena.'

The English are not a steady people. Today all Europe knows that. None the less M. Georges's words had scandalized England. At Heathrow the papers were full of him, even though he had said little more than the Sheffield police. According to Mr Paul Middup, chairman of the South Yorkshire Police Federation, there was 'mass drunkenness' among the 3,000 Liverpool supporters, who turned up at the turnstiles shortly before the kick-off: 'Some of them were uncontrollable. A great number of them had obviously been drinking heavily.' According to Mr Irvine Patrick, a Sheffield MP, the police had been 'hampered, harassed, punched, kicked and urinated on.'

But then the police themselves had behaved ineptly. Seeking to relieve the crush outside the stadium, they had opened a gate and sent an excited crowd—drunks, beasts or otherwise—into a section of the terracing which was already filled to capacity. And then, for some minutes at least, they had watched the crowd's desperate attempt to escape over the fences and mistaken it for hooliganism. They had hardly made a smart move and analysed the situation.

It would have all been familiar to any citizen of Bihar. An underclass which, in the view of the overclass, did not know how to behave. 'Drunks . . . beasts . . . uneducated . . . ignorant.' An antique and ill-designed public facility. A police force which made serious mistakes. Clamorous cross-currents of blame.

At home, I watched television. The disaster excited the medium. For several days it replayed the scene at Sheffield and then moved on to Liverpool, where the football ground was carpeted with wreaths. Funeral services were recorded, football players vowed that they might never play again and political leaders in Liverpool demanded the presence in their city of royalty—a prince, a duke—so that the scale of the 'national tragedy' might be acknowledged. When members of Liverpool's rival team turned up at a burial, the commentator spoke reverently of how the disaster had 'united football', as though the French and Germans in Flanders had stopped bombardment for a day to bury their dead. One football official said he hoped that ninety-five people had not 'died in vain.' Another said that they had 'died for football.'

Nobody in Bihar would have suggested that the dead of Manihari Ghat had made such a noble sacrifice. Nobody would have said: 'They died to expunge corruption, caste and poverty.' Whatever their other faults, Biharis are not a self-deluding people.

GRANTA

Ryszard Kapuściński

The Snow in Ghana

The fire stood between us and linked us together. A boy added wood and the flames rose higher, illuminating our faces.

'What is the name of your country?'

'Poland.'

Poland was far away, beyond the Sahara, beyond the sea, to the north and the east. The *Nana* repeated the name aloud. 'Is that how it is pronounced?' he asked.

'That's the way,' I answered. 'That's correct.'

'They have snow there,' Kwesi said. Kwesi worked in town. Once, at the cinema, there was a movie with snow. The children applauded and cried merrily '*Anko*! *Anko*!' asking to see the snow again. The white puffs fell and fell. Those are lucky countries, Kwesi said. They do not need to grow cotton; the cotton falls from the sky. They call it snow and walk on it and even throw it into the river.

We were stuck here by this fire by chance—three of us, my friend Kofi from Accra, a driver and I. Night had already fallen when the tyre blew—the third tyre, rotten luck. It happened on a side road, in the bush, near the village of Mpango in Ghana. Too dark to fix it. You have no idea how dark the night can be. You can stick out your hand and not see it. They have nights like that. We walked into the village.

The *Nana* received us. There is a *Nana* in every village, because *Nana* means boss, head man, a sort of mayor but with more authority. If you want to get married back home in your village, the mayor cannot stop you, but the *Nana* can. He has a Council of Elders, who meet and govern and ponder disputes. Once upon a time the *Nana* was a god. But now there is the independent government in Accra. The government passes laws and the *Nana* has to execute them. A *Nana* who does not carry them out is acting like a feudal lord and must be got rid of. The government is trying to make all *Nana*s join the party.

The *Nana* from Mpango was skinny and bald, with thin Sudanese lips. My friend Kofi introduced us. He explained where I was from and that they were to treat me as a friend.

'I know him,' my friend Kofi said. 'He's an African.'

That is the highest compliment that can be paid a European. It opens every door for him.

The *Nana* smiled and we shook hands. You always greet a

Nana by pressing his right hand between both of your own palms. This shows respect. He sat us down by the fire, where the elders had just been holding a meeting. The bonfire was in the middle of the village, and to the left and right, along the road, there were other fires. As many fires as huts. Perhaps twenty. We could see the fires and the figures of the women and the men and the silhouettes of the clay huts—they were all visible against a night so dark and deep that it felt heavy like a weight.

The bush had disappeared, even though the bush was everywhere. It began a hundred metres away, immobile, massive, a tightly packed, coarse thicket surrounding the village and us and the fire. The bush screamed and cried and crackled; it was alive; it smelled of wilted green; it was terrifying and tempting; you knew that you could touch it and be wounded and die, but tonight, this night, you couldn't even see it.

Poland.

They did not know of any such country.

The elders looked at me with uncertainty, possibly suspicion. I wanted to break their mistrust somehow. I did not know how and I was tired.

'Where are your colonies?' the *Nana* asked.

My eyes were drooping, but I became alert. People often asked that question. Kofi had asked it first, long ago, and my answer was a revelation to him. From then on he was always ready for the question with a little speech prepared, illustrating its absurdity.

Kofi answered: 'They don't have colonies, *Nana*. Not all white countries have colonies. Not all whites are colonialists. You have to understand that whites often colonize whites.'

The elders shuddered and smacked their lips. They were surprised. Once I would have been surprised that they were surprised. But not any more. I can't bear that language, that language of white, black and yellow. The language of race is disgusting.

Kofi explained: 'For a hundred years they taught us that the white is somebody greater, super, extra. They had their clubs, their swimming pools, their neighbourhoods. Their whores, their cars and their burbling language. We knew that England was the only country in the world, that God was English, that only the English travelled around the globe. We knew exactly as much as they wanted us to know. Now it's hard to change.'

Kofi and I stuck up for each other; we no longer spoke about the subject of skin, but here, among new faces, the subject had to come up.

One of the elders asked, 'Are all the women in your country white?'

'All of them.'

'Are they beautiful?'

'They're very beautiful,' I answered.

'Do you know what he told me, *Nana*?' Kofi interjected. 'That during their summer, the women take off their clothes and lie in the sun to get black skin. The ones that become dark are proud of it, and others admire them for being as tanned as blacks.'

Very good, Kofi, you got them. The elders' eyes lit up at the thought of those bodies darkening in the sun, because, you know how it is, boys are the same all over the world: they like that sort of thing. The elders rubbed their hands together, smiled; women's bodies in the sun; they snuggled up inside their loose *kente* robes that looked like Roman togas.

'My country has no colonies,' I said after a time, 'and there was a time when my country was a colony. I respect what you've suffered, but, we too, have suffered horrible things: there were streetcars, restaurants, districts *nur für Deutsch*. There were camps, war, executions. You don't know camps, war and executions. That was what we called fascism. It's the worst colonialism.'

They listened, frowning, and closed their eyes. Strange things had been said, which they needed time to take in.

'Tell me, what does a streetcar look like?'

The concrete is important. Perhaps there was not enough room. No, it had nothing to do with room; it was contempt. One person stepping on another. Not only Africa is a cursed land. Every land can be like it—Europe, America, any place. The world depends on people, needs to step on them.

'But *Nana*, we were free afterwards. We built cities and ran lights into the villages. Those who couldn't read were taught how to read.'

The *Nana* stood up and grasped my hand. The rest of the elders did the same. We had become friends, *przyjaciele*, *amigos*.

I wanted to eat.

I could smell meat in the air. I could smell a smell that was not of the jungle or of palm or of coconuts; it was the smell of a *kielbasa*, the kind you could get for 11.60 zlotys at that inn in the Mazury. And a large beer.

Instead we ate goat.

Poland . . . snow falling, women in the sun, no colonies. There had been a war; there were homes to build; somebody teaching somebody to read.

I had told them something, I rationalized. It was too late to go into details. I wanted to go to sleep. We were leaving at dawn; a lecture was impossible. Anyway, they had worries of their own.

Suddenly I felt shame, a sense of having missed the mark. It was not my country I had described. Snow and the lack of colonies—that's accurate enough, but it is not what we know or what we carry around within ourselves: nothing of our pride, of our life, nothing of what we breathe.

Snow—that's the truth, *Nana*. Snow is marvellous. And it's terrible. Snow, because in January, January 1945, the January offensive, there were ashes, ashes everywhere: Warsaw, Wrocław, and Szczecin. And bricks, freezing hands, vodka and people laying bricks—this is where the bed will go and the wardrobe right here—people filing back into the centre of the city, and ice on the window panes, and no water, and those nights, the meetings till dawn, and angry discussions and later the fires of Silesia, and the blast furnaces, and the temperature—160 degrees centigrade—in August in front of the blast furnaces, our tropics, our Africa, black and hot. Oh, what a load of shit—What do you mean?—Oh, what a lovely little war—Shut up about the war! We want to live, to be happy, we want an apartment, a TV, no, first a motor-scooter. A Pole can drink and a Pole can fight, why can't we work? What if we never learn how? Our ships are on every sea, success in exports, success in boxing, youngsters in gloves, wet gloves pulling a tractor out of the mud, Nowa Huta, build, build, build, Tychy and Wizów, bright apartments, upward mobility, a cowherd yesterday and an engineer today—Do you call that an engineer? and the whole streetcar bursts out laughing. Tell me: what does a streetcar look like? It's very simple: four wheels, an electrical pick-up, *enough*, *enough*, it's all a code, nothing but signs in the bush, in Mpango, and the key to the code is in my pocket.

We always carry it to foreign countries, all over the world, our pride and our powerlessness. We know its configuration, but there is no way to make it accessible to others. It will never be right. Something, the most important thing, the most significant thing, something remains unsaid.

Relate one year of my country—it does not matter which one: let us say, 1957. And one month of that year—say, July. And just one day—let us say, the sixth.

No.

Yet that day, that month, that year exist in us, somehow, because we were there, walking that street, or digging coal, or cutting the forest, and if we were walking along that street how can we then describe it (it could be Cracow) so that you can see its movement, its climate, its persistence and changeability, its smell and its hum?

They cannot see it. You cannot see it, anything, the night, Mpango, the thick bush, Ghana, the fire dying out, the elders going off to sleep, the *Nana* dozing, and snow falling somewhere, and women like blacks, *thoughts*, 'They are learning to read, he said something like that,' *thoughts*, 'They had a war, ach, a war, he said, yes, no colonies,' that country, Poland, white and they have no colonies,' *thoughts*, the bush screams, this strange world.

Translated from the Polish by William Brand.

Great reads this Autumn from Viking

Lenya: A Life
September
£15.95

The Grotesque
October
£11.95

The Great Indian Novel
August
£12.95

Fludd
September
£11.95

Bitter Fame
October
£15.95

VIKING

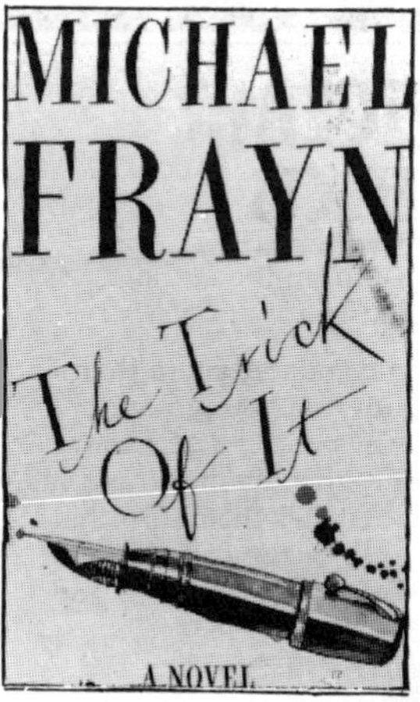

The Trick Of It
September
£11.95

The Floatplane Notebooks
October
£12.95

A Natural Curiosity
September
£12.95

The Pale Companion
September
£11.95

Love, Pain, and the Whole Damn Thing
October
£11.95

Congratulations Granta

CLIVE SINCLAIR
COSMETIC EFFECTS

The explosive new novel from the author of *Blood Libels, Bed Bugs* and *Hearts of Gold.*

'Clive Sinclair has been compared more than once with those two glittering young men of recent fiction, Martin Amis and Ian McEwan. He has their fluency and inventiveness, and his ferocity with language matches theirs. But his eye is all his own . . . not for the squeamish or the lazy. His stories work you hard; tease and torment and shock you.'
Isabel Quigly, *Financial Times* (reviewing *Bed Bugs*)

£10.95

ROBERT McLIAM WILSON
RIPLEY BOGLE

'. . . an assured, stylish debut. It has acrid humour and energetic bravura . . . Ripley Bogle is an impressive read, and Robert McLiam Wilson is undoubtedly a man to watch.'
Peter Bradshaw, *Daily Telegraph*

'. . . a masterpiece of comic writing.'
Jeremy Lewis, *New Statesman & Society*

£11.95

JOHN UPDIKE
SELF-CONSCIOUSNESS

Memoirs

'. . . writing like this wins one's deepest assent; it seems to enlarge the human community.'
Martin Amis, *Observer*

'*Self Consciousness* is a marvellous book, perhaps the best that Updike has ever written.'
Sebastian Faulks, *Independent*

£12.95

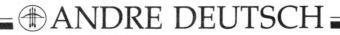

ANDRE DEUTSCH

GRANTA

NADINE GORDIMER
THE ULTIMATE SAFARI

'THE AFRICAN ADVENTURE LIVES ON . . . YOU CAN DO IT! THE ULTIMATE SAFARI OR EXPEDITION WITH LEADERS WHO *KNOW* AFRICA.'

Travel advertisement, Observer, *27 November 1988.*

That night our mother went to the shop and she didn't come back. Ever. What happened? I don't know. My father also had gone away one day and never come back; but he was fighting in the war. We were in the war, too, but we were children, we were like our grandmother and grandfather, we didn't have guns. The people my father was fighting—the bandits, they are called by our government—ran all over the place and we ran away from them like chickens chased by dogs. We didn't know where to go. Our mother went to the shop because someone said you could get some oil for cooking. We were happy because we hadn't tasted oil for a long time; perhaps she got the oil and someone knocked her down in the dark and took that oil from her. Perhaps she met the bandits. If you meet them, they will kill you. Twice they came to our village and we ran and hid in the bush and when they'd gone we came back and found they had taken everything; but the third time they came back there was nothing to take, no oil, no food, so they burned the thatch and the roofs of our houses fell in. My mother found some pieces of tin and we put those up over part of the house. We were waiting there for her that night she never came back.

We were frightened to go out, even to do our business, because the bandits did come. Not into our house—without a roof it must have looked as if there was no one in it, everything gone—but all through the village. We heard people screaming and running. We were afraid even to run, without our mother to tell us where. I am the middle one, the girl, and my little brother clung against my stomach with his arms round my neck and his legs round my waist like a baby monkey to its mother. All night my first-born brother kept in his hand a broken piece of wood from one of our burnt house-poles. It was to save himself if the bandits found him.

Photo: David Goldblatt

We stayed there all day. Waiting for her. I don't know what

day it was; there was no school, no church any more in our village, so you didn't know whether it was a Sunday or a Monday.

When the sun was going down, our grandmother and grandfather came. Someone from our village had told them we children were alone, our mother had not come back. I say 'grandmother' before 'grandfather' because it's like that: our grandmother is big and strong, not yet old, and our grandfather is small, you don't know where he is, in his loose trousers, he smiles but he hasn't heard what you're saying, and his hair looks as if he's left it full of soap suds. Our grandmother took us—me, the baby, my first-born brother, our grandfather—back to her house and we were all afraid (except the baby, asleep on our grandmother's back) of meeting the bandits on the way. We waited a long time at our grandmother's place. Perhaps it was a month. We were hungry. Our mother never came. While we were waiting for her to fetch us, our grandmother had no food for us, no food for our grandfather and herself. A woman with milk in her breasts gave us some for my little brother, although at our house he used to eat porridge, same as we did. Our grandmother took us to look for wild spinach but everyone else in the village did the same and there wasn't a leaf left.

Our grandfather, walking a little behind some young men, went to look for our mother but didn't find her. Our grandmother cried with other women and I sang the hymns with them. They brought a little food—some beans—but after two days there was nothing again. Our grandfather used to have three sheep and a cow and a vegetable garden but the bandits had long ago taken the sheep and the cow, because they were hungry, too; and when planting time came our grandfather had no seed to plant.

So they decided—our grandmother did; our grandfather made little noises and rocked from side to side, but she took no notice—we would go away. We children were pleased. We wanted to go away from where our mother wasn't and where we were hungry. We wanted to go where there were no bandits and there was food. We were glad to think there must be such a place; away.

Our grandmother gave her church clothes to someone in exchange for some dried mealies and she boiled them and tied them in a rag. We took them with us when we went and she thought we would get water from the rivers but we didn't come to any river and we got so thirsty we had to turn back. Not all the way to our grandparents' place but to a village where there was a pump. She opened the basket where she carried some clothes and the mealies and she sold her shoes to buy a big plastic container for water. I said, *Gogo*, how will you go to church now even without shoes, but she said we had a long journey and too much to carry. At that village we met other people who were also going away. We joined them because they seemed to know where that was better than we did.

To get there we had to go through the Kruger Park. We knew about the Kruger Park. A kind of whole country of animals—elephants, lions, jackals, hyenas, hippos, crocodiles, all kinds of animals. We had some of them in our own country, before the war (our grandfather remembers; we children weren't born yet) but the bandits kill the elephants and sell their tusks, and the bandits and our soldiers have eaten all the buck. There was a man in our village without legs—a crocodile took them off, in our river; but all the same our country is a country of people, not animals. We knew about the Kruger Park because some of our men used to leave home to work there in the places where white people came to stay and look at the animals.

So we started to go away again. There were women and other children like me who had to carry the small ones on their backs when the women got tired. A man led us into the Kruger Park; are we there yet, are we there yet, I kept asking our grandmother. Not yet, the man said, when she asked him for me. He told us we had to take a long way to get round the fence, which he explained would kill you, roast off your skin the moment you touched it, like the wires high up on poles that give electric light in our towns. I've seen that sign of a head without ears or skin or hair on an iron box at the mission hospital we used to have before it was blown up.

When I asked the next time, they said we'd been walking in

the Kruger Park for an hour. But it looked just like the bush we'd been walking through all day, and we hadn't seen any animals except the monkeys and birds which live around us at home, and a tortoise that, of course, couldn't get away from us. My first-born brother and the other boys brought it to the man so it could be killed and we could cook and eat it. He let it go because he told us we could not make a fire; all the time we were in the Park we must not make a fire because the smoke would show we were there. Police, wardens, would come and send us back where we came from. He said we must move like animals among the animals, away from the roads, away from the white people's camps. And at that moment I heard—I'm sure I was the first to hear—cracking branches and the sound of something parting grasses and I almost squealed because I thought it was the police, wardens—the people he was telling us to look out for—who had found us already. And it was an elephant, and another elephant, and more elephants, big blots of dark moved wherever you looked between the trees. They were curling their trunks round the red leaves of the mopane trees and stuffing them into their mouths. The babies leaned against their mothers. The almost grown-up ones wrestled like my first-born brother with his friends—only they used trunks instead of arms. I was so interested I forgot to be afraid. The man said we should just stand still and be quiet while the elephants passed. They passed very slowly because elephants are too big to need to run from anyone.

The buck ran from us. They jumped so high they seemed to fly. The wart-hogs stopped dead, when they heard us, and swerved off the way a boy in our village used to zigzag on the bicycle his father had brought back from the mines. We followed the animals to where they drank. When they had gone, we went to their water-holes. We were never thirsty without finding water, but the animals ate, ate all the time. Whenever you saw them they were eating, grass, trees, roots. And there was nothing for us. The mealies were finished. The only food we could eat was what the baboons ate, dry little figs full of ants, that grow along the branches of the trees at the rivers. It was hard to be like the animals.

When it was very hot during the day we would find lions lying asleep. They were the colour of the grass and we didn't see them at first but the man did, and he led us back and a long way round where they slept. I wanted to lie down like the lions. My little brother was getting thin but he was very heavy. When our grandmother looked for me, to put him on my back, I tried not to see. My first-born brother stopped talking; and when we rested he had to be shaken to get up again, as if he was just like our grandfather, he couldn't hear. I saw flies crawling on our grandmother's face and she didn't brush them off; I was frightened. I picked up a palm leaf and chased them.

We walked at night as well as by day. We could see the fires where the white people were cooking in the camps and we could smell the smoke and the meat. We watched the hyenas with their backs that slope as if they're ashamed, slipping through the bush after the smell. If one turned its head, you saw it had big brown shining eyes like our own, when we looked at each other in the dark. The wind brought voices in our own language from the compounds where the people who work in the camps live. A woman among us wanted to go to them at night and ask them to help us. They can give us the food from the dustbins, she said, she started wailing and our grandmother had to grab her and put a hand over her mouth. The men who led us had told us that we must keep out of the way of our people who worked at the Kruger Park; if they helped us they would lose their work. If they saw us, all they could do was pretend we were not there; they had seen only animals.

Sometimes we stopped to sleep for a little while at night. We slept close together. I don't know which night it was—because we were walking, walking, any time, all the time—we heard the lions very near. Not groaning loudly the way they did far off. Panting, like we do when we run, but it's a different kind of panting: you can hear they're not running, they're waiting, somewhere near. We all rolled closer together, on top of each other, the ones on the edge fighting to get into the middle. I was squashed against a woman who smelled bad because she was afraid but I was glad to hold tight on to her. I prayed to God to make the lions take someone on the edge and go. I shut my eyes not to see the tree from which a lion might jump right into the middle of us, where I was. The man who led us jumped up instead, and beat on the tree with a dead branch. He had taught us never to make a sound but he shouted. He shouted at the lions like a drunk man shouting at nobody in our village. The lions went away. We heard them groaning, shouting back at him from far off.

We were tired, so tired. My first-born brother and the man had to lift our grandfather from stone to stone where we found places to cross the rivers. Our grandmother is strong but her feet were bleeding. We could not carry the basket on our heads any longer, we couldn't carry anything except my little brother. We left our things under a bush. As long as our bodies get there, our grandmother said. Then we ate some wild fruit we didn't know from home and our stomachs ran. We were in the grass called elephant grass because it is nearly as tall as an elephant, that day we had those pains, and our grandfather couldn't just get down in front of people like my little brother, he went off into the grass to be on his own. We had to keep up, the man who led us always kept telling us, we must catch up, but we asked him to wait for our grandfather.

So everyone waited for our grandfather to catch up. But he didn't. It was the middle of the day; insects were singing in our ears and we couldn't hear him moving through the grass. We couldn't see him because the grass was so high and he was so small. But he must have been somewhere there inside his loose trousers and his shirt that was torn and our grandmother couldn't sew because she had no cotton. We knew he couldn't have gone far because he was weak and slow. We all went to look for him, but in groups, so we too wouldn't be hidden from each other in that grass. It got into our eyes and noses; we called him softly but the noise of the insects must have filled the little space left for hearing in his ears. We looked and looked but we couldn't find him. We stayed in that long grass all night. In my sleep I found him curled round in a place he had tramped down for himself, like the places we'd seen where the buck hide their babies.

When I woke up he still wasn't anywhere. So we looked again, and by now there were paths we'd made by going through the grass many times, it would be easy for him to find us if we couldn't find him. All that day we just sat and waited. Everything is very quiet when the sun is on your head, inside your head, even if you lie, like the animals, under the trees. I lay on my back and saw those ugly birds with hooked beaks and plucked necks flying round and round above us. We had passed them often where they were feeding on the bones of dead animals, nothing was ever left there for us to eat. Round and round, high up and then lower down and then high again. I saw their necks poking to this side and that. Flying round and round. I saw our grandmother, who sat up all the time with my little brother on her lap, was seeing them, too.

In the afternoon the man who led us came to our grandmother and told her the other people must move on. He said, If their children don't eat soon they will die.

Our grandmother said nothing.

I'll bring you water before we go, he told her.

Our grandmother looked at us, me, my first-born brother, and my little brother on her lap. We watched the other people getting up to leave. I didn't believe the grass would be empty, all around us, where they had been. That we would be alone in this place, the Kruger Park, the police or the animals would find us. Tears came out of my eyes and nose on to my hands but our grandmother took no notice. She got up, with her feet apart the way she puts them when she is going to lift firewood, at home in our village, she swung my little brother on to her back, tied him in her cloth—the top of her dress was torn and her big breasts were showing but there was nothing in them for him. She said, Come.

So we left the place with the long grass. Left behind. We went with the others and the man who led us. We started to go away, again.

There's a very big tent, bigger than a church or a school, tied down to the ground. I didn't understand that was what it would be, when we got there, away. I saw a thing like that the time our mother took us to the town because she heard our soldiers were there and she wanted to ask them if they knew where our father was. In that tent, people were praying and singing. This one is blue and white like that one but it's not for praying and singing, we live in it with other people who've come from our country. Sister from the clinic says we're 200 without counting the babies, and we have new babies, some were born on the way through the Kruger Park.

Inside, even when the sun is bright it's dark and there's a kind of whole village in there. Instead of houses each family has a little place closed off with sacks or cardboard from boxes—whatever we can find—to show the other families it's yours and they shouldn't come in even though there's no door and no windows and no thatch, so that if you're standing up and you're not a small child you can see into everybody's house. Some people have even made paint from ground rocks and drawn designs on the sacks.

Of course, there really is a roof—the tent is the roof, far, high up. It's like a sky. It's like a mountain and we're inside it; through the cracks paths of dust lead down, so thick you think you could climb them. The tent keeps off the rain overhead but the water comes in at the sides and in the little streets between our places—you can only move along them one person at a time—the small kids like my little brother play in the mud. You have to step over them. My little brother doesn't play. Our grandmother takes him to the clinic when the doctor comes on Mondays. Sister says there's something wrong with his head, she thinks it's because we didn't have enough food at home. Because of the war. Because our father wasn't there. And then because he was so hungry in the Kruger Park. He likes just to lie about on our grandmother all day, on her lap or against her somewhere and he looks at us and looks at us. He wants to ask something but you can see he can't. If I tickle him he may just smile. The clinic gives us special powder to make into porridge for him and perhaps one day he'll be all right.

When we arrived we were like him—my first-born brother and I. I can hardly remember. The people who lived in the village near the tent took us to the clinic, it's where you have to sign that you've come—away, through the Kruger Park. We sat on the grass and everything was muddled. One Sister was pretty with her hair straightened and beautiful high-heeled shoes and she brought us the special powder. She said we must mix it with water and drink it slowly. We tore the packets open with our teeth and licked it all up, it stuck round my mouth and I sucked it from my lips and fingers. Some other children who had walked with us vomited. But I only felt everything in my belly moving, the stuff going down and around like a snake, and hiccups hurt me. Another Sister called us to stand in line on the veranda of the clinic but we couldn't. We sat all over the place there, falling against each other; the Sisters helped each of us up by the arm and then stuck a needle in it. Other needles drew our blood into tiny bottles. This was against sickness, but I didn't understand, every time my eyes dropped closed I thought I was walking, the grass was long, I saw the elephants, I didn't know we were away.

But our grandmother was still strong, she could still stand up, she knows how to write and she signed for us. Our grandmother got us this place in the tent against one of the sides, it's the best kind of place there because although the rain comes in, we can lift the flap when the weather is good and then the sun shines on us, the smells in the tent go out. Our grandmother knows a woman here who showed her where there is good grass for sleeping mats, and our grandmother made some for us. Once every month the food truck comes to the clinic. Our grandmother takes along one of the cards she signed and when it has been punched we get a sack of mealie meal. There are wheelbarrows to take it back to the tent; my first-born brother does this for her and then he and the other boys have races, steering the empty wheelbarrows back to the clinic. Sometimes he's lucky and a man who's bought beer in the village gives him money to deliver it—though that's not allowed, you're supposed to take that wheelbarrow straight back to the Sisters. He buys a cold drink and shares it with me if I catch him. On another day, every month, the church leaves a pile of old clothes in the clinic yard. Our grandmother has another card to get punched, and then we can choose something: I have two dresses, two pants and a jersey, so I can go to school.

The people in the village have let us join their school. I was surprised to find they speak our language; our grandmother told me, That's why they allow us to stay on their land. Long ago, in the time of our fathers, there was no fence that kills you, there was no Kruger Park between them and us, we were the same people under our own king, right from our village we left to this place we've come to.

Now that we've been in the tent so long—I have turned eleven and my little brother is nearly three although he is so small, only his head is big, he's not come right in it yet—some people have dug up the bare ground around the tent and planted beans and mealies and cabbage. The old men weave branches to put up fences round their gardens. No one is allowed to look for work in the towns but some of the women have found work in the village and can buy things. Our grandmother, because she's still strong, finds work where people are building houses—in this village the people build nice houses with bricks and cement, not mud like we used to have at our home. Our grandmother carries bricks for these people and fetches baskets of stones on her head. And so she has money to buy sugar and tea and milk and soap. The store gave her a calendar she has hung up on our flap of the tent. I am clever at school and she collected advertising paper people throw away outside the store and covered my school-books with it. She makes my first-born brother and me do our homework every afternoon before it gets dark because there is no room except to lie down, close together, just as we did in the Kruger Park, in our place in the tent, and candles are expensive. Our grandmother hasn't been able to buy herself a pair of shoes for church yet, but she has bought black school shoes and polish to clean them with for my first-born brother and me. Every morning, when people are getting up in the tent, the babies are crying, people are pushing each other at the taps outside and some children are already pulling the crusts of porridge off the pots we ate from last night, my first-born brother and I clean our shoes. Our grandmother makes us sit on our mats with our legs straight out so she can look carefully at our shoes to make sure we have done it properly. No other children in the tent have real school shoes. When we three look at them it's as if we are in a real house again, with no war, no away.

Some white people came to take photographs of our people living in the tent—they said they were making a film, I've never seen what that is though I know about it. A white woman squeezed into our space and asked our grandmother questions which were told to us in our language by someone who understands the white woman's.

How long have you been living like this?

She means here? our grandmother said. In this tent, two years and one month.

And what do you hope for the future?

Nothing. I'm here.

But for your children?

I want them to learn so that they can get good jobs and money.

Do you hope to go back to your own country?

I will not go back.

But when the war is over—you won't be allowed to stay here? Don't you want to go home?

I didn't think our grandmother wanted to speak again. I didn't think she was going to answer the white woman. The white woman put her head on one side and smiled at us.

Our grandmother looked away from her and spoke—There is nothing. No home.

Why does our grandmother say that? Why? I'll go back. I'll go back through that Kruger Park. After the war, if there are no bandits any more, our mother may be waiting for us. And maybe when we left our grandfather, he was only left behind, he found his way somehow, slowly, through the Kruger Park, and he'll be there. They'll be home, and I'll remember them.

GRACE
Maggie Gee
£3.99

A CROWD
IS NOT COMPANY
Robert Kee
£3.99

GLASSHOUSES
Penelope Farmer
£3.99

SHACKLETON
Roland Huntford
£6.99

M31
A FAMILY ROMANCE
Stephen Wright
£3.99

1939:
THE YEAR
WE LEFT BEHIND
Robert Kee
£5.99

NEW WRITING AVAILABLE FROM ABACUS AND CARDINAL

ABACUS

CARDINAL

GRANTA

DAVID GOLDBLATT
THE STRUCTURE OF THINGS HERE

David Goldblatt

In our structures we South Africans tend to declare ourselves quite nakedly, sometimes eloquently, and rarely with dissimulation. There, for all to see, in the geology of what we have built, and of what we have destroyed, are the accretions of our history and the choices we have made.

Opposite: Dutch Reformed Church, Quellerina, Johannesburg.

On following pages: Dutch Reformed Church, Op Die Berg, Koue Bokkeveld; Memorial to the late prime minister and leader of the National Party, J. G. Strydom, and behind it, the headquarters of Volkskas, the Afrikaner banking group, Pretoria; House under construction in Verwoerdburg; House in the black 'homeland' of Qwa Qwa; Apostolic Multiracial Church in Zion, Crossroads Camp, Cape Town; 'Site and service' shacks with high-level lighting masts, Site B, Khayelitsha, Cape Town.

All photos: David Goldblatt

APOSTOLIC MULtRAC
CHURCH iNZION OF S
CAPE TOWN CROSSROADS

Cambridge

Orwell and the Politics of Despair

A Critical Study of the Writings of George Orwell
ALOK RAI
Drawing on a wide range of Orwell's writing, Alok Rai demystifies the idea of Orwell's writing as 'transparent', simply concerned with basic human values. Rather, he considers Orwell as a literary artist as well as a political writer.
£25.00 net 0 521 34519 7 208 pp.

The Theatre of Andrzej Wajda

MACIEJ KARPINSKI
The first account of the theatre work of the Polish director Andrzej Wajda, better known as one of the leading film-makers in contemporary European cinema. Maciej Karpinski focuses especially on such milestone dramatic productions as the internationally acclaimed adaptations of Dostoyevsky.
£30.00 net 0 521 32246 4 153 pp.

The Cuban Condition

Translation and Identity in Modern Cuban Literature
GUSTAVO PEREZ FIRMAT
This book provides a new understanding of Cuba's literary and national identity through revisionary readings of works by Juan Marinello, Fernando Ortiz, Nicolas Guillen, Alejo Carpentier and others. The author examines the way in which Cuba has assimilated its Old World cultural inheritance.
£27.50 net 0 521 32747 4 193 pp.

Poetry and Phantasy

ANTONY EASTHOPE
'There is now no alternative to reading literature in some relation to psychoanalysis.' This is the challenge posed by Antony Easthope in his controversial new study of the English poetic tradition. His examples are drawn from the poetry of Milton, Dryden, Pope, Tennyson, Arnold, Eliot and Pound.
£27.50 net 0 521 35598 2 240 pp.

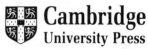

Cambridge University Press
The Edinburgh Building, Cambridge CB2 2RU

GRANTA

RICHARD RAYNER
A DISCOURSE ON THE ELEPHANT

SM
STICK NO BILLS

Yesterday I met a woman, very beautiful, it was in one of those groovy modern art galleries, you know the kind of place, all grey paint and grey steel chairs with big holes where you're supposed to sit and a grey-jacketed assistant whose haircut seems to be part of the exhibit, and I looked her up and down, thought I'd give it a try, so after I had smiled and introduced myself, noting—casually—that her eyes were those of Leonardo's Madonna, her grace was that of a Degas and her cool allure would have left Renoir powerless, while her intellect, her intellect shamed the Tate Gallery's entire twentieth-century collection, after I told her that my one remaining desire, the only thing of any consequence to me now, was to beach my life, wreck it forever if she should only wish, so I could spend a few moments, an hour, perhaps a night, even a *lifetime* in her company (oh God, I exclaimed, I'm out of control, I don't believe I'm saying this, I adore you, it's everything, from your thick, dark eyebrows which don't quite meet to your slim legs tucked into blue socks and Doc Martens, I have a pair also, no, not legs, though obviously I do, no Long John Silver me, but shoes like that, cue: cheesy chuckle) and after I had produced the yellow carnation bud kept behind my back until this moment, she smiled in return and asked me to repeat my name which was the cue for further word-play (it was like fencing, I swear: lunge and thrust, parry, thrust again with one hand and with the other beat death aside, *rinverso tondo*, ELA!) and then off to a hotel, it was easier than her flat, she lived in Baron's Court or somewhere beyond the back of beyond, where we drank cool wine from tall glasses, slowly, undressed, slowly, kissed slowly but with a growing and eager passion, and whispered and laughed and licked and bit, then fucked each other to oblivion.

Didn't happen.

Another of those rare occasions: me, telling a lie. That's not what I want. This is not the story of my life, at least not the story of all of it, but it is the story of my father. And what a story!

At last the time has come for me to tell this, and what I want is an honest job, no tricks; well, not many tricks. Honestly. The truth is like apple pie and mother. Nobody could be against it. Right? True, there is a problem, but it has nothing to do with the truth, it's this: I don't know where to start. That's not true. I know precisely.

Photo: Barry Lewis

The story begins where it ends, and the point of arrival and departure is not an event, not a conversation or a remembered emotion or a portentous moment in history, but the name of my birthplace.

Composure. Composure is not, of course, the name of the place in question, or the name of any place as far as I know (a sleepy hollow in the American heartland, perhaps—Composure, Iowa, pop. 637, it could be home to an evangelical church of unusual fanaticism or the township chosen by alien pod-people to begin their conquest of earth), but I would like to say a few words on the subject, on composure, and on the fact that I used to have it and now I don't. Time was when I would sit alone in a restaurant or a railway carriage, and my composure would be remarked upon. 'Look at that fellow over there,' it would be said, 'doesn't it strike you how *composed* he is.' I had many friends. I didn't approach people; they approached me, attracted by my composure. Now it's different. On a bad day I'm like the bums you see in the street. I talk to myself and fidget and feel lost, and there is a spot in the dripping damp corridor of the hotel where I live which fills me with such terror and despair that when I pass it I no longer know who I am.

What am I saying?

My name is Headingley Hamer.

Absurd, I admit, but that statement is true.

I was born in the noble Scottish city of Edinburgh.

And that one isn't. Listen to what my life would have been if it were. As a small child I would have been raised in a strict but comfortable Protestant faith. I would have played with ancient clockwork toys, drunk warm milk with wholemeal biscuits crumbled into the cup and secretly shot paper-darts at my grim but kind nanny. She would have had a face like an animal which bites and cannot be shaken off without loss of flesh; that's it, she would have looked like a ferret. On wet afternoons she would have taken me to many of the places described in the less sensational fiction of Edinburgh's favourite son Sir Walter Scott; not, of course, that even the more sensational fiction of Sir Walter Scott could be described as racy. But then that's the point about Edinburgh.

Adolescence? It would have brought neither acne nor grubby masturbatory fantasy but rather the wearing of the coarse but durable family tartan, Saturday afternoons on the terraces at Murrayfield watching rugby football and mathematics lessons on an oak desk (an item of Scottish furniture that could be traced back to the Jacobite rebellion) carved with the names of generations of former pupils of the distinguished academy I would without doubt have attended. My life would have continued to be a catalogue of comforting detail and later I would have married the plain but, yes, yes, red-haired girl whom I had known since I was twelve and who played the violin with moderate skill. With her I would have discussed ballooning property prices and our shared outrage at the melting down of whales for margarine. Later still it would have been children with names like Jack and Alice and Ben, lunch-time concerts of Mozart and Bach and Vivaldi (that modern stuff? like cats fighting), and each year on Hogmanay and never on any other night, a binge involving real ale and rare brands of high-grade malt whisky.

In Edinburgh, I would have been filled with an Edinburghian sense of tedium and contentment. In Edinburgh, I would not have become notorious.

I'll explain.

I was born in Deptford and I could have joined The Rolling Stones.

All right, that's a bit much, but it's true, I *was* asked, in the summer of 1969, eight days before Brian Jones was found face down and drugged and dead in his swimming-pool. Jagger and Richards had already decided that Jones was on his way out, which was why they came to me. My reply: 'My father thinks it would be an unwise career decision.' That was telling them. Disaster then smacked into my life with the inevitable impact of a bus with no brakes.

I had been living in London with a woman called Jane, doing the things people of our age were supposed to dŏ: fucking, dancing, smoking dope. We discussed the revolution. We speculated on whether it would be a month or a fortnight before it arrived. In preparation we read the Marxist works of Herbert Marcuse and the necromantic ones of Aleisteir Crowley. Remember, this was 1969.

Frisbee-ownership was the mark of intellectual achievement.

I was on the way up: a guitarist in the rhythm-and-blues band that would later become famous as Dr Feelgood, the lover of a woman with full lips and hair the colour of Pacific sand. Everyone was agreed: The Rolling Stones needed me, not me them. I was going to make it big on my own, and while basking in the radiance of this certainty I returned to the flat one afternoon to find the living-room empty, the kitchen empty and the bedroom—empty. Not so the bathroom, and here I saw: sodden towel snaked across the floor, mirror misty with steam, water dripping from a dull brass tap, one splash and then another, bouncing into the bath where Jane lay with a movie smile on those Monroe lips. Her head rested on her left shoulder, as if there were fur or something else soft there—she liked soft things—and she was wanting to rub her cheek against it. I saw the colour of the water and my first thought was that she was trying a new bath oil. My first thought was wrong. Cuts ran up the inside of her arms, straight and deep, and not red now but almost black: like looking inside an ants' nest. I reacted predictably. That's to say, I felt sick, I thought I would faint, my legs did buckle at the knee. She had opened her veins. I remember asking myself what had happened to the razor. I pictured, down there below the surface, its edge lying against the enamel of the tub or against her wet and still-warm flesh. To this day I can't touch a razor-blade without a tremor.

There was no note. Thirty minutes later, the police arrived. A sergeant with breath like a lager and vindaloo hangover asked if she had been drunk or doped or pregnant, and if we had been arguing. He picked up a spoon from the kitchen table and lifted it to his nose. He sniffed ostentatiously.

'Do you do H?'

'Excuse me?'

'H. Horse. Heroin, sonny.'

I laughed. Couldn't help it, have always enjoyed the ironic, the absurd.

'You think this is a joke?'

'Excuse me,' I said, 'it's just that we weren't into drugs. But I don't know for sure. You never really can. She says she's happy, she says she wants to be married and have our children, she says she's got everything to look forward to. Then, this. I don't understand. But imagine it. Understanding everything about another human being. Each thought, each memory, each detail of every experience. Your head would explode.'

He gave a weary sigh, saying: 'Isn't it the truth?'

Except it isn't. The truth, I mean.

I didn't have a girl-friend named Jane, who therefore did not kill herself in the patrician manner. Never played the guitar, didn't meet Jagger and Richards, never—believe it or not—smoked dope or had opinions on the imminence or otherwise of a second English revolution. Never wanted to be a rock star, was not invited to join The Rolling Stones.

Oh dear. Another of those rare occasions.

It's not that I don't want to tell this story. It's not that I feel forced to do so. It's not that I'm calculating these fantasies. I don't know where they come from. Do you? It's just that I'm having trouble getting going. I'll start again, and this time it'll be the whole truth.

I was born in London, the only child of prosperous parents who had voted Conservative at every election since 1945. But that doesn't mean I equate West Indians and Asians with muggers, cruisers, spliff-smokers, dealers in hard drugs and thieves with lists of video-hiring homes so long they can't remember whether they did or didn't. Not in all cases. I have noticed, however, that these blacks with their funny haircuts and radios which resemble suitcases are *responsive to the moon*. I watch and see that when the moon is full they drop to their knees and howl like wolves. Or Alsatians. I don't say violence is the answer; I say ballots not bullets, and the time I was involved in the public castration and crucifixion of a black steward on the York-Inverness Express (I had endured a less than adequate lunch of Chicken Kiev; he wore trousers the colour of an acceptable burgundy; the train was on time) was an unfortunate case of mistaken identity. I say that truth is: SPADES GO HOME AND IRA PSYCHOPATH OUT.

I also say: ALOHA FROM ELVIS IN HAWAII.

Did that get you going? I bet you guessed. It wasn't the whole truth or even a bit of the truth. In fact, none of it was true. I am no racist, fascist, National Front groupie or admirer, closet or otherwise, of the John Birch Society. My white hood and robes are forgotten in a drawer. It is quite a time since I was involved in either a castration or a crucifixion. Whew! That's the good news. Now for the bad. My story is utterly immoral, by which I do not mean that it consists merely of sex and comedy and thrills but that it has no message, nothing to prove.

I'll tell you something. Morality is not a regular fellow. Morality makes promises which he doesn't keep. Morality makes demands and gives nothing back. Morality does not buy his round. Now I'm returning the favour. The race issue, for instance, is granted the briefest of walk-ons and only appears at all because I would never have met Maclaren and therefore would never have followed him into the hellish back-room of a pub called the Hand of Glory and therefore would never have received a gun from the blackest black man I ever met had the police not shocked an Indian cook into heart-attack and death while searching for looted silverware in the gurgling curry cauldrons of his Lumb Lane restaurant, thus precipitating the worst riot in the history of Bradford.

I've said it.

Bradford is the place I've been trying not to mention.

I was born in Bradford.

Bradford is in the north of England, a city of mill chimneys and grotesque Victorian statuary. But for me Bradford isn't a city but a dream of a department store at the top of a hill so vertiginously steep it seems that the whole building is about to break loose and roll down at any moment. I am on the top floor, lost, wandering among lawn-mowers and garden furniture, and then I am in the lift where the operator works a wheel with a shiny brass handle as we descend, at first smoothly from floor to floor, but then dropping at alarming speed and at last free-falling with no hope of a stop. My feet are stapled to the floor.

For me Bradford is fear. I think of the place as a personal enemy and I know I am right. In Bradford it was always a damp, drizzly November of the soul, and Bradford is where it starts.

But let me tell you about where I am now. I live in 'Wonderland', a crumbling hotel at the north end, the end populated by muggers and screamers and mad poor people, the *wrong* end of the Holloway Road in London. I'm alone most of the time. Scrape a razor down my cheek alone, brush my teeth alone, wash my hair alone with a mild anti-dandruff shampoo (it says you can use it as often as you like, no split ends), spend much of the day alone in my room, take a solitary drink in a pub and talk to no one, sleep by myself and dream dreams which involve only me. It hasn't always been this way. I've been married, I've been in love, I've been so alive that I wanted to shout for joy in the street. Now I suffer what the poet Goethe called *Weltschmerz* (dissatisfaction with the world) and *Ichschmertz* (dissatisfaction with the self). Only someone possessed of a truly Teutonic thoroughness could have thought up the combination; that Goethe, well, I don't know, I tell you, I have my doubts. He must have been a barrel of laughs.

Back to business.

I was born in Bradford, and at night Helen slept among the coffins downstairs.

Helen was my sister, and that's not meant to be another of those flashy first sentences, though I admit I love beginnings, the way they promise all that is to follow and propel the hero—unaware of his chances of success or failure—into the world.

Where was I?

It was the winter of 1959, the winter our mother hadn't died, and at night Helen went downstairs to sleep among the coffins. She would pick one at random and climb inside.

Let me tell you about heroes. A hero should do his heroic stuff and make his exit, otherwise he finds himself tempted to become boss of the new order he has created, turns himself into a tyrant and spends nervous years looking over his shoulder for the next hero in line. Look what happened to Perseus, Theseus, Oedipus, all those Greek fellows: betrayed by a wife, thrown from a cliff, eyeballs punctured. No good, that's what happened, because they didn't stride into the Greek sunset when they had the chance. Think what Jesus would have been like thirty years on: alone and lonely in a palace of cool white marble built by followers in honour of His successful revolution, worrying that He can't quite manage the tricks with the water and loaves and fishes which used to engage the populace so, worrying that the Christian splinter groups are getting uppity in Northern Judea and that each hand He touches could be an assassin's, that He can no longer control His bladder, that the last few drops always leave a stain on His kingly robes and that, most of all, the bitch Mary Magdalene is at it again with Peter. What a drag! The Son of God's best move was getting Himself up on that Cross, where He actually begged the Romans to do the business with the nails and thorns and spear. They had no idea, those witless helmet-heads; they were dupes of His scheme to die and become immortal. That's the trouble with heroes, you see: you can't trust their motives. Not like me: you can trust mine, but then I'm no hero.

It was the winter of 1959, the winter our mother and so on. At night Helen would go downstairs, etc. She would pick one at random and climb inside. She was only four years older than me, yet she had already experienced many lifetimes. At least, that was her story.

I didn't believe a word of it. At the time Helen was eleven and I was, well, work it out for yourself. No, please don't bother. I dare say you're too lazy to go back and I certainly don't want to risk losing your attention. So, you win, I was seven and my sister reminded me of Joan of Arc. All right, I'm giving to childhood the judgements and language of—oh, dear—maturity, but that's what she was like. She had a pale face and short black hair. Her voice was solemn and deep, filled with passion. She told me that our grandfather invented the submarine, that the River Aire flowed through Bradford on a bed of diamonds, that the Nazi dagger with the swastika sawn off which our father had was in fact a sword with magic powers, and I believed her. But not about the coffins. I couldn't allow myself to believe what she said about the coffins. I dared not think about it.

She had other scary ideas. For instance, she read the stories of Edgar Allan Poe and believed them as if they were newspaper reports, dispatches from a battlefield or a pit disaster. Her world was made up of derelict mansions, the fear of being buried alive, razor-edged pendulums which descended towards helpless victims and a plague which was not a matter of fiction but raged in fact in Busby's department store at the top of Manningham Lane, transmitted among the glass counters—from hosiery to perfumes to ladies' lingerie—by hissing pneumatic tubes normally used to convey cash and change.

During daylight, she said, our house seemed normal: a tall Victorian building of soot-blackened stone, on a hill overlooking the city, with gables and a big white door and steps leading down to the outside entrance of a cellar. During daylight you could look through the windows and see curtains, light-fittings, glass bird ornaments on the mantelpiece and our brother Keith's bike propped against the living-room wall where its chain had spread an oily smear on the paint. But at night, she said, at night it was transformed and filled not only with singing corpses, but with candles lit to protect dead souls from demons, non-corporeal women demanding satisfaction from equally non-corporeal lovers and an aborted foetus pickled in a jar in the kitchen.

Gosh!

Then, on the day with which I begin my story, Helen came up with an extra twist.

She said, 'Remember the pendulums I told you about?'

I did.

'There's one in the cellar. Our Dad's had it fitted, down there with all the coffins.'

She imitated the pendulum's long and terrifying arc. '*Swish* down, and *swish* up and, *swish* down and *swish*, cut out your heart, I'll eat it from a dish.'

My sister could talk in rhyme.

'You're a laugh,' I said.

'Is that right? Imagine choking on a fly. Its wings are in your throat, rattling and buzzing. You feel its life. It's *there*. And then it's gone, you've swallowed it. You don't feel it any more. But it's not gone really, its life has just become part of your life. The fly is *you*.'

'Get lost.'

She tapped a finger on her temple, saying, 'The show is in our heads, you see. It's not ghosts in white and skeletons that walk around going *clank-clank-clank*. The big show is in our heads. You've not got a clue, our kid. Not one single clue.'

I knew she was right, that was how I felt, clueless. In those days I had no character. So adults said. For them character was the conceptual opposite of bad reports, skipping school, leaning forward to kiss the back of girls' necks in class, spending too much time scared by Helen's stories and being clueless. 'You're like your father,' I was told. 'No character.' Later I would develop lots, too many perhaps, different characters for different situations, a sweep of characters such as Mr Charming, Mr Melancholy, Mr Passionate, Mr McLiberal-Feminist (a Scot—yes, I can do voices) and Mr Disgusting After Eight Pints and Three Greasy Hamburgers. Even I didn't like *him* very much. And that's enough of those Comic Capitals. Just to say: I was able to twist my soul at will. My soul was, is, made of rubber. This was, is, especially so with women. I expect you want to know how this has affected my love-life. Well, later. You'll have to wait.

For now it's back to Helen. 'You'll see,' she was saying. 'There's a man down there now, in the cellar. He's waiting, he's not ready yet, not opening up his valves. And you ought to see them, they're huge things like on the organ in the church at the bottom of the lane. He'll be ready one day soon, we'll go down there, you'll see the pendulum swing, hear a dead man sing.'

I didn't argue. You couldn't disagree with Helen. She thought things, therefore they were so; always the totalitarian metaphysician, my sister. None of which would have been of the least concern—it wouldn't have mattered at all—had it not been for a curious fact: there *were* coffins in the cellar, towering stacks of them, black and smelling sweetly of varnish.

I went to see my father. I would ask him about the cellar. But to get to his office I had to go first through the garage where Billy Crow had a bucket between his boots and was washing the black Rolls-Royce. He saw me and held a sponge over his head as if it were a trophy. A vast fist squeezed and soapy water came in a torrent, gushing over his head, down his cheeks and neck, rolling from his bare shoulders and puddling on the floor. I said, 'You're an idiot, Billy,' which was true, though I didn't know it then. At the time Billy Crow was just something else I was scared of. My father called him the Human Horse, said he had once carried a piano on his back all the way from Bradford to Blackpool, over forty miles. I was scared of his shaggy size and strength, scared of his lurching walk and his lumpy arms, scared most of all of his cavernous, crack-toothed grin. 'You're daft, Billy,' I called as I ran up the wood steps to the office, not looking over my shoulder to see if Billy was grinning the grin, which I knew he would be.

My father lay on the floor, surrounded by books and bills and magazines. His hands were clasped behind his head and he glanced mournfully at an empty glass which rocked on his chest. The phone was ringing.

I said, 'Dad, what about the phone?'

'Fellow I knew spent £2,000 on whisky in 1947. In *1947*, Headingley, can you believe it? Forty pounds a week, thirty-six shillings a bottle, two bottles a day. That's what I call drinking.'

The phone stopped. I said, 'Dad, I wanted to ask you something.'

'Birds or fish, Headingley, what do you think?'

'Dad?'

The phone started up again. My father took a hand from behind his head and waved it vaguely. 'Would you mind?'

I was about to pick up the phone when he protested, 'Not the phone, Headingley, *the bottle*.'

I poured whisky into his glass.

'There's a fellow in Manchester sells birds' eggs. But not just any birds, oh no, these are extraordinary birds. Eagles and peacocks. Vultures and kestrels. Condors. And not just any eggs. We could have an aviary up in the loft, because these eggs are *fertilized*. Birds will hatch from them. Huge exotic things. We'll have to train them so they'll always come back. Think of the feathers, yellow and black. Or red, burning like poppies. And think of the beat of their wings. What a picture!'

'Dad,' I said, 'Helen's been saying something. About the cellar.'

'Or fish. We could get a big tank. They make one in the shape of a Sputnik. They do, there's a picture in one of the magazines. Think of that, Headingley. Local fish, tropical fish, fighting fish. *In orbit*.'

I realized it was no good trying to talk to him at the moment. My mother had an expression for when he was like this: she would say that he had gone to see the elephant.

'It would be amazing,' he said, and went into a reverie, sipping at the whisky and ignoring the phone which had started to ring yet again. He was silent for some moments. Then: 'Indeed it would.'

I said, 'Dad, the phone is ringing.'

'Fish, yes I think so, definitely fish. It's the more practical option. In the Sputnik tank.'

'Dad,' I repeated, 'the telephone's ringing.'

'Of course it is, old chap. But not to worry,' he said, examining his watch. 'It's time for an adventure.'

Thus: my father. It's right that he should make his entrance this way, with a big lunatic close-up. He had a thin moustache and a flair for melodrama. Loved cricket, hated work. Cultivated an air of suave indifference borrowed from Fred Astaire and the musical comedies of the 1930s. Was interested in any woman who wasn't my mother. He had been a pilot in the war, flying bombers, Blenheims and Lancasters, first from a desert airfield in North Africa and then from the chalk escarpments of Lincolnshire. His memories of that time were not what you would expect. No comic-book heroics. He remembered that in the air his feet had always been cold, that between missions in England he had driven a battered Alvis along roads built faultlessly straight by homesick Romans nearly two thousand years ago—'Think how old this country is, Headingley. No wonder it's tired out,' he said—that he had spent his twenty-first birthday in Alexandria, where he had his own three feet of polished zinc at a bar and the lager was pulled into frosted glasses and he ate and drank all night for ten shillings.

My first memory? We are in a car; he is driving fast and a little recklessly, driving (in fact) like a lunatic. He grins, nods in the direction of the speedometer—it reads 105 miles per hour—and lifts his hands from the wheel. Then he laughs the laugh which I have inherited from him, a joyful and raucous and out-of-control sound, the laugh of someone who senses his trolley could spin off the rails at any moment. And he sings: '*Yes, we have no bananas, we have no bananas tod-a-a-ay*.'

That's not true. It's true that it happened and true, certainly, about the laugh and the song, but my first memory of him is something else and concerns not him but rather his absence. I am four years old and he tells my mother he is stepping out of the house. We need some milk, he'll only be five minutes, he won't even take his coat, but soon it's six hours, twelve, a day later and still he hasn't come back. A policeman comes to the house and stares at my mother's legs as she gives her report, and smiles uneasily when he sees I'm staring at *him*. He squashes my hair with a fat hand and asks if I would like to wear his helmet. It drops over my head on to my shoulders and suddenly I am in a bell tower, dark and echoey, listening to his booming voice: there is nothing he can do, it's a family affair and in any case all Bradford knows Jack Hamer is a bad 'un but he always turns up in the end, more's the pity. After a week we're short of money. While Helen and Keith are at school, my mother and I act as guides for an Irish piano tuner, blind, going with him from house to house to earn extra cash. One afternoon, as reward, my mother takes me to Lister Park where there is a zoo and a snake, a python I think, its once opulent skin now resembling a mouldy rug. Perhaps it doesn't like the cage. Perhaps it doesn't like Bradford. I remember thinking that either way I'd rather be the python than the hamster, white and gold and with brown eyes, and each hair standing on end, which is backed into a corner waiting for its co-tenant to wake up and start contemplating tea. After twenty-two days my father comes back, with no explanation but with a bottle of milk in either hand.

He says, 'I got two, just to be on the safe side.'

What else? Oh yes.

He was in the death business. It doesn't seem accurate to describe him as an undertaker, a word which suggests stove-pipe hats, pale faces like watery mashed potato and long black coats ballooning in the wind. That was scarcely my father's style, though he *was* an undertaker. In 1945, aged twenty-three, he had inherited the business from his father's brother, my Great Uncle Willy. One war was over and for him another had begun. The problem was that Bradford had a surfeit of undertakers, men who had been doing the job for a long time with great skill, career undertakers with undertakerly names: Twiggy Fawcett, Amos Bass, Hirsh

McMahon, Ebenezer Crier and (I'm not making this up) Herbert W. Tristram Coffin. For more than ten years stubborn Bradfordians refused to die in sufficient numbers and the result was a race for each corpse and the sabotage of funerals. My father was unconcerned. He did not dream the diligent undertakerly dreams of Amos Bass, whose heavy boots were always the first to creak up any mourner's path, or the devious undertakerly ones of Twiggy Fawcett, who carried no flesh on his bones and whose skeletal frame stalked moonlit cemeteries with a spade filling in graves which had been dug in advance. Instead he dreamed of a coup. Like Napoleon, he believed the opposition could be dealt with at a stroke, once and for all, *spectacularly*. But in 1959 business was at a low and he was still waiting for Austerlitz. Hence the coffins, bulk-bought from a carpenter in Goole and piled high in the cellar. My father was stocking an arsenal for the campaign.

They were filming at Taylor's Mill. That's the adventure my father mentioned, which begins the story that ends with my mother's death. She was tall, black-haired and dressed in red, a wicked queen from a fairy-tale. No, not my mother—be precise, Headingley—I'm not talking about her any more, but about the film star Diana Farrell. She stood among a crowd of technicians and other actors, laughing and talking with them, yet somehow apart, stamping her feet on the slick and shining cobbles, crossing her arms over her chest and hugging her shoulders as if she were cold. My father offered his coat.

Not an innocent gesture.

'Come with me,' he said.

Nor an innocent command.

The brown eyes of one of Diana Farrell's companions looked my father up and down. He was tanned and handsome, and wore a natty tweed suit. He said, 'And w-w-w-h-at have we here? B-b-bradford's Sir Walter R-r-r-r-alegh, I presume.'

This stammered pronouncement brought laughter from the rest, including Diana Farrell. It wasn't that my father ignored this amusement; he didn't even notice. He was back in the war, landing a plane in dodgy weather. She was the beacon from which he dared not look away; all else was fog. He had gone to see the elephant.

He said, 'You must come. There's something you have to look at.'

The man said, 'Oh, Diana, for God's sake, this one looks like R-r-ronald Colman after two g-gins t-t-t-oo many.'

The others hooted, but this time Diana Farrell did not join in. Instead she gave a casual twirl to the bag which hung from her wrist. She looked at me, saying, 'And you? Who are you, soldier?'

My father did not take his eyes from hers. He said, 'He's my better half, my trouble-shooter. I'd be lost without him. I tell you, he's quite a fellow my kid brother and an invaluable adviser on my business affairs.'

'I bet he is,' she said. 'And what is that business?'

'I'm an architect. Come with me. I'll rebuild your life, you'll see.'

I heard the languid and honeyed voice once more. 'That's r-r-ight, Diana. You go slumming. See where it lands you. N-n-n-eck deep in it I shouldn't wonder. Bloody yokels. They resent everything we stand for. Beauty, wealth and t-t-talent.'

But by then my father had already taken Diana Farrell's arm, and we had already turned our backs; so much for the brown-eyed handsome man.

We went to the cooling tower. Not every mill had one but because there were so many mills it seemed that the city was dominated by these hourglass structures of black brick, 150 feet high, looming over the terraces and streets and over the men and women who trooped to work each day in flat caps and formless coats.

My father said, 'These things are miracles of design. The safest shape for a building of this size, the most economical shape for a building of this size, the most *practical* shape for a building of this size. It was proven by a team of engineers. Swedish fellows I think they were.'

He paused before we went in. 'Which is funny when you think about it,' he said, and his hands made a mime of the female form. 'Because *that's* what they remind me of. A regiment of monstrous women, standing guard over Bradford. Everywhere you look.'

'Are you an architect or a comedian,' she said. 'Or just a woman-hater.'

He told her he was a criminal millionaire, and I groaned

inwardly. Even now I can think of few greater embarrassments than hearing someone else lying while in pursuit of sex. Or telling the truth while so engaged. Then she asked the question I was asking myself.

'And what would a criminal millionaire want from me?'

My father, of course, did not answer.

In the cooling tower we found piles of cinders and smoking ash, charred bales of spoiled wool, and pieces of old machinery, almost unrecognizable now, their shapes distorted and made wild by the heat that blasted them when the mill was working. High above us was the sky, an oval of luminous grey, and the light was strange, a faint clouding, almost like steam, as if it had struggled hard to get down this far and then given up, but not before exhaling a last, dying breath.

She said, 'What is this place?'

'I love you.'

'Is it dangerous?'

'I have always loved you.'

'Is it dangerous?'

'I will always love you.'

'Where do those go?' she said, pointing to steps which ran round the inside of the tower, up and up in a dizzying spiral towards the sky.

'Do you still do theatre? Or is it just films now that you've hit the big time.'

'I hate theatre. It's just some man in black swanning around doing this,' she said and issued a theatrical sigh, *aaaaaghhh*. 'Let's go to the top.'

My father made a face. 'You want to go to the top?'

'I want to go to the top.'

So we did. I assure you it wasn't as easy as it sounds. Minute after minute went by and still we trudged on and on, up and round, round and up, until my shins began to ache and my father's breath became a wheezing pant. Diana Farrell was unconcerned. She moved ahead, her step light as a dancer's.

I said, 'Dad, what are we doing?'

He paused on the heat-cracked brick. He told me he'd been asking that himself. He was developing a theory. It concerned his own character. There were situations, he realized, when he found himself behaving in a way that seemed to have been predetermined. These situations concerned women and were not questions of mere lust or momentary infatuation. True, he did sleep with some of the situations and some did last only a single night. But others went on for years. My mother, for instance, was one of those situations. He had known it the first time he saw her, realized he was just a bear led on a chain, unable to help himself. The other mystery was that he never knew when they would finish. It could happen slowly or as suddenly as a gunshot: *bang*, mortally wounded situation. While they lasted, though, they were exhilarating. He invited me to consider what we were doing: climbing steep and perilous steps in pursuit of an actress whose fascination was not her beauty so much as the fact that she reminded him of what it was to be younger and fresher to the world. And perhaps the fascination was not even that, perhaps it was just that she was a face he would not routinely see in Bradford. Perhaps he had no idea of the true nature of her fascination, but he was impelled. She was a situation, a chance to see the elephant. The erotic can turn to farce very easily, he told me, but he was prepared for that. His passport listed his occupation: sexual fatalist.

Of course, he said nothing like that.

He really said, 'Orgasm, no slapstick.'

No, no, no.

'Striking a spark.'

Nor that. In fact, he said nothing, because I was too tired, too intent on the trudge, too nervous of his reaction to ask the question.

We made it at last. We were dirty and out of breath. Diana Farrell had somehow kept her red dress spotless and had almost finished smoking a cigarette. The pack and lighter were on a ledge and as my father approached she made a slight adjustment of their position, not a nervous gesture, but quite conscious, as if she were building a protective wall.

My father was the gesture's equal. He crushed the wall and took her hand. I could sense the closeness of the elephant: *thump-thump-thump*.

'So,' he said, still gasping. 'Will you marry me?'

'You're barmy. Besides, you're married already and I'm filming in South America next month. Me and Carmen Miranda.'

He sang, '*Braaaaaa-zzzil.*'

'You are barmy,' she said. 'You were barmy all those years ago, and you're still barmy now.'

'I didn't know if you remembered.'

'Nineteen fifty-one. In London. You'd been in some car race. You were wearing a big bath towel like a toga. Drunk, of course. As a lord.'

'I heard you married.'

'My agent. Turned out he was fucking one of the cocktail girls from the Moonlight. Remember that place? The barman had a sleepy eye and chewed everything in multiples of twelve. I didn't say a word. Just waited for a couple of weeks then cleaned out our joint account. Took the cash and went to Paris for a month. Before I left I hit him hard enough to make his clients' book dizzy. We're divorced, thank God.'

'Another man?'

'What did you say your job was now?'

'I work for the devil. I walk the streets of Bradford with a case full of contracts and a wallet full of cash. Souls at a fiver a time.'

'You don't say.'

'I'm an undertaker.'

'Now I really don't believe you.'

Enthusiastic confirmation from me: 'It's true, miss. There are coffins in our basement. My sister says there's a pendulum as well, with this sharp edge like a sword, for torturing people.'

'Your sister says *what*?'

'So you two are a double act.'

'Haven't you noticed? Headingley and I are such terribly gloomy fellows. Just like undertakers.'

Diana Farrell was laughing now. 'You had a son,' she said, 'and you called him "Headingley". Why didn't you just tie a rock round the poor little devil's neck?'

Did I explain about my name? It was—need I say?—my father's idea. With my mother it would have been something respectable and unremarkable, like Mark or Matthew or

Christopher, that was what she wanted, and it was while she lay in bed recovering from my birth that my father slipped along to the registration office at Bradford Town Hall, a building whose design resembles nothing so much as a Venetian dream palace of the late Baroque period. Once there he played out an ornate fantasy all his own. You see, it was his theory that there was a magic in Christian names. Who, he said, would dream of calling their child Adolf? To do so would be the guarantee of such contempt and mockery that the child would certainly turn out, if not such a rascal as Hitler, at least a rotten fellow. Conversely, he argued, the right sort of Christian name could act as inspiration, and since he was obsessed with cricket, it was his only ambition for me that I should play for Yorkshire and aged nineteen score a maiden century against one of the despised southern counties, he called me not Herbert or Leonard (after Sutcliffe and Hutton, great batsmen) as those names had meanings beyond the game, but Headingley, which has one association only. Headingley is the home of Yorkshire County Cricket Club; I am named after a cricket field.

At this point, Diana Farrell was jack-knifed over the edge of the tower, waving with enthusiasm. The brown-eyed handsome man was below, not bothering to gesture in reply. 'The director,' she explained. 'We've been having a fight.'

'I suppose that means,' said my father, 'that you're fucking him.'

'Is there something wrong with your lips? They seem stuck to your gums.'

'It was my smile. I was thinking that it's nice to see you again.'

And then he leaned forward to kiss her, but she moved away, saying, 'It's nice to see *you*. But I won't sleep with you. That was then and now I have a policy not to sleep with men while their children are in the stalls.'

'Who says I want to sleep with you? Who says he's my child?'

The cock crowed for the second time.

'Still the Don Juan, aren't you?'

'Don't talk to me about him. He was just an over-publicized Spaniard. Bloody fellow would have resented everything I stand for.'

'And what's that?'

My father smiled: 'Beauty, wealth and t-t-alent.'

I've told that as it happened. I had no idea my father already knew Diana Farrell until we were on top of the cooling tower. After that I became his alibi on frequent elephant-viewing expeditions. It went on for weeks. Went on in haphazard fashion because he refused to make arrangements, saying that people who did that needed lines on writing-paper and squeezed toothpaste from the bottom of the tube. So each afternoon he'd collect me from school and we went down to Taylor's Mill where the first question was always: would we find her? Sometimes the answer was quick, there she was, a slender arm raised high in greeting if she wanted to see him or in dismissal if she didn't. Sometimes the answer took longer: she wasn't on set, or they were shooting, and we would have to hang around. It didn't seem to bother my father either way: he was content to wait and then try to seduce her all over Bradford.

He took her to the reservoir at Wrose, where he got out of the car and lay in the mud in front of the wheels, saying he wouldn't move unless she told him she loved him in return. She said he knew it was impossible, because he was married with children and she was worried about James, her director, the brown-eyed, etc.

My father: 'I dreamed he killed us both. With his camera. Just crushed us with it. There we were, strawberry jam, underneath the arc lights.'

Her: 'I *am* sleeping with him.'

Him: 'Loot. I need to get my hands on considerable amounts of the stuff. I need loot. Or boodle. Do you think James can help?'

He told her, smiling, that he was suffering somewhere, that he had always suffered, that yes, he was very jolly, adored the colour red, that his bird was the hawk and his aeroplane a Merlin-roaring Lancaster, but that the moral engines were going and he was about to drop from the sky.

She said, 'You talk too much,' which he did, and so do I, another habit I picked up from him. But how was she to suspect, and how was I, that in this case what seemed lies was truth?

Or was it?

By the time he took her to the cricket ground at Windhill where my grandfather once played with Learie Constantine, the West Indian who wore silk shirts buttoned always at the wrist, even on blazing summer days when the five poplars on the northern boundary stood motionless in the heat, the weather had turned into Bradford weather, brutish and black. We sat in the car. Rain thumped on the roof. My father had a half-bottle of whisky. The bottle was in the shape of a bell. He said, 'I'm going to do something very strange. I'm going to be completely honest.'

Oh, very smart that, very casual indeed.

'I'm in bad trouble. There's a fellow called Gannister. He's after my neck.'

Diana Farrell was unmoved. She wore a thin-lipped smile, as if she'd heard it before. Father pressed on. The elephant.

'Gannister made a fortune after the war, selling cars with nylons stuffed in the gearbox. Muffled the noise, you see, so you couldn't tell what a mess the whole crate was. He's got a garage on the Leeds Road, a lock-up in Guiseley, a farm up Bingley way. Something else somewhere else. Drives a Cadillac with a shotgun in the boot. Says he's shot three men, and I bet drool was coming out of his mouth while he did it.'

She said, 'Sounds like the booze talking.'

'I don't drink so much, you know,' he said, taking another life-size swig. 'Just enough to keep a couple of shots ahead of reality. And Gannister.'

'Sounds like self-pity.'

But my father shook his head and had another drink.

'I was wrong. You have changed. What happened to you, Jack?'

'I became an undertaker.'

'You were always an undertaker.'

'I remember when I met you. You wore a green satin hat and a dress like an explosion in a firework factory. Not a week has gone by when I haven't thought of you. Not a single week. I lived for a moment when I knew you. I need you.'

Really! I assume he had heard that line in a film. In the car there was a smell of whisky and warm leather. The elephant was close. He laid a hand on her cheek. He stroked her arm. They kissed. I remember how I thought of it: like pulling a toy arrow from glass, the rubber sucker resisting at first then coming away with a wet plop.

'Headingley, old fellow, wouldn't you fancy a bag of crisps?' said my father, looking at me over Diana Farrell's shoulder. He winked and gave me a two-shilling piece.

I was on the cricket square in the rain. My father, I realized, had a life beyond the one I knew. It involved secrecy and deceit. I wonder what my father cared for really? Did he care about the simplicities, the decencies of the human heart. Do I? I was resentful and thrilled. I found a rotting apple and off-breaked it, imagining that it had fooled Constantine and sent him back to the pavilion, silk sleeves fluttering.

Looking back, I saw rain bouncing from the windscreen of the now gently rocking car.

It was the night of the *conversazione*. I was with Helen, Keith and my mother, and we were on our way to Saltaire.

'Headingley,' said my mother, 'I want to ask you something.'

I knew what was coming.

She said, 'Have you seen your father in the last few days?'

What did I do? I'll tell you, but first let me ask: what was the most important moment in the history of our species? I imagine I am a professor in a lecture hall, faced by students whose suggestions I have graciously invited. What do they think was the most important moment? The blonde at the back, whose shoes rub and whose heels are covered with wrinkled plaster, raises a plump and enthusiastic hand. From her it's . . . the invention of the wheel. *Oh yeah*? I let her know what I think, namely that the wheel was just the first of those gimmicks whose purpose was to allow people in white coats to give bragging press conferences and make a lot of money easily. The wheel was only science, I say, and science was only Frankenstein and his monster. The blonde blushes. Then it's the birth of Christ, *you must be joking*, I shout, *that fraudulent Jew boy*? The gift of fire . . . *blind man at the helm* . . . and the formation of the first social group, which doesn't even merit comment but is dismissed with an imperious punching motion. There's a silence after that, and I'm careful to give the message—it's a beam I send them from my eyes—that I'm not in a temper. True, their proposals have been banal so far, but I'm sure . . . what? I smile at the flame-haired temptress who dresses always in short tartan skirts and who says it was the distillation of the first single malt whisky, *yes that's more like it.* We laugh and there is another silence before I at last divulge. The most important moment in the history of the species? Was the telling of the first lie. It's true, I say, the human genius is for fabrication, for the creation of that which is not. As an Irish poet once said, false representation is the critical difference between man and horse.

So, on that night when my mother asked if I'd seen my father, what did I do? I examined the lemonade which Keith had spilled moments before on the rubber mat beneath our feet in the car; the liquid was spreading through the grooves, assuming the shape of a V. I demonstrated that I am no quadruped.

I said, 'No, mum, I haven't seen him at all.'

She glanced at me then, saying, 'Are you sure?'

'Yes, mum, I haven't seen him for ages.'

'He hasn't been picking you up from school?'

'No, mum.'

Helen pulled a face, Keith made an exaggerated coughing sound as he suppressed a laugh, but my mother sighed. 'I'm sorry, Headingley. I didn't mean to accuse you of lying.'

Shake, rattle and roll! I like those Irish poets.

The party was on the first floor. When we were half-way up the stairs I could hear it and as we got closer, the music and conversation grew loud. I grasped Helen's hand.

We entered the ballroom. A band thundered. A fat man in a tuxedo was trying to sing like Frank Sinatra. He had a red carnation in his buttonhole and the face of a murderer. My mother looked around and saw him at the other end of the room; my father, I mean, not the villainous crooner.

'Jack,' she said, 'I might have known I'd find you here. Never miss a party.'

But my father was smiling and already surrounded, busily

ignoring the shouts of various others. She was just one more.

Billy Crow and his sister were there. 'Us need that money, Mr Hamer,' the sister said. 'Us need it now. It's not reet you not givin' Billy 'is wages.'

Diana Farrell was there. 'Weren't you keen to show me how well you can rumba?'

And the brown-eyed handsome man: 'Can you imagine what Bradford m-m-ust have looked like to the V-v-v-v-ikings when they came through? Not exactly like stumbling on M-m-mayfair, is it?'

'Yer've bin reet good tah Billy, Mr Hamer, and ahm grateful. But bills'll not wait. Rent'll not wait.'

'If you won't dance then I'll find someone who will.'

'C-c-oming all the way from D-d-enmark in their helmets with h-h-h-h-orns on. Three m-m-onths in a bloody cold longship to f-find this. Or was it N-n-n-orway?'

'If you think I'm going to put up with much more of this, Jack, you're wrong. You're dead wrong.'

He spoke at last, but not to my mother. Instead he addressed Helen, Keith and me. 'What would you say if we moved from Bradford? We'll have a big house and a cellar for disposing of unwanted guests. A house so huge that we will never run into each other and can meet only by appointment. A house so huge we'll need a map. I'll buy you each a compass. What do you think?'

'Will there be dead men in the cellar?'

That was Helen, of course, but then it was my mother once more, saying: 'Jack, you haven't introduced me to your lady friend. That's rather rude, wouldn't you say?'

'Ah can't insist, yer knows that, Mr Hamer, and Billy'll allus do yer work 'cos Billy's like that an' don't know no better an' you're 'is friend.'

My father took out his wallet and, without counting, handed over its contents. He said, 'I hope it's enough. I have been remiss. You have my apologies. Billy, I'm very sorry.'

I looked down . . . Billy's grin.

'D-d-d-iana. Shall we trip the light f-f-fantastic?'

'There's too much 'ere, Mr Hamer.'

'Please. Take it on account. I'm not sure when I'll be able to pay Billy next.'

'Oh, very generous, Jack. Always the grand gesture. Meanwhile you haven't seen your family for a week.'

'Are we going to rumba, or aren't we?'

My father pressed the palms of his hands to his temples. 'By all means we will rumba,' he said. 'But first I must be social secretary. Muriel, may I present Diana Farrell? Diana has a degree in philosophy. From Heidelberg University. We speak only of metaphysics and lager beer. And Diana, I'd like you to meet Muriel, another of my business associates. Isn't this what Saturday night should be? A regular do.'

He looked at them both and attempted what I imagine he thought was a winning smile, which makes me wonder what my father understood about women. The answer, of course, is everything. And I understand even more. That's one of the issues at hand here, how well we have understood women, my father and I.

My mother hit him across the face. The blow sounded like a gunshot. Not that I know what a gunshot sounds like. That's not true, I do. Anyway, it was a violent unexpected sound and everything hushed. Even the singer paused from his butchery of 'Come Fly With Me'.

'Oh yes,' she said, 'it's a regular do all right. Fasten your safety belts, we're in for a bumpy night.'

'B-b-bravo, Bette Davis. I just adore amateur th-th-theatricals.'

There was laughter and the band started up again.

'Now then, what's this? Happy soddin' families?' said another voice, one we hadn't heard before, with a strong Yorkshire accent. And thus, unannounced—typical, an important character makes his entrance: *Gannister*, Captain Ahab, harpoon at the ready, in sullen and insane pursuit of something he nearly caught so long ago. The whale, the whale! Where is the whale? Here he comes.

My father said, 'Bloody hell, it's Gannister,' and slid an arm round my reluctant mother's shoulders. 'Nasty, nosy, noisy in everything but the way he comes up behind you and that's because he's worried about wasting leather on his shoes. And that's because he's worried about money. Gannister likes money, don't you old chap? If you drop it, presto! It doesn't break!'

'You're a card all right, Jack,' said Gannister with a chuckle. 'I like that about you. You're a bloody card all right.'

'But my dear fellow. That's not so. You're the one. With that fabulous American car of yours. Bradford's Jimmy Cagney. You know you are. Drive around with your molls in the back, waving to your wife and kiddies at the bus stop. Damned cool. And I'll tell you something else. Not only am I not a card, at the moment I'm sorry I'm the only man in Bradford who is not not Jack Hamer. Do you follow? Tell my associates here . . .'—pause for nod in our direction—'that I want to change. I do. I want to live quietly, away from all this. Give me the Highlands. Do you know the Highlands, old man?'

Gannister did not know the Highlands.

'Or perhaps the Islands. There's always those. Do you know the Islands?'

Gannister did not know the Islands.

'Neither Highlands nor Islands?' My father let go of my mother and took him by the arm. He said, 'Tropical fish.'

Smiling, Gannister took a cigar from his pocket and rolled it slowly along a tongue black as Bradford. He told my father to go on for as long as he liked. He loved to listen, he said, he didn't mind at all. Spit gleamed and bubbled on the cigar.

'Guppies, sword-tails. Zebras and Siamese fighting fish. Isn't there one called a Red Molly? I need to know all you know.'

Gannister just grinned.

And I grinned too, until I looked at Helen. She had turned white and was pointing. 'I've met you before. You're an evil man,' she said. Her voice shook: Joan of Arc, recently introduced to the executioner. That was how it turned out. I loved you Helen, I never told you, not really, but I did.

Gannister was still grinning. I had a dizzy sensation. I too felt sick and afraid. Though then I could not know how dangerous he was. He would do anything to achieve his goal. Yet nothing of this was visible, except perhaps in his cigar. Alight now, it was like Gannister: sleek and slightly plump and glowing with purpose. I am very much like Gannister, it seemed to say, I am Gannister, a born boss among cigars.

I hate people like that: tyrants with torture in their smiles. Don't you wish you could smash their complacency? I hate also those who are weak and so confused by their weakness that they can do nothing but wish everyone was as weak and confused as they. Spineless shits! And the people in between, I can't stand them either, the ones who carefully tread the line, neither too cocky nor too unsure, like a fellow I knew who wore a shiny grey suit and on Friday nights in subterranean wine bars grinned enthusiastically at his employer's bad jokes, you know how to get a nun pregnant, you *fuck* her, and whose life was tied up in the question of whether he could dump his girl-friend and thus afford to trade in his fast red car for a faster one of even greater redness. Mediocrity, worthless scum!

I am Hamlet!

Where was I? With Gannister, saying: 'You get nowt for nowt, Jack.'

And Keith, jumping up and down, shouting: 'And you've got a face like Boris Karloff after plastic surgery in a horror film.'

Gannister did not take his eyes from my father. 'We've got an arrangement, Jack. Remember. Nowt for nowt.'

'Lend me a fiver, will you, old man?'

Still Gannister smiled as he handed over the note. My father held it up to the light and, with the deft motions of a magician, turned its crispness between his fingers. He said, 'I have enchanting visions of what this could buy. Two bottles of Scotch. Delectable foods. A ticket for Lord's and a Dexter double-hundred. Wonderful, isn't it?'

He pulled out a cigarette lighter and turned this between his fingers with equal wonder. 'You know Gannister, someone asked me a question: "What once lost, is never found?" The answer she wanted was "the truth". But the correct answer was of course the one I gave: "A Dunhill lighter."'

There was a flame and the banknote was a butterfly of fire, hovering for a moment, then turning black and fluttering up towards the ceiling. My father said, to no one in particular, 'Shall we dance?'

Then it was more magic. Having invited Diana Farrell and the brown-eyed handsome man to our house for tea the next day, my father didn't show up. And nor did Diana Farrell. While I played a game, rolling a coin along the floor and diving to catch it in front of the floor-length glass windows,the brown-eyed handsome man talked to my mother.

I realize I haven't told you much about her. She looked like she should have been in films herself: eyes of Garbo, legs of Dietrich, mouth of Hayworth. So I exaggerate. She was small, tough and determined, and pretty, though the most remarkable feature of her appearance was her red hair. Bradford people remarked on it. 'Joost tek a look at that carrot top. Like a Roman candle on bleedin' bonfire night.'

My father took pride in her strength of character. That may seem curious. But he did; he told stories. Once, for instance, he had arranged to meet two members of the Yorkshire cricket team only to be kept waiting all night because they were with my mother, drunk in the Oddfellows Arms. Another time she thought he was with another woman in a Scarborough hotel room and arrived bent double in the dumb-waiter, leaping out with poker in hand. And then there was the occasion when mourners drove forty miles from Skipton to pay their respects to a dead relative in the Hamer Funeral Service Chapel of Rest (our living-room) and she found that the body was not there, had been buried in error the day before. So she improvised, came on strong and serious, told them there was a crisis, she'd just had a warning from the Bradford Infirmary, a fever was being transmitted by a South African bug found in the orange boxes from which coffins were sometimes made. Dangerous dead men! Sick stiffs! She told them that the house was in quarantine and after that you couldn't see them for dust.

'Why do you put up with it?'

'What?'

'Your husband.'

'This morning I took all Jack's clothes, every stitch, and threw them off the Pottle Street bridge in Shipley.'

'Women. Fiendish in search of revenge.'

'Sod that. I'm not interested in revenge.'

'What would interest you? Some sordid business in your bedroom. With me, mmm?'

She said, 'Your stammer, it's gone.'

The brown-eyed handsome man arched an imperious eyebrow. He didn't, but he did say, 'I'm a preposterous character all right, but please don't assume I'm the fool I sometimes pretend to be. And your husband thinks I am.'

'Well, I'll be buggered.'

'If such is your preferred *modus operandi.*'

That was when I dived for the coin one more time, missed, and it was goodbye window, hello deep cut in my upper arm. The drive to the hospital featured me leaking blood on Jaguar upholstery and him begging to see her again. They could take a drive, he said, or go to the c-c-c-cinema.

She said, 'I'll take the sordid bedroom business.'

My mother and the brown-eyed handsome man: there's an unexpected development. This question of men and women. Big, isn't it? And difficult. Here, for instance, is my mother, not being a mother at all. Possibilities occur to me.

1. Men do not like women, fear that they are a widely distributed species of beast of prey, know that feminism is merely the equivalent of the medieval witch's *grand grimoire* and are therefore more determined than ever to teach them not to talk or think.
2. Men like women, find that the reality is somewhat different from the expectation, discover that beyond a certain point women assume a different self, as water changes when boiling, and therefore try to teach them not to talk or think.
3. Men understand women. This sounds reasonable. Men are cool customers.
4. Men do not understand women. To confront one is to be faced with another person saying, 'I am me, I am me, I am me, I am me, I am me.' Men are themselves self-infatuated and self-deceiving and

thus certain to be shocked and outraged by this proof of the existence of un-me.

5. Men are interested in getting women to do impossible things. To do this it is necessary to find that bit of themselves which matches a bit of whichever woman they are talking to. Then, bingo! Which raises another question? Why do women suck men's penises? What could conceivably be in it for them? Search me. I mean: would you like to be force-fed tepid oysters?
6. Men are regular fellows. Women are not. Women, like morality, are reluctant to buy their round. Men know this and understand that women are capable of all sorts of beastly behaviour. A man could not have betrayed Christ, for instance. Iscariot, that miserable fuck, was a cross-dresser.
7. Men are quite right to want to spoil the fun. Women are planning a series of outrages against society. Men have played the fool for quite long . . .

Moving quickly now to the crisis. My father came back. There were no arguments about where he'd been. It was as if my mother had given up caring. But there were arguments about Gannister, who had taken to waiting outside our house in a big black American car which had a ton of polished chrome and fins leaping from the rear. Then my father went away again and Gannister didn't come any more.

One night I dreamed I was in a morgue. A corpse lying next to me asked how I died. I said I bled to death. He asked why no one came to help. It was because I was locked in the boot of a car after I'd been shot in the stomach. And him? He drowned, he said. A little girl on a slab said she had drowned too. She bet her sister that she could hold her breath for two minutes in Shipley beck. She lost the bet. Then from way down the morgue there was a huge butcher saying he'd always liked a flutter himself. He wanted to know who'd won the last race at York .

I woke up. I went downstairs. The house seemed hollow and silent. Helen was knitting in the kitchen, a grey jumper she gave me later. I liked that jumper.

She said, 'It's show time.'

I must have looked blank.

'Tonight's the night. I knew you'd come.'

I tried to continue looking blank.

'There's one down there now. I can feel him. He's tall and thin with black hair. He looked like death even when he was alive and he died horrible. His wife strangled him with a silk stocking.'

I can't remember what I felt. Yes, I can: the neon light buzzed in the silence and everything in the kitchen assumed a terrible life. Helen's knitting needles moved in clicking metallic patterns, zigzags of fear. I felt terror.

'Just a filmy thing. But it did the job. Life's so fragile. Now he wants to sing to you.'

I tried to laugh. Couldn't make a sound.

'You'll remember tonight for the rest of your life.'

That was no lie.

'Are you scared?'

'Don't be daft,' I said.

In the hall moonbeams came through the skylight. There were squares of brightness on the floor; it seemed to me that the squares were dreams, intense and peaceful dreams which did not involve going into the cellar where coffins rested on stone slabs alongside cobwebbed gas meters and jars of pickle and raspberry jam.

Helen walked on tiptoe like a cartoon burglar, pausing after each step on the black-and-white tiled floor, admiring the silence of her motion. My own walk was loud. I slapped my naked feet hard into the squares of brightness. The strategy was to wake up everyone in the house. I imagined myself sitting by the stove in the kitchen sipping cocoa from a white porcelain mug while my father lectured Helen on the importance of respect for the dead. Not to worry that he wasn't even in the house and that I had never witnessed him in any such tutorial display. He didn't bother about the dead one way or the other. It was a fine strategy.

It didn't work.

We were at the cellar door, shiny black with a knocker in the shape of a leering gargoyle. No it wasn't. It was an old, oak door, an ordinary door, but it led to the cellar and I hoped my father had locked it up tight and tossed away the key.

He hadn't.

Helen turned on her torch. A yellow beam shot into the gloom, and we followed it, past flaking whitewashed walls, down worn and creaking wooden steps. There was a smell of mildew and something rotting. Fruit, I hoped. The cold damp of the cellar was all about me like iced water.

Down and down and down, each step taken slowly, carefully, until we were at the bottom. Helen turned and made another of her cartoon burglar gestures, this time raising her finger and tapping it against her lips to signal silence. I imagined mice burrowing and spiders tensing their legs as they heard our approach. It was possible there were rats beneath the flagstones. Or on top of them. It was very possible. The cellar was filled with a gnawing life.

Helen swung the torch and its beam picked out a coffin. It was long and black and shining, with carved panels and handles of polished brass. Expensive: someone wanted to surprise the neighbours with a final, unanswerable act of one-upmanship.

She whispered, 'That's fifty quid's worth of box with a dead man inside.'

'There isn't really a body, is there?'

'Don't be so namby-pamby,' she said, shrugging. It's true, she did, but then Helen was always so sure of herself.

'I think we'd better get back upstairs before someone wakes up.'

'I think we'd better get on with it.'

I walked towards the coffin. My heart thumped so that I lost my breath. I thought my lungs would explode. I reached for one of the coffin handles, and the feel, in my palm, of the cool brass, calmed me, slightly.

'Push off the lid.'

There was silence. My chest shook. Time was rubber so stretched that I could see through it as it became thinner and thinner, like being at the dentist when it seems the tooth-plumbing will never stop and your mind reviews your life moment by moment. Then time snapped. I screwed shut my eyes and pushed.

'Go on, our kid,' said Helen, and now her voice was urgent yet gentle, a team coach encouraging a nervous rookie, as if she understood what I felt. 'Look into the box.'

So I opened my eyes. And saw forbidden knowledge, Gilles de Rais hanged for satanism and the murder of a hundred children, Adam in despair and the serpent in the garden but Eve to blame as well, and a woman in Bluebeard's back room, the one painted after his name, face to face with the circumstances of her own death.

I saw nothing of the kind. I saw a body, a man dressed in black in the coffin. I couldn't see all of his face because the forehead was wrapped with a white cloth and two pennies shone where the eyes should have been.

From behind, Helen said, 'His hair will go on growing for weeks yet. There are parts of the body that are stubborn. They won't give up the ghost. Like the parts that sing.'

She moved the torch, and a figure, grotesque and hunchbacked, appeared on the wall; my shadow. Then the torch was directly beneath her chin, shining up, giving her face a white and ghostly look. 'And you thought I was lying,' she said. 'From now on you'll know I don't tell lies.'

I thought of the man. Imagine your breath being cut off: a rattle in the throat while you still smell the apple that is still cut in two on your plate. I thought about his last supper.

There was a noise from the coffin. It was as if the man had read my thoughts and wanted to send a message. I told myself I must have imagined it. I said, 'Did you hear that?' Helen did not say whether she had or not. Then, incredible as it seems, and it did seem incredible, the man in the coffin began to speak.

He said, 'Are you sitting comfortably.'

Helen and I stared at each other. She looked as scared as I was. 'The voice,' she said, 'it sounds different. It's not usually like this. It's usually wonderful, like a voice from heaven.'

There was another sound—metal bouncing on stone—and rolling, as if two pennies . . . I knew without looking. The man was getting out of the coffin.

I imitated a gesture I'd seen made by a teacher at school, a woman who said I could be charming when I chose, that I knew how to get what I wanted if only I put my mind to it. I made the sign of the cross. It didn't get me what I wanted. The coffin-occupant was still there, talking again. 'Man has come into the forest,' he said. 'Bambi, your mother cannot be with you any more.'

I knew that voice, and I saw from Helen's face that she did too. She shone the torch. The man was looking at the corner where one of the pennies still rattled and then he raised his eyes. It was our father. Our father. He loved Walt Disney. Thus 'Bambi'. I remembered the time he had taken Helen, Keith and me to see the film. I had hidden under the seat when Bambi was lost in the forest, and he had joined me, saying, 'I say, Headingley, don't blame you at all, bit strong this.'

'Dad,' Helen said, 'you're dead, aren't you?'

What if it were true?

'You're dead and you've come back.'

'No, sweetheart, I'm not. Dead people don't talk.'

'But they do. They sing.'

He was crying. He told us dead people did not sing. It was a beautiful idea but, like many beautiful ideas, untrue. He told us our mother had died, it had happened that morning, they'd taken her to the infirmary, a blood vessel broken in the brain, we were all going to have to help each other and be very brave. He stopped suddenly as if hearing a noise. The cellar hummed.

There was nothing, just Helen whispering, 'She's dead?'

GRANTA

George Steiner
Noël, Noël

That one sound is different.

So many sounds at this time of year. I have noted twenty-seven. That of Father's footstep before he opens the front door. Lighter as the holiday nears. His stair-step, dragging when it's been a long day. That of his slippers, the furry scuff towards the tinkle of the whiskey decanter, and then the slosh in the glass. Mother's gait: quick in the dark of the morning, changing, a touch heavier after lights-on. The drum-roll of her heels, in and out. And that queer weightlessness, the pent-up breath of her step before she enters the bedroom. I won't try and list the child-music. The scamper, right to the blown tip of her hair, when off to school. The skip at the gate. She dances to herself, at times, in her room. Tap and turn. Her laughters. Stuff my ears and I can still tell you of seven sorts. They ripple across one's skin.

There are, of course, the sayings of the house. When the heating clanks on or the rain dribbles. The flushings, the wince and quease (how would you put it?) of the stair-well. More door-voices than there are registers of wind. Warmth has its sound when it slides under the kitchen door. I know them all. They prickle my scalp. But this one is different.

I may be in error. Exceeding care is in order. Like that of the rat-catcher, arched and knit to hear the faintest creak, the cut whisper in the roof-beam or trestle. Error would be unforgivable. Come Christmas, sounds mix and multiply. And are shot through with smells. The shiver of the dwarf-pine with its green smell and hiss of needles; that of the post lurching through the slot in the door, heavier now with the waxen sound and scent of the glossy brochures and catalogues; the crackle of wrappings and the whole house chiming, like the chandelier. Even the lone light in the attic sounds crystal gay. But here I must be prudent. Not only the candles in the window and on the mantelpiece give off a savour of felt and old copper; so do the electric bulbs, hung with pine-cones and holly, and on so much longer during these short days. One inhales sound and smell at one breath. Confusions may arise. (Days too soon I muddled the tide and ebb of voices from the school-yard—Penny does not have far to go in the morning, 'Not far to drop,' says Father, at which she pretends to flinch—with that of the carollers.) One cannot be too precise. I may be in error.

Photo: Allan Titmuss

Yet that sound *is* different.

When did I first hear it?

I don't remember exactly. Not exactly, that is. To which uncertainty blame attaches. Is my memory weakening? It has been formidable. Not a whistling in the street or in the house that I ever forgot or confused with any other. Last spring's early thrush, the show-off, crotchet-semi-quaver-crotchet and the rubato on the trill. Ask me when Father bought the new wellies, the lined ones, or Mother burned the roast with the guests—I caught Mr Blakemore's rancid breath, those dentures, even before he banged the door-knocker—with the guests (did I already say that?) at the front steps. Ask me about Penny's mumps and their hot smell in the room, and the time (it was years ago, wasn't it?) when I heard her at the top of the landing, without slippers, passing her fingers and then her braids through the moonbeams, trying to count them one two three, sing-song, in her night-dress. With its odour of camphor, meaning start of school and leaves falling. Ask me. I will call up memory. How, then, is it that I don't recall, not exactly, the first time I heard the sound?

Could it have been when Mother was looking after her aunt—bronchial flu, was it?—and was away for the weekend? There are such sharp holes in the air when she is out of the house. Father and Penny had been to the movies. Four steps on the gravel. But then only two and the key fumbling in the lock. Because he was carrying her into the house, skipping, laughing. Penny was laughing too. And there were chocolate éclairs for tea, which Mother thinks bad for our teeth. So I was sworn to secrecy. 'Hi-ho the gang,' said Father and put rum in the tea. Only a drop for Penny and, at first, she wrinkled her nose and wouldn't. But then she sipped and coughed and giggled. The taste hung on our breath like warm gold. After which Father put on his favourite cassette, the *Pirates of Penzance* highlights, and he danced his hornpipe and knocked over the delphinia. So we were sworn to secrecy again and had raisin slices on top of the éclairs. Do you know what he did then? Put the raisins and bits of walnut to the edge of his lips and blew them out, in a high arc, telling Penny to catch them in her mouth. But they fell on the carpet and I was quicker. 'O Daddy, Daddy-O,' hummed Penny, spluttering and rounding her mouth. 'Daddy's duck,' he said. And she asked again when Mother would be back and why Auntie May had no one else to look after her, and couldn't Mum come home tonight. 'She would smell the chocolate éclairs,' said Father, *basso profundo*, and we would be in serious trouble, '*mucho* serious, Ducky.' Which made Penny giggle more.

Could it have been that night I first heard that sound?

Or was it at Nubb's Point?

I do detest picnics. Those ants; drawing-pins in my ears. But could it have been there? Consider the broad daylight. The herd of people about, squealing, snoring, licking wax-paper, huffing at one another, flying kites and screeching after them. Consider the loud slap of the lake against the piling. And the transistors. In all that squelch and flailing one can scarcely hear oneself sleep. True, there is the tunnel of shadow and of mildew behind the boat-house; and that odd thick spread of high grass and scrub downwind, away from the benches and the ices. But even there children swarm and couples cling (why else do they go on a picnic?). So it could not have been there, the sound I mean. Or could it? The time we dozed till twilight, till the early chill came off the water and Mother got up shivery. To pack the hampers, to shake the sand and dead grass out of the bath towels. Which was just when Father looped the beach-ball high and challenged Penny and me to the chase; beating us to its first bounce and punching it again with his fist so that it arched into the late light and over the tea-stand. Where I lost them. There was muck in my eyes. I could hear them racing, breathing loud, and laughing. 'Penny for your thoughts, sweets for a penny,' Father's voice sliding away. I don't think it was then. And how could it have been, with Mother calling and starting towards the car-park? Revving motors and klaxons confuse me, like the yawp of gulls. I did say that I loathe picnics and the candy-drops underfoot.

What sound?

I find myself asking. Asking myself. Which is a muddle. Have I been imagining it, as I might certain smells? Does fear really have that scent of sodden cardboard? Is it in my head? I have seen old men tweeze out their hearing-aids and shake them bitterly, forgetting that the bat's piping is inside their skulls. It could just be, you know. I don't claim to be as sharp as I used to be. Other sounds, yes: twangings after the heavy winds, scratches as from somewhere behind my teeth, trills when I'm very thirsty. I might muddle or imagine those. But not that sound. It is too . . . Too what? I do have an especial ear. Too *other*. I don't know that that makes sense. *Other*. Like nothing else in earth or air. And there might just be something in the word *other* which is like the shape and shadow of the sound. The 'O' at the outset, the soft thud and the rasp. I can't have imagined that soft scratching, like a hand through stubble. Night-beings, they say, move to that sound. Broken bits of us loosed to the air when the moon is down.

But does it matter? I mean, does it matter where when I first heard their sound? I am hearing it now. Now.

What a day it has been. The house caught in a bright wash of bells. The door-bell: deliveries. A registered parcel—the annual smoked ham from Father's cousin in York. Bells pealing on the radio and at Evensong, on the box, out of some vaulted nave, and those white voices of little boys chiming Latin. 'Bluebells, tinklebells, twinklebells, Santa's a-coming.' And the bird in the oven, crisping, crackling, simmering like handbells in the far wood. If only the house wouldn't ring so. It makes it hard to be certain. The door being shut.

Daddy dancing the evening long. Not literally, to be sure. But walking, turning, standing as if always on his toes. Taking the stairs at a bound. Whistling away the whiskey on his breath. Not leaving me be for even a minute. Calling, rubbing his hot cheeks against mine. 'Old King Cole,' off-tune, incessant, making the sitting-room rock. That 'merry old soul!' over and over and over and Daddy-O slurping at me: 'Merry! Do you hear me, you sad brute, merry! That ole King Cole, a goner, high, on the trip of his boozy life. Jinglebells, *mon ami*. Heading for our chimney. Merry! The soul of him bursting like grilled sausage. You don't understand, do you, *mon ami*, with your sad old eyes.' I do hate it when he speaks to me in French. Dancing. I tell you the man was treading air. And those stage-whispers: 'No peeking, Katkins. Off with you. Upstairs, Penny and I have business. Wrappings to wrap. Ribbons to tie. For a certain special little lady. Off with you. I'll keep a weather-eye on the oven. Not to worry. For all manner of things shall be well. But nooo peeking, Slyboots. Not till tomorrow morning. Mummy's Christmas. Mummy's own very special Christmas. Right, Penny?' And Father swung Mother around the settee as if she were a child. I heard the light-switch clicking off as she went upstairs. But the darkness wasn't dark. You understand, don't you? It pulsed, somehow. There was no stillness in the silence. After he and Penny had trimmed the tree, I mean, and put out Mummy's gifts, the chintz house-coat, the acacia plant, the toiletries in their starry mantles and tinsel. The darkness just wouldn't go quiet. You do know what I mean, please.

The thread of light under Penny's door. Pencil-thin and dark-pink as is the shade on her bed-lamp. At first I couldn't make out the tune, the little old record-player which they rescued for Penny out of the attic last spring being so low. Then I caught the lilt of it. The *Snow White* medley. 'Whistle While You Work.' A favourite of hers. And somewhere somehow out of that soft piping, out of the filament of light under that door, came sound, the oh-ing, so faint I could barely pick it up, the Daddy-O O-Daddy-waddy and the scudding breath, as through his mouth, the soft soft laughter, but more like a slipping out of key, sideways, out of true, the sound that is other. That is on the other side. Of what? I don't really know. On the other side of what can be borne. 'A penny for the guy. And mum's the word. Mum.' And this time the glassiness was out of his laughter. It was everyday. As if morning had come and the time for gifts. But it hasn't. Not yet.

My hind-legs ache. Badly. I am not as strong as I once was. But strong enough, still. When he opens the door—I love him so—I'll go for his throat. He is wearing his flannel house-shirt. The plaid one, with the broken collar button. I shall aim for his throat. And the sound will cease. I have no choice. You do see that, don't you? It being Christmas.

ROUTLEDGE CULTURE

FLASHPOINTS
Studies in Public Disorder
David Waddington, Karen Jones** and **Chas Critcher,
all at Sheffield City Polytechnic
A topical study showing how and why seemingly trivial incidents act as flashpoints for widespread disturbances by investigating the underlying causes.
June 1989: 220pp 216x135 Hb: 0-415-01238-4: £30.00
Pb: 0-415-01239-2: £8.95

HARDY IN HISTORY
***Peter Widdowson,** Middlesex Polytechnic*
'Hardy of Wessex' is an important cultural figure – filmed and televised, and an asset to the tourist industry. Who invented this Hardy and why? Peter Widdowson examines how a 'great writer' is produced in sociological terms, and considers the cultural factors involved.
June 1989: 264pp: 216x138: illus
Hb: 0-415-01330-5: £30.00 Pb: 0-415-01331-3: £8.95

Routledge

Available from most booksellers. In case of difficulty or to order a catalogue contact Rachel Maund, 11 New Fetter Lane, London EC4P 4EE

Originals, classics and the cream of new fiction

BLACK SWAN
IN A CLASS OF ITS OWN

The liveliest line in paperbacks

DON'T ▸ AVOID ▸ THE ▸ ISSUES

Subscribe to Granta and you need never miss another issue. You'll get free delivery to your home and save up to 28% off the bookshop price!

Name

Address

Postcode

BI281

Please enter my subscription for:

☐ one year £16 ☐ two years £30 ☐ three years £43

Please start my subscription with issue number ________

Payment:

☐ cheque enclosed ☐ I will pay later: please bill me

☐ Access/American Express/Diners Club no:

(Please note: we cannot accept Visa/Barclaycard)

OVERSEAS POSTAGE. Europe: please add £4 per year. Outside Europe: £8 per year air-speeded, £12 per year airmail.

UP TO 28% OFF

DETACH HERE

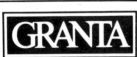

GRANTA

DON'T ▸ AVOID ▸ THE ▸ ISSUES

Subscribe to Granta and you need never miss another issue. You'll get free delivery to your home and save up to 28% off the bookshop price!

Name

Address

Postcode

BI282

Please enter my subscription for:

☐ one year £16 ☐ two years £30 ☐ three years £43

Please start my subscription with issue number ________

Payment:

☐ cheque enclosed ☐ I will pay later: please bill me

☐ Access/American Express/Diners Club no:

(Please note: we cannot accept Visa/Barclaycard)

OVERSEAS POSTAGE. Europe: please add £4 per year. Outside Europe: £8 per year air-speeded, £12 per year airmail.

UP TO 28% OFF

GRANTA

No postage
necessary
if posted
in the UK

Granta
FREEPOST
Cambridge
CB1 1BR

No postage
necessary
if posted
in the UK

Granta
FREEPOST
Cambridge
CB1 1BR

GRANTA

WALTER ABISH

FURNITURE OF DESIRE

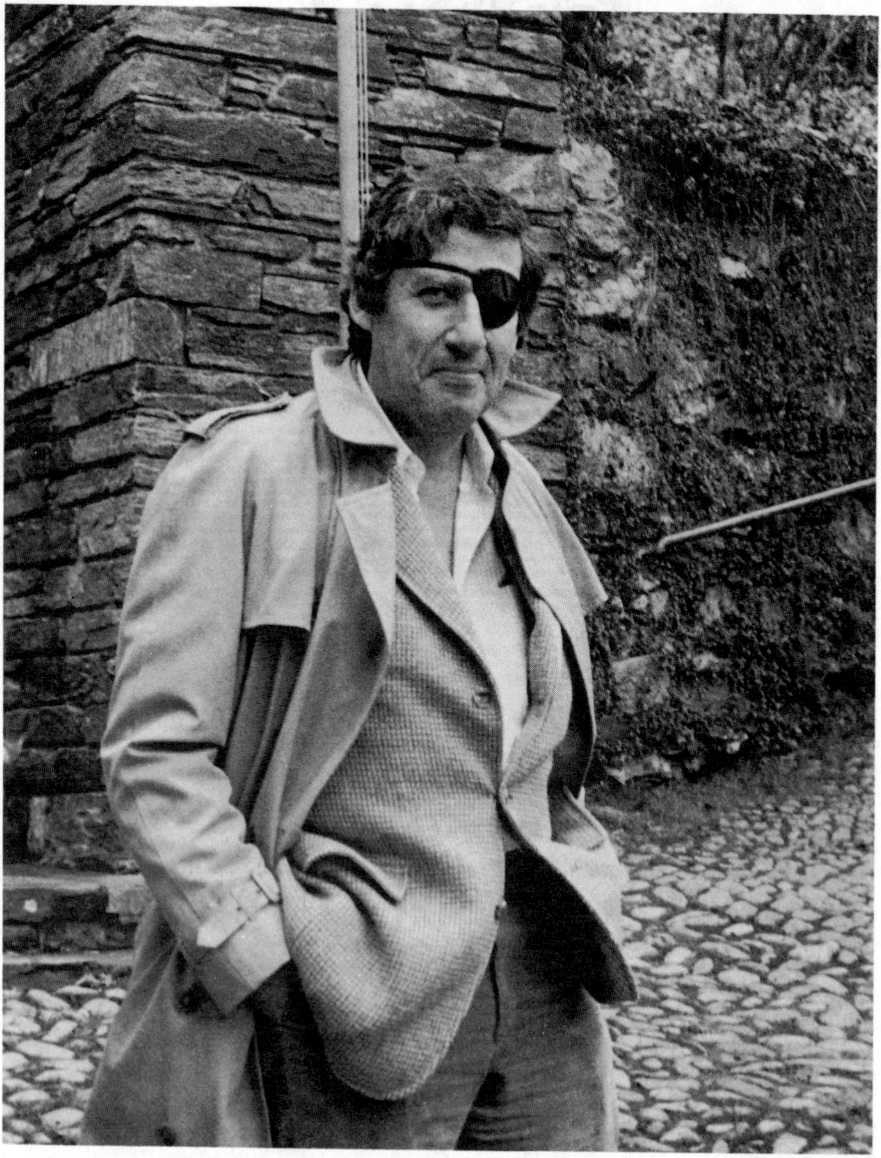

At some level, he was able to marvel at his very audaciousness. Their eyes, a doll's blue, disconcertingly blank, bright, unblinking—both of them on their way to catch the local bus, gazing at him, he instantly realized, without having come to any conclusion . . .

It took him only a moment to eliminate all doubt. The opportunity was ripe. Detecting an air of availability, he concluded that this situation, put crudely, was worth pursuing. Wasn't he Merkweise's chauffeur, in proximity to the heart of authority—so to speak, one soft leather car seat removed from its dominion—the executive car serving, in more ways than one, as an icon of its prerogatives? And he, now, smiling cockily, cap aslant, confidently standing next to the immaculate black and chrome mirrored exterior to which he had that morning contributed at least an hour's attention, stood waiting for the exact moment in which to frame in his mock salute the two in their snug, skimpy skirts and enticing low-cut blouses. One glance sufficed. Grabbing the initiative, instantly communicating to this enchanting pair, irresolutely waiting, like an as-yet-undelivered package, that he was confident—reliable, trustworthy, experienced—not just a husk, a shell, not just a uniform with gleaming buttons bearing the insignia of Durst Chemi, but someone ready to throw all caution to the wind. No room for hesitation. Fearlessly advancing . . . Isn't that something women are able to discern in a man at one glance? Momentum, confidence? From childhood—aren't they taught to read the tell-tale signs of weakness, equivocation, self-denial, as they relentlessly scan shoes, finger-nails, mouth, moustache, shirt collar? They can spot indecisiveness as readily as they can anticipate the rapist's first move, the molester's hesitant overture. With uncanny astuteness they're able to trace a man's anticipation of a rebuff to the involuntary quiver of eyebrows. With the precision of a surgeon, they peel back the outer layer, no matter how thick or coarse the skin, to detect the indecisiveness beneath.

He communicated his conviction as he raised his visored cap with a practised: *Guten Tag, meine Damen*, the half-ironic pitch intended to place doubt as to the courtesy but not the intent—thereby emitting a sexual thrill, like a mating call. Irresistible! For they, to all intents and purposes, in their tight skirts and nipple-revealing blouses ablaze with the passion of a flowery design, were

Photo: Cecile Abish

nothing less than a blatant walking sexual message, even though their faces remained somehow stern and aloof. Confidently, he asserted: Oh, yes, let me show you . . . A stream of *non sequiturs*, clusters of cloudy meaning, stimuli to entrap their heady emotional response. Testing, testing. Each word an independent scanning device.

I was just on my way to the airport when . . . Hallo! . . . I caught sight of you both and said to myself: Who are these gorgeous . . .

A pyramid of lavish phrases. Concocting as he went along, obtrusively showing his teeth in a raffish grin. Testing, testing. Shrewdly applying words like so many stimulants—duty-free perfume, raw silk, airport, first class lounge, nightclub—to set the stage, keep them mesmerized, no hasty or nervous motions: holding open the car door, as if their acquiescence was assured.

In a gravelly voice: May I have the pleasure? The half-irony, a little clumsy, a little obvious.

Then as they settled cosily into the front seat, cushioned by seventeen layers of fine black leather, expectantly eyeing him—an audience waiting for the curtain to rise, he confidently slammed the door shut, a deep satisfying sound, still talking: the unpredictable weather, the superb 1987 Niersteiner Hipping Riesling Kabinett he had tasted, Mediterranean coast, nude beaches, moving briskly to the driver's side of the car, settling in behind the wheel. No longer the uniformed subordinate, *Direktor* Merkweise's lackey, but inwardly metamorphosed into his true self: the autonomous driver, risk-taking playboy, reckless gambler.

Starting the car, while—as if to test their credulity—persuasively contending: You might not suspect that this top-of-the-line Mercedes is a temperamental beast. Intentionally saying beast not animal. It unfailingly responds to its passengers. It's so sensitive. Smoothly pulling out of the driveway, as if he had executed this precise scene a thousand times. Can you hear? That slight hum is a gauge of its mood.

They giggled nervously.

It speaks to me.

Rina, her sharp face impudently tilted: What does it say?

Valuable cargo, this side up, was the instant reply.

Now heading for the Mürenwald district—the abduction!

Easy, easy. Offering them Merkweise's cigarettes: Dunhill. Put aside for just such an occasion.

Admitting: I prefer them.

A light from the silver pocket-lighter. A chauffeur's perks? Or just rewards? Let's face it, without the car he'd make no headway: the smooth black leather upholstery, the smell of leather, the soft head rest, that protective interior calm of privilege was half the trick.

And Rina, responding more overtly to his propositions, her long legs thrusting themselves into his view like a promise. With contrived innocence she pressed the glove compartment button, pretending to be startled when, with a subdued snap, it sprung open—the light in the glove compartment came on.

What did he keep in that inner recess?

Letting them, both giggling unrestrainedly, explore the illicit space, his private space—appraising and commenting on the pair of gloves, the pocket-knife, the miniature flashlight, the first-aid kit, *Die Welt* folded to the sports page, the bar of hazelnut chocolate . . .

Ah, he's got a sweet tooth! Rina breaking off a piece of the chocolate bar. Hesitantly Betty took a piece.

Go on, he urged.

Rina coolly probing: Where are we going?

Attempting to divert her: You've not been taking acting lessons, have you?

The question registered. Rina, flattered. No. No. I've wanted to. I've been told that I have both the figure and . . .

He, seeking to include Betty: I can tell . . . You've both had some stage experience. To anyone who—

You'd be surprised, admitted Betty, by how much acting experience a waitress is required to have. Turning to Rina: Wouldn't you say what we do comes close to . . .

Ridiculous, Rina said with a sharp-faced look of annoyance.

Something about the way you move, he insisted. Not prepared to give up such a promising topic. You both have a natural . . . searching for the right word, finally settling on talent. Yes, talent.

Betty kept exploring the contents of the first-aid kit. While Rina, frowning, leaned forward, to see if she might have overlooked something of significance in the glove compartment. What's this? Holding up the tiny bottle of perfume, a sample he had received and put away, for it might come in handy.

It's yours. You can have it.

Betty pouted, feeling left out as Rina unscrewed the cap and, having dabbed the perfume on the inside of her wrists, waved them in the air. Betty following suit, faithfully executing every one of Rina's exaggerated gestures. Then, both delicately sniffing each other's wrists, and finally baring the inside of their wrists to him.

Keeping an eye on the road, he leaned sideways. Marvellous. His nose grazing Betty's wrist. A performance? Could they possibly be putting him on? By taking the roundabout route to Mürenwald, he avoided the traffic and any untoward impression of being in a single-minded rush. They were having a good time. Out for a drive!

Inserting a tape into the cassette player—*Die eine in Havana, die andere in Hawaii*—he alluded to the eccentricities of his boss.

Ah, *Direktor* Merkweise.

I've seen him do Tai Chi exercises in the car.

What is Tai Chi? Betty wanted to know.

Rina, with an impish smile: Does he know that you are here?

Caution! Carefully selecting his words: We tend to see eye to eye!

That's what they all say, Rina claimed.

He likes music, said Betty, as if in Merkweise's defence.

Yes, he admitted.

What else? Go on. Tell us, urged Rina.

My lips are tightly sealed. Turning the key to the lock of his mouth, while rolling his eyes skyward. Peals of laughter.

I bet! said Rina.

I've seen a lot . . . In his mind running down a list of 'convenient' local hotels, narrowing it to Hotel zum Grünen Heinrich as the least likely to offend, the least likely to put off the pair. By now feeling like a successful jewel thief about to undertake another exploit. The audaciousness of his venture pleasing him. To have come this far. Please, please. He wasn't asking for too much, was he? Driving, one hand on the wheel, an appearance of being relaxed, brain ever so alert, as he kept trying to maintain the banter. No strain. No sweat! Their indulgent acquiescence, their failing to press him on where he was going—something they had been conditioned to do—was in his favour. Afternoon—singing along: *Er heisst Waldemar und hat Schwarzes Haar, er ist weder stolz noch kühn. Aber ich liebe ihn. Er heisst Waldemar und ist kein Star . . .* Their faces, capable no doubt of a disquieting and shrill indignation, stayed trustingly relaxed, and—what? *Er heisst Waldemar und küsst wunderbar.* Once he might not have pressed his luck. Now driving at a sedate, measured pace, *Heute nicht und morgen nicht, So und nicht anders, so und nicht anders . . . So soll es sein für mich!* Buoyed by the music that soothingly drifted out of the car's interior to pacify the rest of Selten. Strictly speaking—ha, ha—no anxiety about his sexual competence—his performance. To think that they had appeared, the two of them—on pay day! Fortunately he'd had the presence of mind to cash his pay-cheque. He was careful to give them room to respond to what he was saying—a measure of his discernment. Nodding. Yes, yes, though he only caught every second word. All childish prattle. Caught them exchanging glances. No fools, they! He'd be all right as long as he was able to refrain from touching on the remote past. Years ago, he'd mindlessly refer to his favourite episodes of history—compulsively. Now, as soon as he inadvertently uttered any one of those heartfelt words, really the rhetoric of the vanquished, be it *Waffen SS* or *Kriegskamerad*, his brain's censor came slamming down, in time to prevent the listener from drawing any conclusions to his role in that all too recognizable past, now the domicile of grievous losers. How distressing to come face-to-face with someone ancient enough to have experienced—could it be Hitler's entry into the Sudetenland? God! And to have the same birthday, 20 April, as Hitler to boot.

Could he be mistaken, but less than twenty minutes in the car and their youthful trusting faces seemed to have acquired—was it an attempt to conform to the lavish interior of the car—a less spontaneous, a more hardened veneer. Finding a parking place on the side-street alongside the hotel, he triumphantly tossed his cap on the back seat, as if nose-thumbing *Direktor* Merkweise's sanctified place.

You should have seen this place seven years ago!

Instantly kicking himself. Seven years ago they were still in grade school. The grey stucco hotel had a new coat of paint—Selten's sign of upgrading. On the new glass door over half a dozen colourful stickers, American Express, Visa, Euro travel clubs. Triumphantly. Look at that! Pointing to the familiar emblems of hotel approval and respectability. Anything to lure them, convince them. My preferred locale. Convinced that once they crossed the threshold, victory was within his grasp. Both suddenly overcome by inertia, taking their time—as if to reconsider. One stifling a yawn, causing him immediate concern. As it was, the sallow-faced desk-clerk gave a sign of recognition. Of that he was reasonably sure. The radio playing: *Immer wenn ich glücklich bin, glücklich bin, glücklich bin, kann ich mir nicht helfen, ich muss weinen.* All it took was the mention of tears to make him want to weep.

It was still early, though once swallowed by the lack-lustre hotel wouldn't they be on eternal third- and fourth-class, dimly illuminated hotel time? Music turned low. *Immer wenn ich lustig bin, lustig bin, lustig bin, kann ich mir nicht helfen, ich muss weinen.*

The swing-door to the kitchen was wide open. He, staying jovial, steering them into this fake oak, varnished, inhospitable interior—we're having fun, aren't we?—acknowledging, no, encouraged by their compliance, reassured that the place had not deteriorated, did not smell worse. The fragrance, a rich beer bouquet impregnating the heavy dark table-top marked the hotel's losing struggle with fresh cucumbers, cauliflower, string beans.

Having placed the scuffed plastic-encased menus on the table, the waiter waited to take their order.

Is Hans here? Was it his intention to indicate by means of the question a prior familiarity with this establishment?

His day off, was the lustreless response. The waiter slowly rocked on his heels, not impatient, merely sizing them up. The sorrowful jackdaw face, eyes roving, had seen everything.

Barely glancing at the familiar German menu—which he knew inside out—not wishing to delay this ceremony, he looked winningly at the waiter. Slow smile: We would like a spread, stretching his arms wide to indicate the vastness of their appetite.

Oh no, said Betty anxiously, as if this would place her under an obligation—only to receive a jab from Rina.

Encouraging, he thought.

The waiter, then taking their order for drinks: White wine for the ladies?

A decanter! The best, mind you.

The waiter trotted off to the kitchen, while a tall woman in an apron, arms crossed belligerently, appraised them from a distance.

As he placed the wine glasses on the table the waiter, perhaps intending to make conversation, inquired: On vacation? A harmless enough question, yet to the waiter's mild bewilderment, it sent the pair into peals of laughter.

We've just come back from an inspection of Disney World.

And the waiter, nobody's fool. Ah, by way of Selten?

More hilarity.

President Reagan and I are on the best of terms. Whenever he visits Germany, I drive him around.

You're not staying abreast of world news. They have a new President.

Oh, sure, he said airily, turning to Betty and Rina for approval. But we are loyal to the old, aren't we? Lifting his glass. Let's drink to Reagan. Then, placing thumb and forefinger between his lips, shrilly whistling, loud enough to bring the cook to the kitchen door. Ronny Reagan! Whee. Raising his glass of beer to their glasses of white wine.

To Reagan, they chimed, pleased by his ready response. Barely started on his beer he ordered another round . . . advancing his manoeuvre, by introducing the 'siesta'. How, on his visit to the Middle East, where he advised the Israelis on where to dig for oil—

That's a good one, said Rina.

He took to sleeping in the afternoon. My German colleagues would have preferred to play poker, but the Bedouin—

Isn't siesta Spanish? Betty inquired.

Rina kept showing her legs no matter where she sat. A signal? The sexuality of the situation was contagious. Excusing himself, he walked to the lobby finding the tall, emaciated desk-clerk engrossed in a book.

That's the best way to pass the time!

The clerk did not even look up.

Franz did not give up easily: I once read *The Tin Drum*. Everyone was raving about it. But, let me tell you, that's not

Germany. Well, we love to disfigure ourselves, don't we?

The clerk kept on reading, but Franz was undismayed: Glad it didn't rain in Hamburg.

When the desk-clerk looked up at him uncomprehendingly, he explained: Hamburg is playing Frankfurt. Not getting a response from the washed-out face, he leaned against the desk, still beaming goodwill. I think we might want to rest before going on our way.

No expression. No response.

A room to stretch out, catch forty winks, eh?

Extracting a twenty from his wallet, rolling it between his fingers as if it were cigarette paper, before offering the man this cigarette. It was accepted without a word. One had to use initiative.

We'd like a large room, preferably with bath. Then, adding with a painful grimace: Only for a short duration . . . Out by nightfall. Ha, ha. His wallet, in readiness, permitting the desk-clerk a glimpse of the thick wad of hundred Mark notes—a rare enough occurence.

One hundred, said the clerk promptly, without blinking.

What? Discomfited, he made eye contact. In an injured voice: You don't—

One hundred, the man repeated.

Urging him, man to man—something a little more reasonable, perhaps.

Not with a bath.

And without?

Grudgingly he looked down at a chart: We have a smaller room for eighty.

Exorbitant . . . Trying once more: Come on. There must be a—

No. Anything with a bath—

But it's only . . .

The man gave him a take it or leave it shrug.

Now, plaintively: Last time I was here I paid fifty. I swear . . .

We haven't had anything for fifty in years. When were you last here?

With a look of incredulity. But for five hours or less? Finally realizing that he had no choice and that every minute's delay was a minute lost. The best you have, he urged . . .

With a marked lack of enthusiasm, the man slid a registry card in his direction.

When we leave, Franz promised.

It's required.

I'll take care of you, he promised.

I can lose my job.

Franz extracted a ten . . .

The man took it as if it were his due. You have to fill out the form. Then, reassuringly: We don't check any papers.

Hurriedly he jotted down Wagner, the first name that came to mind. Residence. Frankfurterstrasse 31, Wiesbaden. His companions became Ilse and Margot Wagner.

Grumbling that everyone was taking the law for granted, the desk-clerk handed over a key to which was attached a heavy oversized plastic disk bearing the number seven in return for the one hundred Deutschmarks. A brand new bill that might never see the interior of the cash register.

To his alarm Betty and Rina looked bored. They needed constant stimulus. Constant attention. Do you know the joke about the VW car salesman who finds himself at a reunion of Mercedes salesmen? When that one was received with laughter, he launched into one about the mountain climber who accompanied his best friend on his honeymoon.

No one would agree to that, said Betty emphatically.

Why don't we party upstairs . . . No hesitation now. His loquaciousness oiling the way.

I'll take you both to the lake next Sunday. From there we can head for the mountains.

Betty showing interest. Not Rina. Not a glimmer from her.

Despite a minimal resistance, he bundled them upstairs . . . Let's party upstairs. It will be nice to stretch out—painstakingly avoiding the threatening, the ever dangerous word, bed.

To the waiter: Supply us with refreshments—beer and cold cuts. Waving the key, room seven. Astounded by the ease.

Somehow the three of them squeezed into the tiny elevator. He breathed in the scent of their hair, his mind impatiently racing ahead. Everything, in the hotel, from the green wallpaper, to the worn bannister, the dim lighting in the hallways, the locks on the room doors that would not keep anyone out who wanted in—or conversely, anyone in who . . . conveyed a reassuring history.

Betty at once opened the window. To let in the fresh air. Stuffy here. Both critically eyeing this new interior, their faces clouded. Was it by an inkling of impropriety? But the dangerous moment passed as he, sensing another hurdle, playfully tackled them both—as they were standing in front of the huge mirror. Admittedly the huge mirror somewhat threw him off his stride, as he exuberantly kissed one then the other, tongue darting in and out—a transition to the next stage? Then, as if to diminish the sexual intent and demonstrate his boisterous, ageless, fun-loving capacity, he tried to stand on his head—not quite succeeding—falling to the floor with a resounding crash. Intoxicated? I can, believe me . . . Face red with exertion, he tried again with like result, but at least he had succeeded in making them laugh.

Betty, then accomplishing what he had tried, followed by a graceful cartwheel. He gripped her in a bear hug: My God. She's good. Releasing her when she began to squirm. He was astounded by her acrobatic skill. Fantastic.

And she, modestly: I like gymnastics.

Rina, earnestly: In East Germany she'd have it made.

Only then, noticing how muscular Betty's legs were. Bending to kiss Betty. To his dismay she kept her lips tightly compressed. Rina was more accommodating. On being kissed, she awkwardly raised one leg backwards. Was the gesture from a coquette-replay of an embrace from the TV soaps? She was more absorbed with the way she looked in the mirror, until finally her initial resistance gave way and she fell on the bed—exhausted by his testosterone insistence, his swelling persistence.

How could they not become aware of this protruding bar that announced his bursting intent? Wasn't this his true universe, to pay homage to these creatures? On his knees, he showered them with compliments—touching, holding, hands gliding up and down their legs. Kissing the white kneecaps, as they—Isn't he a silly?—serenely and complacently gazed down at him, their trusted mentor. On the bureau a large brown vase containing dried flowers . . .

After how many diversions and kisses and extravagant

compliments, did he, at long last, manage to place himself between the parted legs of—was it Betty or Rina?—who was still wearing her blue undies. But the material was loose so that with a certain awkward positioning he was able—but only after an uncertain heave and the unexpected giggly assistance of the obliging onlooker—to insert himself into Rina . . . Astonished.

Why her?

Always that innate desire to prolong the pleasure—determined that this has to last, trying ever so hard. He fondled the milky white breast of one, then turned to the smaller and firmer breast of the other, attempting to memorize the exact geography of this moment. An explosion of German details? Wasn't it good to be alive? Uneasily aware of a threatening deposit of doubt and gloom lodged in the recess of his mind, as he permitted a defeatism to worm its way into the narrow passage of his brain. Was it worth all that effort and money? Really.

Is your son still AWOL from the army?

Startled. Bad enough to have his son mentioned. But to have them comment on his desertion. Betty, half-naked on the bed, seeing his wary expression, changed the subject. And he, winding a towel round his head, stood up, strutting.

I am a Spanish conquistador.

Their laughter cheering him up. A knock on the door. He went to it, opening it a crack.

Yes.

Room service.

About time. In his shirt and socks, taking the tray from the stony-faced maid. She had neglected to bring the beer. Never mind. To their amusement, running to his trousers for a two-Mark piece. The tiny refrigerator was stocked with tiny bottles of vodka, whiskey, but, to his chagrin, only two beers. There were the mixers—tonic, tomato and orange juice in tiny bottles, several bars of chocolate—Betty was crying . . .

What's the . . . Why is she crying?

She does it all the time, Rina said, matter-of-fact voice.

The tears, so large they seemed artificial, coursed down her cheeks.

Betty, said Rina with adult asperity. Don't put on so.

Did I? he began, Tell me! Did I? Suddenly overwhelmed by the memory of his dead daughter. Falling to her death. No, leaping. Why are you crying? You can tell me.

But she wouldn't say. So he, solicitously, embraced her, and this time, the second time, he made love to her; it went with greater ease, though she kept weeping throughout. For him it entailed a much greater exertion.

The sound of the late afternoon traffic, a constant reminder of time, made him increasingly edgy. People on their way home. The sound below of cars being parked. A police car, siren at full pitch, passing by. When it stopped, he felt a moment of panic. Even as he was making love, he couldn't put the Mercedes, with its all too familiar three-digit licence plate, out of his mind. Everyone recognized Joachim Merkweise's car.

Later, when he playfully suggested to Betty that she move in with him, she hesitated, then said, Yes.

You dummy. Can't you see, he's a tease? Rina said.

And Betty, drying her tears, asked: Who's better?

What wouldn't he give for a nice snooze. Then coffee in the garden. Instead, in the hotel mirror, watching himself, ponderously, painfully once again insert this semi-erection into a fleshy brunette whose brightly painted lips formed an O in response.

When he maintained, there are so many things a German will never consider, he was instantly challenged: For instance?

Head cocked, eyeing their bodies, he regretfully declined—No, no.

He's a prude.

Fancy that.

All that talk.

What do you like?

I like good, honest . . .

Bullshit, said Rina, nothing you like is honest.

He, the avid reader of signals, was confounded by their unembarrassed nakedness—a certain matter-of-factness that initially raised and now somewhat dampened all expectations. Sneaking a look at his watch. One more hour. Trying to decide if his throbbing head permitted him once more . . .

Look, shrieked Betty, pointing to a cat, tail upright, that had strode in from the balcony. Rina rising from the bed to investigate, walking naked to the glass door. Standing on the threshold for all the world to see.

You're not dressed, he scolded.

Look at him. Our SS man. This said condescendingly.

Eyes narrowed: Whoever told you that?

Betty giggling. We know everything about you.

He was overcome by a choking sensation in his throat, pointedly: Everything?

Almost, Betty said airily.

Tell me.

And what we don't know we can find out, if we take the trouble.

And what may that be?

If you . . .

Oh, shut up, said Rina.

The cat entered, sniffed his trousers, jumped on the dresser, purring, as she squatted next to his wallet.

By now he had spent one hundred for the room, thirty-two in tips. The cold cuts were thirty, drinks totalled forty-two, which added up to . . .

Rina, confidingly: We've been to the *Hilton* in Frankfurt, and the *Vier Jahreszeiten* in Munich.

What? He could accept the *Hilton*, but the *Vier Jahreszeiten*? With whom? Looking at them, as if to reappraise his afternoon. Was there more to this . . .

That would be telling, laughed Rina.

Just the *Hilton*.

Rina, outraged: What do you take us for?

You can tell me.

Whatever it sounds like, said Betty firmly. It was quite innocent.

I bet.

Rina was running the water in the none-too-clean, chipped bath-tub. The drain had a reddish, rusty stain, but both were unconcerned. The room filled with steam. Rina primping in front of the mirror, staring at herself, as he sat on the round rim of the tub, examining the tile floor.

Has your son really returned? Betty wanted to know.

What? Again taken aback. Dieter? To Selten?

Someone said he's back.

I don't wish to . . . Then overcome with curiosity: Who said so? But they refused to say. Lowering his head into his hands: My son is bad news. No self-discipline. Always opposed to accepting the norm.

What's the norm? Betty wanted to know.

He's cute, said Rina, turning around.

How would you know?

We've seen his picture.

What picture?

It was a clipping . . . a newspaper.

What paper?

How should I know?

He went to Cuba as a revolutionary, Betty chirped in.

Revolutionary, my ass. Then looking at his watch. Get ready. I'll be back shortly.

Are you rushing us? grumbled Rina.

Can't we have dinner before we return? Betty asked.

I want you both dressed, *pronto*! Leaving the bathroom, he quickly dressed and walked down the hall to the elevator. Groggily pressing the down button, counting his expenses as he made his slow descent. Seeing half a dozen people in the lobby, he rushed out, to check the car. From a phone booth calling the office: I've had a flat . . . No, no . . . I fixed it myself . . . I'll explain.

Then back to the room, this time using the stairs, impatiently telling them to hurry up. I thought you'd be ready by now.

I don't like to be rushed, snapped Rina.

As soon as I get the job in the executive dining-room, I'll have you there as well, Betty promised her.

Oh, sure, said Rina.

Have I ever let you down?

I'm not all that sure that you'll get it.

It's in the bag, said Betty, the more trusting one.

Driving back, this time taking the highway, he talked effusively of German metaphysics. What, for instance, do we retain of any given situation? The day after, less and less. Finally the brain is barely able to hold on to more than a fragment. By tomorrow, I'll no longer remember what I've said. If I strain myself, I may be able to recall the furniture, the third-rate hotel furniture.

And Rina enraged: You're a shit-head.

While Betty resigned: They're all the same. We are just the furniture to their pleasure.

To drown out their voices he played: *Davon geht die Welt nicht unter, sieht man sie manchmal auch grau, einmal wird sie wieder bunter, einmal wird sie wieder Himmelblau* . . . Join in, he bellowed in a drill sergeant's voice. Join in. And they did!

RANDOM HOUSE UK LIMITED

PEOPLE OF THE BLACK MOUNTAINS
Raymond Williams
£13.95
0701128453
Chatto & Windus

BEGINNING
Kenneth Branagh
£12.95
0701133880
Chatto & Windus

TALES OF THE CITY
Armistead Maupin
£14.95
0701134291
Chatto & Windus

ADVENTURES ON THE WINE ROUTE
Kermit Lynch
£12.95
0370313623
Bodley Head

HENRY V
William Shakespeare
Adapted by Kenneth Branagh
£7.95 0701135360
Chatto & Windus

LEWIS PERCY
Anita Brookner
£11.95
0224026682
Jonathan Cape

LONDON FIELDS
Martin Amis
£11.95
0224026097
Jonathan Cape

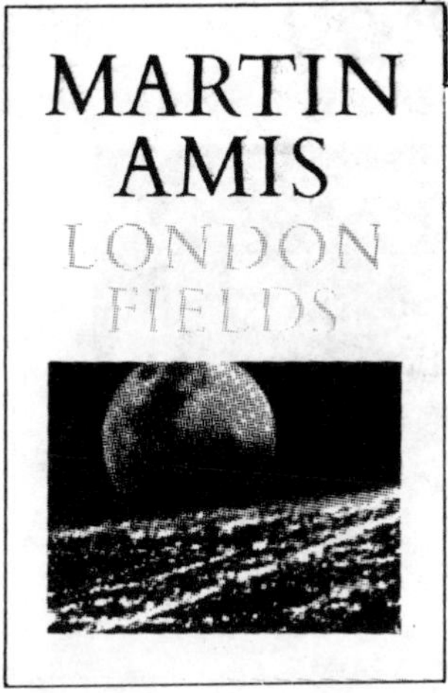

A SECRET COUNTRY
John Pilger
£12.95
0224026003
Jonathan Cape

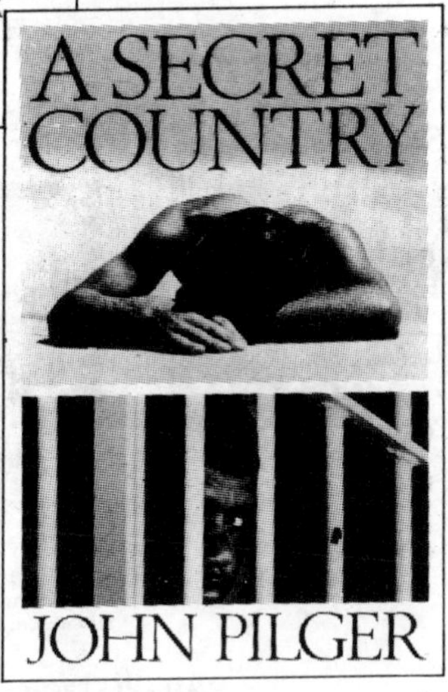

Waterstone's Guide to Books
1989–1990

An ordering service for readers for only £5.95

Available from over 30 branches of
Waterstone's Booksellers and from
Waterstone's Mail Order Division
4 Milsom Street, BATH BA1 1DA, (0225) 448595

W
WATERSTONE'S
BOOKSELLERS

Waterstone's Booksellers
London · Edinburgh · Dublin

OLYMPIA
Compact Discs Ltd.

RIMSKY KORSAKOV

U.S.S.R. Academic Symphony Orchestra, conducted by Y. Svetlanov

OCD 158
Symphonies No. 1 in E Minor
and No. 3 in C Major.

OCD 211
Russian Easter Festival Overture.
Sadko op 5. Fantasia on Serbian
Themes op 6. At the Tomb op 61.
Sinfonietta in A Minor. Overture on
Russian Themes.

OCD 227
Dubinushka op 62. Skazka op 29.
Suite Le Coq D'Or.
Capriccio Espagnol.

AVAILABLE FROM ALL LEADING RECORD SHOPS.

Olympia Compact Discs are manufactured exclusively by Disctronics (Europe) Ltd.
Produced by: Olympia Compact Discs Ltd, Southwater, West Sussex, RH13 7YT, England. Telephone: 0403 732302, Telex: 878118G.

GRANTA

GUY DAVENPORT
COLIN MAILLARD

For Cigarettes
Virginia Tobacco is the Best
Piedmont

Colin Maillard

Down the slope of the knoll by the river a group of boys were driving another, smaller boy before them. His every attempt to break and run was thwarted by blocking shoulders and quick footwork.

—Stand, Aage said to Tristan, still and easy. I'll do the rest.

—Martin and Peder, Bo said, are going to fight.

—Not till after, Martin said.

—And not here, Peder said. Back of the hill, and in our underpants, so's not to get blood on our clothes.

—Crazy, Ib said.

Aage unbuttoned Tristan's shirt and took it off with a flourish.

—Hang it on the post, he instructed Martin.

Aage worked Tristan's undershirt up. His voice was calm and menacing. A few more unfastenings and pulls, and Tristan stood mother-naked, cheeks and ears the colour of a radish.

—Here in the sack, Peder said.

He shook out a dress, blue with dots, a frilled hem and a pink ribbon through the lace at the collar.

—Sexy, Bent said.

—Looks more like a night-gown, said Bo.

—You're going to make me wear a dress? Tristan asked.

—We told you not to talk, Aage said. Stick your arms through the sleeves.

—It's only a game, Martin said. Isn't it, Ib? Ib doesn't tell lies.

—Not only a game, Ib said, but a game with the rules backwards. You're It, we decided last night, and instead of you having the blindfold, we are the blindfoldeds.

—Except for the haircut, he looks like a girl.

—What for? Tristan asked.

—The more you talk, Aage said, the worse it's going to be for you, squirt.

—Pigeon to the Master, Bo said, and you'll wish you were dead.

—This is the drill, Bent said. We're blindfolded, you're not. If you were to get clean away, slim chance, you can't go back, not in a dress.

—What happens when you catch me?

—We told you not to talk.

Photo: Guy Mendes

Aage looked at Bo, merry with a secret, and Bo flipped his fingers against his blue sweat-shirt. Bent zipped down the fly of his short pants and crossed his eyes. Ib guffawed. Martin glared at Peder, Peder at Martin.

A skipper on flixweed opened its wings twice before darting off, with a dip, zigzag and fluttery.

—*Sylvestris Poda*, Tristan said. I don't care. Gives me the sniffles, this dress.

Aage bound Bo's eyes with a scout kerchief, Bent's, Ib's and on around until they were all blindfolded, except Tristan, who stood miserable and confused in his dress. Bo's white quiff stuck up like a grebe's tail from the scarf belting his eyes, and they all moved like wound-up toys.

In every direction there were green and brown fields, and a silver sliver of sea to the west.

—You're there, somewhere, Aage said. If you talk or holler, we'll know where you are and get you.

They began to mill, with stiff arms and open hands.

—It's me you've got, smugger, Bo said. Feel for a dress.

—There was an owl, a Great Grey, *Strix nebulosa*, on a limb, Bent said, on the fir.

Tristan ducked Ib's flailing grope.

—Outside my window.

—We could all be frigging each other, Peder said, in brotherly bliss.

Tristan nipped under Aage's reach, changing course like a rabbit.

—Not Peder and Martin: they're going to fight.

—Same thing, Bo said.

It was not bright to think of green graph paper and algebra when who knew what was about to happen to him, but Tristan did.

—Everybody stand still. Blind people can feel what's around them.

Or of the yellow willow by the river and the heron that stood on one leg downstream from it.

—Wind.

—Arms out.

—Turn slow, all of us in close.

—We could hold hands, in a circle, and move in.

—If he's inside.

—Silence.

He could see. They couldn't. No reason why they should ever catch him.

—The owl was looking in at our window.

—Which blinded him.

Thing was, to make no noise and to account for every direction at once. Stay on your toes, stay down, keep turning.

—Who groped my crotch? Martin asked.

—Peder, probably, Bo said.

Bent, squirming away from Ib, made a wide opening in the circle, through which Tristan nipped, and walked backwards, on his toes. Then he turned and ran as fast as he could. From the dip on the other side of the knoll he could see a woman with her butterfly net, a farmer burning off his field. The shine had gone off the sea. He minded being barefoot more than the dress. The dress was like a dream, and no fault of his, but to have let his shoes be taken away from him was lack of character.

—Bullies, he said out loud. And unfair.

But he'd fooled them, there was that. And he would never know what they would have done to him if they'd caught him.

—Don't think like that! he said, stomping his foot.

If he made a big circle, he could get back to the school without being caught, provided it was a good while before they realized he'd given them the slip.

If he were in Iceland or on Fyn, there would be ponies he could commandeer and ride. If he were on the other side of the school, there would be a road, with cars. It would be grand if a helicopter choppered down, with police or soldiers, to rescue him, deliver him in glory to the school, having kindly given him a flight jacket to wear over his miserable dress. And the woman netting butterflies was too far inside the long way around he had to circle. If his luck held, he could be a long way ahead of them before the pack was on his heels.

He kept to the sides of knolls. His breathing was wet and sharp, as when you're taking a cold.

Heather and bracken and gorse and knot grass, and all as fast in rubble as a cat's tail in a cat. All people with socks and sneakers were rich, didn't they know? And pants. And did his balls feel good because he was free? If he was: they might be tearing after him, with longer legs, and with shoes, and here he was crying, like a baby.

He didn't dare look back. For one thing, every direction now looked the same. For another, he didn't want to know if they were behind him in a pack, or worse, fanning out, to come at him on all sides.

A stitch in your ribs goes away, he knew, if you keep running, and there was second wind, good old second wind. And luck, there was luck.

Had the sky ever been emptier or everywhere so far away?

Luck, he felt in his bones, had a warrant for his safe passage over these scrub meadows. The wood's edge would be just beyond the next rise or the next. Then he could go along the wood, even disappear into it, if need be. There was a longish stretch of open fields after that, before the next wood, but that one had paths in it, and through it he could get back to the school.

But he had to go around hills, not over them, where they could see him.

What was all this about, anyway? Playing Colin Maillard with the rules reversed and him in a dress? Aage he'd suspect anything of, always ready for a jape as he was, especially if it was a way of sucking up to Bo. Bent was a mean little rat to be in on this. How did Ib get mixed up in it?

His nose stung inside, and the back of his mouth.

He'd cut the underside of two toes, the little one on his left foot, the long one beside the big toe on his right. His knees hurt. His shins hurt.

He stumbled and fell sprawling.

I will not cry, he heard himself saying. I will fucking not fucking cry.

When he got up, he couldn't believe that the use of his left ankle was not his any more. The pain would go away. Luck wouldn't do something like this to him. It absolutely wouldn't. He needed all the luck he could get.

Worse, he heard voices.

The voices made him angry. It was wonderfully easy now not to blubber, not even to think of defeat. He was going to get away. A wonky ankle wasn't going to stop him.

The voices were to his left. They weren't a hue and cry. They were mingled in with each other. Ib's he recognized, and Aage's. He heard *all this crap about a fair fight* and *we won't stop you.*

He forgot that his ankle wouldn't work and fell again. Where *were* they?

On the other side of the knoll to his left. He remembered: Martin and Peder were to fight. He hated fights. They were more senseless, even, than making him wear a dress to play *blindebuk* backwards.

The whole stupid world was crazy. Plus it didn't seem to notice.

He gave up hopping and crawled towards the top of the knoll. There was a big rock he could lie flat behind and look. Their minds, at least, weren't on him any more. There was sweet relief in that. And they wouldn't pick on him when he had a hurt ankle.

Aage and Bo were with Martin, who was stripped down to his undershorts. Peder was undressing, throwing his clothes to Ib and Bent. He had smaller undershorts than Martin, blue with a white waistband. They'd left on their socks and sneakers, as the ground in the hollow where they were was as rocky and scrubby as the fields he'd run so fast over.

The late afternoon was filling the hollow with shadow. Aage was whispering in Martin's ear. Bo sat, Martin's clothes in his lap.

Peder walked over and stood nose to nose with Martin, talking very low between clenched teeth. His hands tightened into fists. Martin was breathing fast, his chest jumping as if he'd run farther and harder than Tristan.

But they hadn't run at all. He saw that he'd apparently been making a steady turn to the left, when all the while he thought he was running in a straight line. The post where they'd played Colin Maillard was the next knoll over. Talk about unlucky.

He was scared. He hated what he was seeing and didn't want to see. Martin and Peder almost touching, breathing into each other's mouths, looking into each other's eyes as if trying to look into each other's heads. Aage stood eerily still, waiting with a strange expression on his face. Bo's knees were quivering. Ib had his hands on his hips, legs wide apart. Bent was licking his lips.

Peder hit first, a jab into Martin's midriff that sounded like a melon splitting and doubled Martin over. Before he could straighten up, Peder kicked him in the chest, a fierce football punt of a kick that made him fall backwards.

Tristan closed his eyes and pushed his face against the ground. He heard grunts, ugly words, scuffling.

Aage, Bo, Ib and Bent said nothing at all.

When he dared a look, Peder was on top of Martin, pummelling his face with both fists, which were bloody. Martin's legs were flailing against the ground.

Tristan was half-way down the slope, running with a dipping limp, before he realized that he had moved at all.

—Make him quit! he was shouting.

Bo looked up at him in surprise. Aage grinned.

—Keep back, he said. A fight's a fight.

With a porpoise heave and flop, Martin twisted from under Peder, jabbed his knee into his crotch and pulled free. Peder's face was white with pain, his mouth making the shape of a scream. Martin was bleeding from the nose in spurts and he was sobbing in convulsions, his shoulders jolting. He wiped the blood from his mouth and fell on Peder with both fists hammering on his terrified face.

Tristan locked his arms around Martin's waist and pulled.

—Help me get him off, you ass-holes! he shouted. You fucking stupid shits!

—Stay out of this, Aage shouted. It's none of your fucking business.

—Where'd he come from, anyway? Ib asked.

By tightening his arm-lock and pushing as hard as he could, Tristan rolled Martin off Peder, who got up with a paralytic jerk, gagging. Backing away on knees and elbows, he retched and puked.

Bo said quietly: I think they've fought enough.

—Me too, Bent said.

—O, shit, Aage said. They haven't even begun. Shove Tristan baby there towards the school with a foot against his ass, so's we'll have boys only again, and let's get on with it.

—I think they've fought enough, Aage, Bo repeated. Something's wrong with Martin. There's too much blood.

—How can we get them to the infirmary, Bent asked with a scared voice, without all of us getting it in the neck?

—Cripes! Ib said. Peder's konked out.

—Fainted.

—Knocked out.

—Shake him.

—Get the puke out of his mouth.

—Let the bastard die, Martin said, spitting blood. Turn me loose, Tristan.

Bo and Ib lifted Peder by the shoulders, trying to get him to sit up.

—Don't like the way his head lolls, Bo said.

—He's coming around. Look at his eyes.

—They'll never get cleaned up and get back to school looking as if they haven't had a fight. It's a fucking war, here.

—Who says the fight's over? Aage asked.

—O, shut up, you stinking sadist, Tristan said. You're mental, you know that?

Aage, pretending speechlessness, covered his mouth with both hands.

—Peder! Bo hollered, are you all right?

—Look, Ib said, we've got Peder unconscious and maybe bleeding to death, huh, and we're acting like morons. Let's do something.

—Do what?

—Carry him to the infirmary for starters.

—Let him die, Martin said.

—Wipe some of the blood off with Tristan's dress, Bo said. Take it off. Go get your clothes, on the post next hill over.

—Can't, Tristan said. Turned my ankle running from you pigs and can't go that far.

—I'll get them, Bent said.

—So off with the dress. Let's rip it in two, half for Martin, half for Peder.

—Peder's opening his eyes.

—The whole point of the fight, Aage said, was for somebody to win it. You can't have a fight without a winner and a loser.

—Stuff it, Ib said.

—And fuck it, Martin said. I've had it. If Peder has too. He, by God, looks it.

—No way, Ib said, we can't keep this from Master. Looks like a train hit both of you.

Tristan stood naked as an eft on one leg. Ib kept spitting on the wad he'd made of the halved dress, wiping blood off Martin.

Peder waved Bo away, who was trying to do the same for him.

—Stand him up, Bent said. See if he can.

Peder gave him the finger, scrambled up and pitched forward, to vomit again.

—What, Tristan asked, was the fight about, anyway?

—You don't want to know, Ib said. Can you walk on that leg?

—Sure, Tristan said, I think so.

—All we need right now, Bent said, is for somebody to come along to see two of us looking like a slaughterhouse and one naked cripple. Master would eat pills for the next two days.

—Turn anybody's stomach, Tristan said. Turns mine. Fighting's stupid, you know?

—If anybody asked your opinion, Aage said.

—Why did you make me play blind-man's buff in a dress? Look, I'm not afraid of any of you, huh? And I'm not taking any more bullying, OK?

—Would you fucking listen? Aage said.

Bo mopped Martin. Ib and Bent helped up Peder, whose knees were trembling.

—I'm all right, Peder said, his voice thick. Just let me alone a bit.

He pulled off his briefs to wipe his face. He felt his testicles with cautious fingers.

—Still there.

—Bo, Peder said, feel my balls and see if you think anything's wrong. One word out of anybody, and you get it in the mouth, I fucking promise.

—The rules were no rules, Aage said, so you can't bitch about kneed balls.

—Since when were you God? Tristan asked.

—Nobody's whining, Aage, Peder said. You get a knee in your

balls and see if you don't puke.

—Let Martin feel, Bo said. He did it, and that's where it started, and you've got to make up. That's what a fight's for, yes?

—Up on the hill, Bent said, when I fetched Tristan's clothes, which you might put on after I went to the trouble, good deed and all, you know, the woman murdering butterflies seemed to be drifting this way. She's the one who glares at us on the way to the candy store.

—How did whichwhat start with Peder's balls? Tristan asked. All my togs are inside out.

—Do we let Tristan in? Bo asked. We've made him bust his ankle and he did give us the slip.

—Ib and Bo and me, we vote yes, Bent said. Martin? Peder?

—He's too little, Martin said. Or is he?

—Feel my balls, Martin, Peder said. See if they're OK. I'm not mad anymore.

—Let me, Aage said. I'll give you a straight answer.

—No, Peder said. Martin. And there's a damned tooth loose.

—It was you that wanted to fight, Martin said.

—So let's have your opinion as to whether I'm ever going to be a father.

—What's *in?* Tristan asked. I have two toes about to come off, if anybody's interested, to go with my bum ankle.

—There's a poor imitation of a creek on the far side of the wood, you know, Ib said. We can get the blood off Martin and Peder.

—But not the bruises, fat lips and shiners.

—My balls are going to look like a black grapefruit. What do you think, Martin?

—If you come OK, next time you jack off, then they aren't busted, right? Let's see the tooth.

—What am I in? Tristan asked.

—What's your vote, Aage?

Aage shrugged and quiddled his fingers.

—I'm already outvoted. I steal the dress, I solve Peder and Martin's problem, I invent inside-out Colin Maillard, and all at once I'm a clown.

—Life's like that, Peder said.

—Look, Bo said, it's getting cold out here. Let's head out, the shortest way back, and to every question we answer absofuckinglutely nothing. Stare right over the top of the head of anybody asking any question. OK?

All nodded, including Tristan.

They cast long, rippling shadows on the brown meadows, Bo carrying Tristan piggyback, Aage with his hands in his pockets, Martin and Peder each with an arm around the other's shoulders, Ib and Bent skipping along behind.

1979-1989 Lyric HAMMERSMITH
ANNIVERSARY 10th SEASON

PRIN
World Premiere by Andrew Davies starring Sheila Hancock
17 Aug-14 Oct prevs 17-22 Aug press night 23 Aug 7pm

FAITH HOPE CHARITY
by Odon von Horvath translated by Christopher Hampton
18 Oct-9 Dec prevs 18-26 Oct press night 27 Oct 7pm
The play the Nazis banned!

THARK
by Ben Travers starring Griff Rhys Jones
directed by Griff Rhys Jones and Peter James
15 Dec-16 Feb prevs 15-20 Dec press night 21 Dec 7pm

GRANTA BOOKS

Ten years ago, we printed 800 copies of the first issue of the 'new' *Granta*. On the first of September, our tenth anniversary, we will print 150,000. In a decade *Granta* has become the most widely read magazine in the English language. How did we do it? By publishing only the writing we care passionately about.

The first of September marks another special day: the launch of Granta Books.

And perhaps the most important feature of Granta Books is this: the size of the list. At a time when more and more publishers are bringing out more and more titles, we want to concentrate on a select few – ten, twelve, maybe fifteen a year. We want to hold to the principle that has always governed *Granta:* to publish only the writing we care passionately about.

1 0 Y E A R S

THE MEZZANINE

NICHOLSON BAKER

THE MEZZANINE is the story of one man's lunch hour. It addresses the big questions of corporate life in the grand manner:

Why does one shoe-lace always wear out before the other?
Whose genius lies behind the wing-flap spout on the milk carton?
Whatever happened to the paper drinking-straw?

'Easily the best first novel of 1988.'

The Boston Globe

'I love novels with gimmicks. By that I mean novels that are told not through plain old narrative but rather through some enormously complicated technical stunt. The list of great ones is not long; "Tristram Shandy" comes to mind, and Nabokov's brilliant "Pale Fire", a story told entirely in footnotes. Gimmick novels are often parodies, but this is not essential – just look at "Ulysses", which I consider the ultimate gimmick novel. "The Mezzanine", a first novel by Nicholson Baker, has no story, no plot, no conflict. When somebody describes it to you it sounds stupid (which, by the way, is a characteristic of all good gimmick novels). Yet its 135 pages probably contain more insight into life as we live it than anything currently on the best seller lists.'

The New York Times Book Review

Nicholson Baker lives in Mount Morris, New York, with his wife and child. His stories have appeared in *The Atlantic* and *The New Yorker*. This is his first novel.

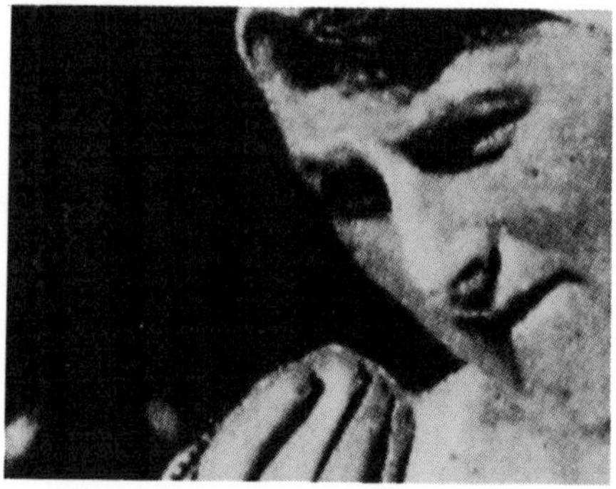

On sale 1 September
from all good bookshops
price £10.95 (hardback)

GABRIEL GARCÍA MÁRQUEZ

Clandestine in Chile

In 1973, a portly, dark-haired, bearded film director fled Chile after the military coup. Twelve years later he returned, slim, fair, clean-shaven, bringing with him a false passport, a false name, a false past and a false wife.

What kind of man trades his own identity for an invented one? What compels an exile to return to the country where he is on the wanted list?

This is the story of Miguel Littin, who risked his freedom to bring the world a truer picture of life under Pinochet. From eighteen hours of taped interviews, Gabriel García Márquez retells, in the voice we know from the novels, the adventures of Miguel Littin, clandestine in Chile.

On 28 November 1986, in Valparaiso, the Chilean authorities impounded and burned 15,000 copies of this book.

GABRIEL GARCÍA MÁRQUEZ has written three collections of short stories. His novels include *One Hundred Years of Solitude, The Autumn of the Patriarch, Chronicle of a Death Foretold* and *Love in the Time of Cholera*. In 1982 he was awarded the Nobel Prize for Literature. He divides his time between Barcelona and Mexico.

On sale 1 September
from all good bookshops
price £10.95 (hardback)

JOHN BERGER AND JEAN MOHR

A Fortunate Man

John Sassall is a country doctor who has chosen to practise alone in an isolated and depressed English rural community. The people he serves trust him almost without question. He is doing what he wants to do.

In this honest and moving book, John Berger and Jean Mohr show the complex relationship between Sassall, his patients and their environment, and question at what social cost Sassall can consider himself a fortunate man.

Available now from
all good bookshops
price £6.99

JOHN BERGER AND JEAN MOHR

A Seventh Man

Why do the industrial European countries depend on importing twenty-two million hands and arms to do the most menial work? Why are the owners of those arms and hands treated like replaceable parts of a machine? What compels the migrant worker to leave his village and accept this humiliation?

Continuing the collaboration begun in *A Fortunate Man*, John Berger's text and Jean Mohr's photographs are at the same time disturbing and compassionate. *A Seventh Man* shows that the migrant worker, far from being on the margins of modern experience, is absolutely central to it.

Available now from
all good bookshops
price £6.99

JOHN BERGER AND JEAN MOHR

Another Way of Telling

With the invention of photography we acquired a means of expression more closely associated with memory than any other. But exactly how and why do photographs move us? What can we learn from family albums and the private use of photographs? Do appearances constitute a code of life, a sort of 'half-language'?

These are some of the questions examined in *Another Way of Telling*, in which John Berger and Jean Mohr lay the groundwork for a new theory of photography. No book of photographs quite resembles this one, with its mixture of stories, theory, portrait and confession. Its principal tale, told without words in 150 photographs, concerns the life of a fictional peasant woman. It is not cinematic and has nothing to do with reportage. It constitutes another way of telling.

Available now from
all good bookshops
price £7.99

JOHN BERGER

Once in Europa

A farmer sits in a barn at night, playing the accordion to himself. Another feeds a bonfire with the corpses of dozens of dead sheep, his entire flock struck by lightning. A woman watches an old man shouting his name from a hillside into the wind.

Around such images John Berger, in his first fiction for six years, builds pictures of whole lives. The narratives in *Once in Europa* are above all love stories, though the love might be the devotion of a bachelor son to his widowed mother, or the hopeless, humiliating infatuation of a solitary farmer for a woman from the town.

But in tracing the course of love and its consequences, these stories do more: they depict precisely, and utterly without sentimentality, the life of a community uniquely determined by the work it does – the annual raising of livestock, the cultivation of the land – its labour governed and dignified by the seasons and elements.

'Marvellous stories, remarkable for their quality of visionary intimacy.'
Angela Carter in *The New York Times Book Review*

JOHN BERGER, art historian, essayist, poet and novelist, was born in London in 1928. His many books include *The Success and Failure of Picasso* and *G*, the novel for which he won the Booker Prize in 1972.

John Berger now lives and works in a small peasant community in the French Alps. This milieu is the setting for *Pig Earth* and *Once in Europa*, the first two volumes of his trilogy 'Into Their Labours' that evokes, in fictional form, the peasant's odyssey from village to metropolis.

On sale 1 September
from all good bookshops
price £10.95 (hardback)

MARTHA GELLHORN

The View from the Ground

Martha Gellhorn's dispatches chart the century: Middle America during the Depression, Spain in the aftermath of Franco's death, Christmas with the down-and-outs in London, a lynching in Mississippi, returning to Cuba after forty-one years. Angry, courageous, full of energy, *The View from the Ground* is a remarkable act of testimony, a memoir of a full life in troubled times.

'One of the most extraordinary women of her era.'
Chicago Sun-Times

'An eloquent, unforgettable history of a chaotic century.'
San Francisco Chronicle

MARTHA GELLHORN was born in St Louis, Missouri. In 1930, aged twenty-one, she talked her way into a free passage to Europe and arrived in Paris with $75 in her pocket and the conviction that she could earn a living as a foreign correspondent. She returned to the United States in 1934 and two years later published her acclaimed book of four linked novellas on Depression-hit America, *The Trouble I've Seen*.

In 1937 she returned to Europe as a war correspondent, and for the next nine years she reported on the wars in Spain, Finland, China and finally Europe in World War Two. These experiences are collected in *The Face of War*. After 1946 her journalism became occasional and freelance, but she continued to report on whatever engaged her interest and concern from Vietnam to the Middle East and the wars in Central America.

Martha Gellhorn is the author of five novels, two collections of stories, four books of novellas and three books of non-fiction. She lives in Wales.

On sale 1 September
from all good bookshops
price £14.95 (hardback)

TIMOTHY GARTON ASH

The Uses of Adversity

Ten years ago Timothy Garton Ash arrived in East Berlin, looking for a library suitable for pursuing his academic research. He found one, but rarely went there. Instead he spent time with *samizdat* publishers; hung around at the polling stations, watching fraudulent elections; talked into the night with the actor ('Dr Faust') who worked for the State Security Police in his spare time. Finally he abandoned his research and wrote about what he saw – in German. When he tried to return to East Germany, he was not allowed in.

He went to Poland and wrote a history of Solidarity. It was translated into Polish and became – and continues to be – an underground bestseller. He is no longer welcome in Poland.

Last year, Timothy Garton Ash visited Prague. He was allowed to stay just long enough to get arrested and thrown out again. His reputation now arrives before him.

Ten years ago Timothy Garton Ash began to discover Central Europe. *The Uses of Adversity* records what he found.

Timothy Garton Ash was born in 1955. His last book, *The Polish Revolution: Solidarity*, won the society of Authors' Somerset Maugham Award and was described in the *TLS* as 'a masterpiece of contemporary history'. His first book, *Und willst Du nicht mein Bruder sein ... Die DDR heute ('And, if my brother you won't be ...' East Germany Today)*, won a diplomatic protest from the East German Government. His is Foreign Editor of the *Spectator* and a regular contributor to the *Independent* and the *New York Review of Books*. He lives in Oxford.

On sale 1 September
from all good bookshops
price £13.95 (hardback)
£5.99 (paperback)

RYSZARD KAPUŚCIŃSKI

The Soccer War

In 1964, Ryszard Kapuściński was appointed by the Polish Press Agency as its foreign correspondent – or, perhaps more accurately, as *the* foreign correspondent – and for next ten years, he was 'responsible' for fifty countries.

He was the only foreign correspondent in Honduras when, after a World Cup qualifying match with El Salvador, the 'Soccer War' was declared. Posted to Africa, he arrived in Zanzibar as revolution broke out; fleeing to what was then called Tanganyika, he encountered a coup. In Burundi he was sentenced to death by firing-squad; in Nigeria he survived by driving straight through machine-gun fire and a series of burning road-blocks. He befriended Che Guevara in Bolivia, Allende in Chile and Lumumba in the Congo. By the time Kapuściński returned to Poland in 1980, he had witnessed twenty-seven revolutions and coups.

'The Soccer War' is Kapuściński's story, his eye-witness account of the emergence of the Third World. The book is as unusual as the experiences it depicts – one that could be described as reportage or autobiography or history; and, finally, as an extraordinarily good read.

RYSZARD KAPUŚCIŃSKI was born in 1932 in the city of Pinsk in eastern Poland, a region that is now a part of the Soviet Union. He was educated in Warsaw and at the age of twenty-three was posted to India, his first trip outside Poland. His first book, *The Polish Bush*, stories of the Polish 'frontier', appeared in 1962 and was an immediate best-seller. He has since travelled widely throughout the Third World – storing up, as he once said in an interview, the experiences for the books that would come later. The first of these books, published in 1968, was based on a journey through Islamic Russia. This was followed by books on Africa, Latin America and South Africa. His first book to be translated into English was the *The Emperor*, based on the last days of Haile Selassie and subsequently made into a play produced by Jonathan Miller. His other books in English include *Another Day of Life*, about the war in Angola, and *Shah of Shahs*, based on the revolution in Iran.

Ryszard Kapuściński lives in Warsaw.

Publication February 1990
Price to be announced

GRANTA

William Boyd
Transfigured Night

Selbstmord

In this city, and at that time, you should understand that suicide was a completely acceptable option, an entirely understandable, rational course of action to take. And I speak as one who knows its temptations intimately: three of my elder brothers took their own lives—Hans, Rudi and Kurt. That left Paul, me and my three older sisters. My sisters, I am sure, were immune to suicide's powerful contagion. I cannot speak for Paul. As for myself, I can say only that its clean resolution of all my problems—intellectual and emotional—was always most appealing.

The Benefactor

I came down from the Hochreith, our house in the country, to Vienna to meet Herr Ficker. The big white villa in the parks of Neuwaldegg was closed up for the summer. I had one of the gardeners prepare my room and make up a bed, and his wife laid the table on the terrace and helped me cook dinner. We were to have *Naturschnitzel* with *Kochsalat* with a cold bottle of Zöbinger. Simple, honest food. I hoped Ficker would notice.

I shaved and dressed and went out on to the terrace to wait for him to arrive. I was wearing a banana-yellow, soft-collared shirt with no tie and a light tweed jacket that I had bought years before in Manchester. Its fraying cuffs had been repaired, in the English way, with a dun green leather. My hair was clean and still damp, my face was cool, scraped smooth. I drank a glass of sherbet water as I waited for Ficker. The evening light was milky and diffused, as if hung with dust. I could hear the faint noise of motors and carriages on the roads of Neuwaldegg and in the gathering dusk I could make out the figure of the gardener moving about in the *Allee* of pleached limes. A fleeting but palpable peace descended on me, and I thought for some minutes of David and our holidays together in Iceland and Norway. I missed him.

Ficker was an earnest young man, taller than me (mind you, I am not particularly tall) with fine, thinning hair brushed back off his brow. He wore spectacles with crooked wire frames, as if he

Photo: Barry Lewis

had accidentally sat upon them and had hastily straightened them out himself. He was neatly and soberly dressed, wore no hat and was clean-shaven. His lopsided spectacles suggested a spirit of frivolity and facetiousness which, I soon found out, was entirely inaccurate.

I had already explained to him, by letter, about my father's death, my legacy and how I wished to dispose of a proportion of it. He had agreed to my conditions and promised to respect my demand for total anonymity. We talked, in business-like fashion, about the details, but I could sense, as he expressed his gratitude, strong currents of astonishment and curiosity.

Eventually he had to ask. 'But why me? Why my magazine . . . in particular?'

I shrugged. 'It seems to be exemplary of its sort. I like its attitude, its, its seriousness. And besides, your writers seem the most needy.'

'Yes . . . that's true.' He was none the wiser.

'It's a family trait. My father was a great benefactor—to musicians mainly. We just like to do it.'

Ficker then produced a list of writers and painters he thought were the most deserving. I glanced through it: very few of the names were familiar to me, and beside each one Ficker had written an appropriate sum of money. Two names at the top of the list were to receive by far the largest amounts.

'I know of Rilke, of course,' I said, 'and I'm delighted you chose him. But who's he?' I pointed to the other name. 'Why should he get so much? What does he do?'

'He's a poet,' Ficker said. 'I think . . . well, no man on this list will benefit more from your generosity. To be completely frank, I think it might just save his life.'

Schubert

My brother Hans drowned himself in Chesapeake Bay. He was a musical prodigy who gave his first concert in Vienna at the age of nine. I never really knew him. My surviving brother Paul was also musically gifted, a brilliant pianist who was a pupil of Leschetitzky and made his debut in 1913. I remember Paul saying to me once that of all musical tastes the love of Schubert required the least explanation. When one thinks of the huge misery of his life and sees in his work no trace of it at all—the complete absence in his music of all bitterness.

The Bank

I had arranged with Ficker that I would be in the Österreichische Nationalbank on Schwarzspanier Strasse at three o'clock. I was there early and sat down at a writing desk in a far corner. It was quiet and peaceful: the afternoon rush had yet to begin and the occasional sound of heels on the marble floor as clients crossed from the entrance foyer to the rows of counters was soothing, like the background click of ivory dominoes or the ceramic kiss of billiard balls in the gaming room of my favourite café near the art schools.

Ficker was on time and accompanied by our poet. Ficker caught my eye, and I gave a slight nod and then bent my head over the spectral papers on my desk. Ficker went to a teller's guichet to inquire about the banker's draft, leaving the poet standing momentarily alone in the middle of the marble floor, gazing around him like a peasant at the high, dim vaults of the ceiling and the play of afternoon sunshine on the ornamental brasswork of the chandeliers.

Georg, as I shall refer to him, was a young man, twenty-seven years old—two years older than me—small and quite sturdily built, and, like many small men, seemed to have been provided with a head designed for a bigger body altogether. His head was crude and heavy-looking, its proportions exaggerated by his bristly, close-cropped hair. He was clean-shaven. He had a weak mouth, the upper lip overhung the bottom one slightly, and a thick triangular nose. He had low brows and slightly oriental-looking, almond-shaped eyes. He was what my mother would have called 'an ugly customer'.

He stood now, looking expressionlessly about him, swaying slightly, as if buffeted by an invisible crowd. He appeared at once ill and strong—pale-faced, ugly, dark-eyed, but there was something about the set of his shoulders, the way his feet were planted on the ground, that suggested reserves of strength. Indeed the year before, Ficker had told me, he had almost died from an overdose of Veronal that should have killed an ordinary man in an hour or two. Since his school-days, it transpired, he had been a compulsive user of narcotic drugs and was also an immoderate drinker. At school he used chloroform to intoxicate himself. He was now a qualified dispensing chemist, a career he had taken up, so Ficker informed me, solely because it gave him access to more effective drugs. I found this single-mindedness oddly impressive. To train for two years at the University of Vienna as a pharmacist and pass the necessary exams to qualify testified to an uncommon dedication. Ficker had given me some of his poems to read. I could not understand them at all; their images for me were strangely haunting and evocative but finally entirely opaque. But I liked their *tone*; their tone seemed to me to be quite remarkable.

I watched him now, discreetly, as Ficker completed the preliminary documentation and signalled him over to endorse the banker's draft. Ficker—I think this was a mistake—presented the cheque to him with a small flourish and shook him by the hand, as if he had just won first prize in a lottery. I could sense that Georg knew very little of what was going on. I saw him turn the cheque over immediately so as to hide the amount from his own eyes. He exchanged a few urgent words with Ficker, who smiled encouragingly and patted him on the arm. Ficker was very happy, almost gleeful—in his role as the philanthropist's go-between he was vicariously enjoying what he imagined would be Georg's astonished surprise. But he was wrong. I knew it the instant Georg turned over the cheque and read the amount. Twenty thousand crowns. A thriving dispensing chemist would have to work six or seven years to earn a similar sum. I saw the cheque flutter and tremble in his fingers. I saw Georg blanch and swallow violently several times. He put the back of his hand to his lips and his shoulders heaved. He rcached out to a pillar for support, bending over from the waist. His body convulsed in a spasm as he tried to control his writhing stomach. I knew then that he was an honest man for he had the honest man's profound fear of extreme good fortune. Ficker snatched the cheque from his shaking fingers as

Georg appeared to totter. He uttered a faint cry as warm bile and vomit shot from his mouth to splash and splatter on the cool marble of the Nationalbank's flagged floor.

A Good Life, a Good Death

I got to know Ficker quite well over our various meetings about the division and disposal of my benefaction. Once in our discussions the subject of suicide came up, and he seemed genuinely surprised when I told him that scarcely a day went by when I did not think about it. But I explained to him that if I could not get along with life and the world then to commit suicide would be the ultimate admission of failure. I pointed out that this notion was the very essence of ethics and morality. For if anything is not to be allowed, then surely that must be suicide. For if suicide is allowed, then anything is allowed.

Sometimes I think that a good life should end in a death that one could welcome. Perhaps, even, it is only a good death that allows us to call a life 'good'.

Georg, I believe, has nearly died many times. For example, shortly before the Veronal incident he almost eliminated himself by accident. Georg lived for a time in Innsbruck. One night, after a drinking bout in a small village near the city he decided to walk home. At some stage on his journey back, overcome with tiredness, he decided to lie down in the snow and sleep. When he awoke in the morning the world had been replaced by a white turbid void. For a moment he thought . . . but almost immediately he realized he had been covered in the night by a new fall of snow. In fact it was about forty centimetres deep. He heaved himself to his feet, brushed off his clothes and, with a gonging headache, completed his journey to Innsbruck.

How I wish I had been passing that morning! The first sleepy traveller along that road when Georg awoke. In the still, pale light, that large hump on the verge begins to stir, some cracks and declivities suddenly deform the smooth contours, then a fist punches free and finally that crude ugly face emerges, with its frosty beret of snow, staring stupidly, blinking, spitting.

William Boyd

The War

The war saved my life. I really do not know what I would have done without it. On 7 August, the day war was declared on Russia, I enlisted as a volunteer gunner in the artillery for the duration and was instructed to report to a garrison artillery regiment in Cracow. In my elation I was reluctant to go straight home to pack my bags (my family had by now all returned to Vienna), so I took a taxi to the Café Museum.

I should say that I joined the army because it was my civic duty, yet I was even more glad to enlist because I knew at that time I had to *do* something, I had to subject myself to the rigours of a harsh routine that would divert me from my intellectual work. I had reached an impasse, and the impossibility of ever proceeding further filled me with morbid despair.

By the time I reached the Café Museum it was about six o'clock in the evening (I liked this Café because its interior was modern: its square rooms were lined with square honey-coloured oak panelling, hung with prints of the drawings of Charles Dana Gibson). Inside it was busy, the air noisy with speculation about the war. It was humid and hot, the atmosphere suffused with the reek of beer and cigar smoke. The patrons were mostly young men, students from the nearby art schools, clean-shaven, casually and unaffectedly dressed. So I was a little surprised to catch a glimpse in one corner of a uniform. I pushed through the crowd to see who it was.

Georg, it was obvious, was already fairly drunk. He sat strangely hunched over, staring intently at the table-top. His posture and the ferocious concentration of his gaze clearly put people off as the three other seats around his table remained unoccupied. I told a waiter to bring a half litre of *Heuniger Wein* to the table and then sat down opposite him.

Georg was wearing the uniform of an officer, a lieutenant, in the Medical Corps. He looked at me candidly and without resentment and, of course, without recognition. He seemed much the same as the last time I had seen him, at once ill-looking and possessed of a sinewy energy. I introduced myself and told him I was pleased to see a fellow soldier as I myself had just enlisted.

'It's your civic duty,' he said, his voice strong and unslurred. 'Have a cigar.'

He offered me a Trabuco, those ones that have a straw mouthpiece because they are so strong. I declined—at that time I did not smoke. When the wine arrived he insisted on paying for it.

'I'm a rich man,' he said as he filled our glasses. 'Where're you posted?'

'Galicia.'

'Ah, the Russians are coming.' He paused. 'I want to go somewhere cold and dark. I detest this sun and this city. Why aren't we fighting the Eskimos? I hate daylight. Maybe I could declare war on the Lapps. One-man army.'

'Bit lonely, no?'

'I want to be lonely. All I do is pollute my mind talking to people . . . I want a dark, cold lonely war. Please.'

'People will think you're mad.'

He raised his glass. 'God preserve me from sanity.'

I thought of something Nietzsche had said: 'Our life, our happiness, is beyond the north, beyond ice, beyond death.' I looked into Georg's ugly face, his thin eyes and glossy lips, and felt a kind of love for him and his honesty. I clinked my glass against his and asked God to preserve me from sanity as well.

Tagebuch: 15 August. Cracow.

If your wife, for example, continually puts too much sugar in your tea, it is not because she has too much sugar in her cupboard; it is because she is not educated in the ways of handling sweetness. Similarly, the problem of how to live a good life cannot ever be solved by continually assaulting it with the intellect.

The Searchlight

I enlisted in the artillery to fire howitzers but instead found myself manning a searchlight on a small, heavily armed paddle-steamer called the *Goplana*. We cruised up and down the Vistula, ostensibly looking for Russians but also to provide support for any river crossings by our own forces.

I enjoyed my role in charge of the searchlight. I took its mounting apart and oiled and greased its bearings. Reassembled, it moved effortlessly under the touch of my fingers. Its strong beam shone straight and true in the blurry semi-darkness of those late summer nights. However, I soon found the living conditions on the *Goplana* intolerable because of the stink, the proximity and the vulgarity of my fellow soldiers. And because we were constantly in motion, life below decks was dominated by the thrum and grind of the *Goplana*'s churning paddles. I spent long hours in my corner of the bridgehouse needlessly overhauling the mechanism of the searchlight—anything to escape the torrent of filth and viciousness that poured from the men. I found my old despair began to creep through me again, like a stain.

One day we disembarked at Sandomierz and were sent to a bath house. As we washed I looked at my naked companions, their brown faces and forearms, their grey-white bodies and dark dripping genitals as they soaped and sluiced themselves with garrulous ostentation. I felt only loathing for them, my fellow men. It was both impossible to work with them and have nothing to do with them. I was glad that I felt no stirrings of sensuality as I contemplated their naked bodies. I saw that they were men but I could not see they were human beings.

Tagebuch: 8 September. Sawichost.

The news is worse. All the talk is of Cracow being besieged. Last night there was an alarm. I ran up on deck to man the searchlight. It was raining and I wore only a shirt and trousers. I played the beam of the searchlight to and fro on the opposite bank of the river for hours, my feet and hands slowly becoming numb. Then we heard the sound of gunfire, and I at once became convinced I was going to die that night. The beam of the searchlight was a lucent arrow pointing directly at me. And for the first time I felt, being face to face with my own death, with possibly only an hour or two of life remaining to me, that I had in those few hours the chance to be a good man, if only because of this uniquely potent consciousness of myself. 'I did my duty and stayed at my post.' That is all I can say about that tremendous night.

The Amputee

Of course I did not die and of course I fell back into more abject moods of self-disgust and loathing. Perhaps the only consolation was that my enormous fatigue made it impossible for me to think about my work.

It was about this time—in September or October—that I heard the news about my brother Paul. He was a quite different personality from me—fierce and somewhat dominating—and he had tackled his vocation as concert pianist with uncompromising dedication. Since his debut his future seemed assured, an avenue of bright tomorrows. To receive the news, then, that he had been captured by the Russians and had had his right arm amputated at the elbow, as a result of wounds he had sustained, was devastating. For days my thoughts were of Paul and of what I would do in his situation. Poor Paul, I thought, if only there were some other solution than suicide. What philosophy it will take to get over this!

Tagebuch: 13 October. Nadbrzesze.

We have sailed here, waited for twelve hours, and have now been ordered to return to Sawichost. All day we can hear the mumble of artillery in the east. I find myself drawn down into dark depression again, remorselessly. Why? What is the real basis of this malaise? I see one of my fellow soldiers pissing over the side of the boat in full view of the few citizens of Nadbrzesze who have gathered on the quayside to stare at us. The long pale arc of his urine sparkles in the thin autumn sunshine. Another soldier leans on his elbows staring candidly at the man's white flaccid penis, held daintily between two fingers like a titbit. This is shaken, its tip squeezed and then tucked away in the coarse serge of his trousers. I think if I was standing at a machine-gun rather than a searchlight I could kill them both without a qualm . . . Why do I detest these simple foolish men so? Why can I not be impassive? I despise my own weakness, my inability to distance myself from the commonplace.

The Battle of Grodek

On our return from Sawichost I received mail. A long letter from David—I wonder if he thinks of me half as much as I think of him?—and a most distressing communication from Ficker, to whom I had written asking for some books to be sent to me. I quote:

> I see from your letter that you are not far from Cracow. I wonder if you get the opportunity you could attempt to find and visit [Georg]. You may have heard of the heavy fighting at Grodek some two weeks ago. Georg was there and, owing to the chaos and disorganization that prevailed at the time, was mistakenly placed in charge of a field hospital not far behind our lines. Apparently he protested vigorously that he was merely a dispensing chemist and not a doctor, but resources were so stretched he was told to do the best he could.
>
> Thus Georg found himself with two orderlies (Czechs, who spoke little German) in charge of a fifty-bed field hospital. As the battle wore on more than ninety severely wounded casualties were delivered during the day. Repeatedly, Georg signalled for a doctor to be sent as he could do nothing for these men except inject them with morphine and attempt to dress their wounds. In fact it became clear that through some oversight these casualties had been sent to the wrong hospital. The ambulance crews that transported them had been erroneously informed that there was a field surgery and a team of surgeons operating there.
>
> By nine in the evening all of Georg's supplies of morphine were exhausted. Shortly thereafter men began to scream from the resurgent pain. Finally, one

officer, who had lost his left leg at the hip, shot himself in the head.

At this point Georg ran away. Two kilometres from the field hospital was a small wood which, at the start of the battle, had been a battalion headquarters. Georg went there for help or at least to report the ghastly condition of the wounded in his charge. When he arrived there he found that an impromptu military tribunal had just executed twenty deserters by hanging.

I do not know exactly what happened next. I believe that at the sight of these fresh corpses Georg tried to seize a revolver from an officer and shoot himself. Whatever happened, he behaved in a demented manner, was subdued and arrested himself for desertion in the face of the enemy. I managed to visit him briefly in the mental hospital at Cracow ten days ago. He is in a very bad way, but at least, thank God, the charges of desertion have been dropped and he is being treated for *dementia praecox*. For some reason Georg is convinced he will be prosecuted for cowardice. He is sure he is going to hang.

The Asylum at Cracow

Georg's cell was very cold and dark, the only illumination coming from an oil-lamp in the corridor. Georg needed a shave but otherwise he looked much the same as he had on my two previous encounters with him. He was wearing a curious oatmeal canvas uniform, the jacket secured with strings instead of buttons. With his big head and thin eyes he looked strangely Chinese. There was one other patient in his cell with him, a major in the cavalry who was suffering from *delirium tremens*. This man remained hunched on a truckle bed in the corner of the room, sobbing quietly to himself while Georg and I spoke. He did not recognize me. I merely introduced myself as a friend of Ficker.

'Ludwig asked me to visit you,' I said. 'How are you?'

'Well, I'm . . . ' He stopped and gestured at the major. 'I used to think I was a heavy drinker.' He smiled. 'Actually, he's being quite good now.' Georg rubbed his hair with both hands.

'I heard about what happened,' I said. 'It must have been terrible.'

He looked at me intently and then seemed to think for a while.

'Yes,' he said. 'yes, yes, yes. All that sort of thing.'

'I completely understand.'

He shrugged uselessly. 'You don't have any cigars on you, by any chance? They haven't brought me my kit. One longs for a decent cigar.'

'Let me get some for you.'

'I smoke Trabucos—the ones with the straw holder.'

'They're very strong, I believe. I don't smoke, but I heard they can burn your throat.'

'It's a small price to pay.'

We sat on in silence for a moment, listening to the major's snufflings.

'It's very cold here,' Georg began slowly, 'and very dark, and if they got rid of the major the conditions would be perfect.'

'I know what you mean.'

'Actually, I have several boxes of Trabucos in my kit,' he went on. 'If you could get a message to my orderly perhaps he could bring me a couple.'

'Of course.'

'Oh, and would you ask him to bring me my green leather case.'

'Green leather case.'

'Yes,' he paused. 'That is essential . . . ' He rubbed his face, as if his features were tired of being eternally composed.

'I think with a good cigar I could even tolerate the major.'

I found Georg's orderly in the Medical Corps' billet in a small village on the outskirts of Cracow. The city was clearly visible across the flat cropped meadows where a few piebald ponies grazed: a low attenuated silhouette punctuated by a few domes and spires and the odd factory chimney. In the indistinct grainy light of the late afternoon the bulk of the Marienkirche had the look of a vast warehouse. I passed on Georg's instructions: two boxes of

Trabuco cigars and his green leather case.

'How is the lieutenant?' the orderly asked.

'He's very well,' I said. 'Considering . . . Very well indeed.'

Georg died that night from a heart seizure brought on by a massive intravenous injection of cocaine. According to his orderly, who was the last person to speak to him, he was 'in a state of acute distress' and must have misjudged the dose.

Tagebuch: 10 November. Sawichost.

The simplest way to describe the book of moral philosophy that I am writing is that it concerns what can and cannot be said. In fact it will be only half a book. The most interesting half will be the one that I cannot write. That half will be the most eloquent.

Tea at Neuwaldegg

It is springtime. After a shower of rain we take tea on the terrace of the big house at Neuwaldegg. Me, my mother, my sisters Helene and Hermine—and Paul. I am on leave; Paul has just been returned from captivity as part of an exchange of wounded prisoners. He sits with his right sleeve neatly pinned up, awkwardly squeezing lemon into his tea with his left hand. I think of Georg and I look at Paul. His hair is greying; his clothes are immaculate.

Quite suddenly he announces that he is going to continue with his career as a concert pianist and teach himself to play with the left hand only. He proposes to commission pieces for the left hand from Richard Strauss and Ravel. There is silence, and then I say, 'Bravo, Paul. Bravo.' And, spontaneously, we all clap him.

The modest sound of our applause carries out over the huge garden. A faint breeze shifts the new spring foliage of the chestnut trees, glistening after the rain, and the gardener, who has just planted a bed of geraniums, looks up from his work for a moment, smiles bemusedly at us, clambers to his feet and bows.

The Listener

27 APRIL 1989 · £1.00

MIKE TOMLINSON
Why your office makes you sick

ROGER BOLTON
George Blake, history and suppression

GILLIAN REYNOLDS
Diary of a Sony judge

PETER FOGES
The decline of the US networks

BOB WOFFINDEN
Flouting the critics

9 770244 392001 17

WILLIE'S WILES
MY LIFE WITH MARGARET

THE VERY BEST OF BRITISH BROADCASTING

Plus topical coverage of books, theatre, cinema, music, food, drink and painting. The Listener is comprehensive, authoritative, informative and, some say, provocative. Above all it is stimulating. You can buy your copy each week at your newsagents or call 0442 876661 to purchase a 1 year subscription by credit card for £48. Either way, you can't afford to miss it.

The Listener

MORE THAN MEETS THE EYE

GRANTA

Jeanette Winterson
The Architect of Unrest

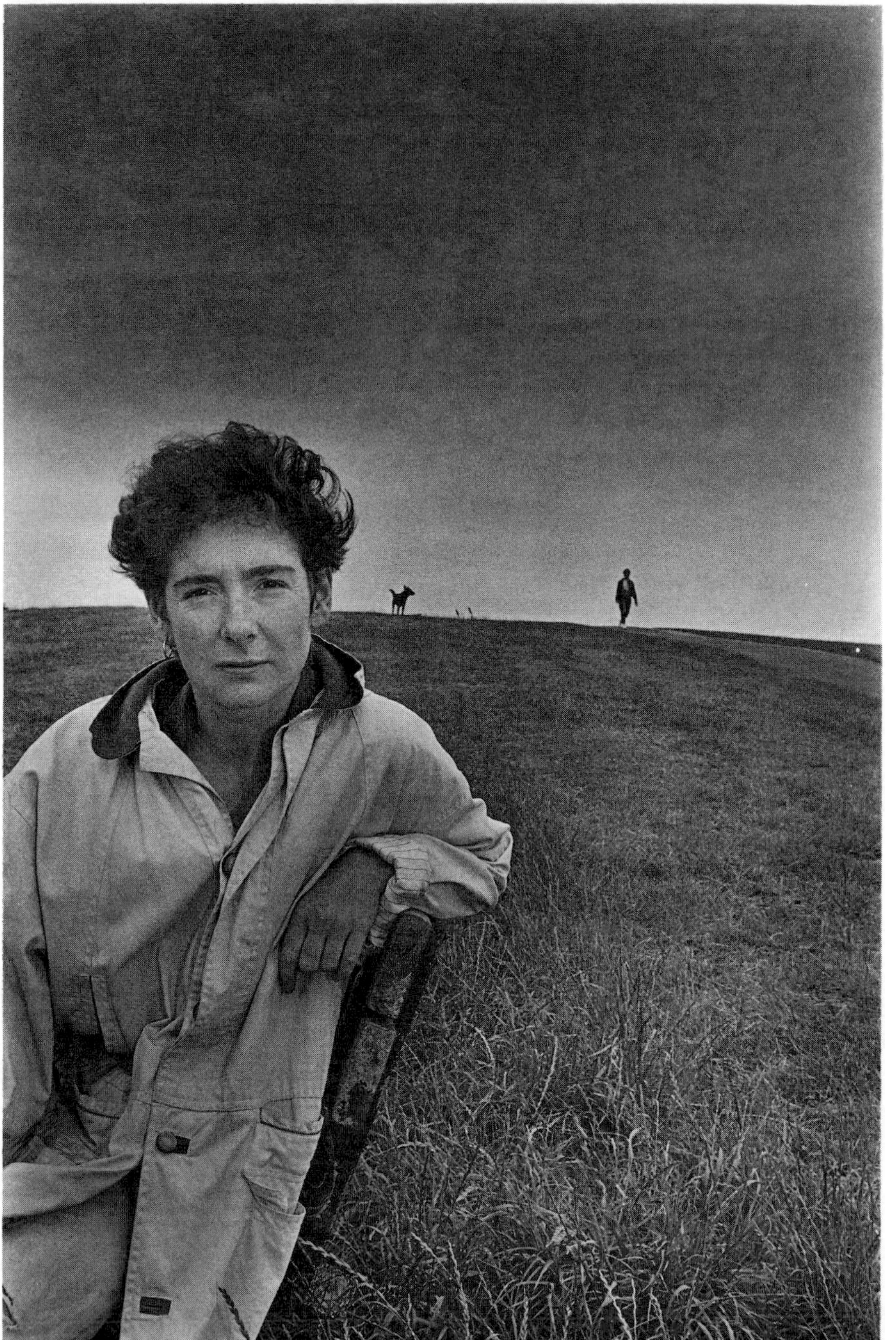

Gilbert Howard

I am an architect. I am redesigning the City of London by the consent of the people with money, whose views are imperative. My predecessor, Sir Christopher Wren, had a similar brief and similar constraints. Mammon is not a new god.

There have been other architects in the three centuries that separate me from Sir Christopher, but none who have been so perfectly placed to profit from the accidents of nature. When the Great Fire destroyed so much of London in 1666, it took with it the last vestiges of the Middle Ages and the worst excesses of Elizabeth.

You imagine I am talking only of buildings and rush to correct me. I am not talking only of buildings, if by that you mean a thing of foundations and solid walls. I am talking of invisible cities; the attitudes that allow buildings to materialize at all. The cast of mind, the habits of thought, the fancies and the daydreams. Most of all, the terror and horror. Buildings keep inside them what we love. And outside them? Who knows what lies beyond their walls, within their hollows?

And so when I talk of the spaces created by that purgatorial fire, I mean the vast acres lost to prejudice and superstition. Shakespeare, whatever his merits, was a man more interested in magic than in science. Indeed, the transforming spirit of the Renaissance was alchemical not scientific. I think of the Renaissance as the apotheosis of the primitive. Magic's last stand. A knot of coloured handkerchiefs and from the filthy window-sill a flight of doves.

Pretty. Very pretty. Conjurors, however, are for children's parties and in the late seventeenth century England began to grow up, to become the rational man of the glorious eighteenth century. No doubt it was romantic to try to transform urine into precious metal and to make a metaphysics out of this, but at last we were able to see that if we wanted the streets to be paved with gold we first had to wash away the piss.

Like Sir Christopher, I am designing the hearts and minds of men. My banking halls and art galleries are inspired by a new understanding: that if we make provision for the poor, the poor will always be with us. There is no room for the hideous philanthropy of

Photo: Barry Lewis

tower blocks and mission halls. We must not riddle the future with the diseases of the past. I know you have been thinking this secretly for some time. At last we are not afraid to air our secret thoughts.

For 300 years, the rational man has sought to be heard above the chants and howls of the savage. We have made progress and the dominant voice is at last the level tone of reason. A revolution has run its course and we are on the brink of a world where superstition and religion will be museum-pieces only. In the West and gaining ground in the old citadels of the East is the philosophy of the free man; independent in thought, unfettered in heart and sensible in love. For the first time in history the self we long to be has a technology equal to it.

There is a danger, though. Turn to your Poe and you will see how troublesome the buried life can be. Whatever is walled up, mutilated, whatever is only partially destroyed, its tongue cut out, its heart still beating, will be heard scraping at the coffin-lid, laughing behind the wall. Many have killed the thing they fear only to find it alive and well inside them. We must be sure then, as we build our brighter future, that the past is gone.

Sir Christopher was fortunate with his fire. I have been just as lucky. The common lament of architects is that you cannot build beautifully for the many. The many are dying now. AIDS has seen to that. How admirable nature is that when the earth groans under the weight of senseless feet, a volcano, a fire, a war, a plague comes to redress the balance. In the tradition of our future (a phrase I have coined myself) we are working with nature not against her. We are allowing the virus to spread, though only in a controlled way, throughout those sectors of society that most need a little trimming. Think of it as pruning a rose. We calculate that population levels will fall by roughly one half in Great Britain and a little less than that in the United States of America. Other countries are cautiously and most secretly joining our brave enterprise and I am confident that in the next twenty years we will begin to see the kind of utopia, a one-world utopia, that writers have always imagined but never expected.

My plan for London begins with the square mile of the City. I am pulling down little shops and tower blocks alike. Listed buildings are on the whole exempt, except where the future is more pressing than the past. Churches, for instance, are not to be saved. I am very anxious that no meeting-house for hypocrites should survive the life to come. For personal reasons and ones you will readily understand, St Paul's will remain. I have permission to redesign the interior as an architectural museum. A fitting homage to both of us, I think.

The demolition work has begun in every quarter, and some of my buildings are ready for glass. In a few years we shall see the independent heart of a mighty city. Readers of Dickens will have to forgo their guided walks. As a boy, trotting beside my uncle, who liked to mudlark along the Thames reaches in search of coins and clay pipes, I was astonished at how fitfully London had shaken off her past. The houses, the streets, the river itself seemed nothing more to me than a collection of ghosts. How can a people who live literally in what lies behind them design for themselves a present in keeping with their development? We have been to the moon and put a baboon's heart in a baby and soon the babies themselves will be born in little tubes. All the things we thought we couldn't do we have done and now we know that any wild adventure of the brain will soon become the schooldays of our children. When I was a boy, computers were as big as wardrobes and not half so good at containing things; now infants carry lap-tops in their satchels and plug into the moving mind of the world. It is time that our buildings caught up with our thoughts.

You suspect me of being against history. Not at all. Indeed many of our group are historians of one kind or another. How may we learn about ourselves without knowing who we were? You will acknowledge that any true revolution seems barbaric to those who do not understand its aims. What of the French who deposed their monarchy, despised their calendar and instituted under Napoleon an astonishing programme of building works with the purpose of doing away with what had been?

After the last war, we in Europe had an unprecedented opportunity to rebuild but we turned away from it into a welter of preservation orders and cage-like apartments. I was a young man then and the rubble and open spaces of the Blitz seemed like the acres of Heaven to me. I submitted a plan to the Government, but of course it was turned down. No, they didn't even do me that courtesy; they ignored it.

Ah well. That young man has vanished. Where is he now? There is no trace of him, nor of his charts and daydreams. You might call at his lodgings and no one would know his name. Why should the lodgings live longer than the lodger?

It was in those days, when I was all passion and high belief, that I first started to read Ruskin. I found a copy of *The Stones of Venice* in a second-hand bookshop and sat up for a day and a night learning the nature of things. I began to realize what Jesus meant when he warned his disciples that if the people did not praise him, the very stones would cry out. They do cry out. They vibrate with individual life. Do not bother me with poured concrete. I build with true materials.

Today, while I was inspecting the building work between Broadgate and the river, an awful thing happened. I noticed that part of our demolition work had uncovered an old window previously lost behind a shield of concrete. The window was intact: frame, glass, leaded parts, wooden angels at each corner and a cracked lintel beneath. It appeared to be from a modern office block, a kind of disused annex, though how it had escaped a preservation order I don't know. Still, the last thing I wanted was any delay and I ordered my foreman to smash through it at once. He hurried away to make the arrangements and I stood alone looking up.

After a moment, the window opened and a man in a curly wig poked out his head and surveyed the sky. He kept one hand on the latch of the window and in the other he held a quill pen. His cuffs were dirty. His gaze fell in my direction, though whether he addressed the following remark to me is uncertain. '*Gloria cum laude*!' he exclaimed and, bobbing back in, slammed the window shut.

I was very much put out, and when my foreman returned I asked him to lift me in the crane so I could look in through the window.

We rose in our yellow monster and were soon on a level with

the lintel. I gave the order to hold steady and rubbed one of the dust-thick panes. There was nothing, nothing. The wall, the window, were like Hollywood flats, sets with nothing behind. It was folly, a mistake. A walled-up wall. Whoever heard of such a thing?

The foreman was clearly disturbed by my attention, so I had him take me down at once and I let him get on with his task. I walked towards the river, ignoring the traffic and the ant-like streams of workers on their way home. I walked and walked, along my boyhood routes and eventually to the house of Sir Christopher Wren, still standing with its garden intact, though few know of the narrow alley that leads to a gate in the wall, or of a little grate in the gate to peep through. At the grating I stood on tiptoe and pressed my face to the iron like a lover at a convent. In the garden I saw Sir Christopher tending his roses.

I fell back against the opposite wall, glad of the cold stone and the overhead shade of an oak tree. After a few moments I regained myself sufficiently to try again. The garden was empty.

Tonight I have not turned to Poe. I am alone in my sitting-room, the clock is ticking, a glass of port sits on the table in front of me. There is much to be done but whenever I turn to my work I see the events I have outlined to you and my hands tremble. I have the sensation that this room is shrinking, that the walls are moving closer and closer. The bookcase seems nearer than it was. Footsteps tread softly in the corridor outside and I think I can hear my daughter calling. She cannot be calling, she is dead, and there is no one outside except my cat. I have not seen my cat this evening. Have you, perhaps? I long to sleep but fear sleep. What dreams may come? Rouse yourself, Howard, put on all the lights. Look, the room is brilliant now, a ballroom full of dancers. Work while you have light . . .

White tie and tails. Some things don't change. At last I am to be honoured for my work and the people who ignored me must praise me now. If only they knew how much they owe me. Naturally the countless deaths are lamented but the lamentations are niceties only. After the funeral we throw off our weeds and play. London is much less crowded than it was. Indeed it is becoming a pleasant place to have a house.

I am my old self again. The sweats and tremors of the recent past are over and I have not been troubled for a few weeks now. No doubt I have been experiencing in my body what the body of the world is experiencing as it seeks to throw off the last grasp of the primitive. Progress is everywhere. I am happy for posterity to point the finger at me. I have left my testaments and for the rest of this lifetime I am content to be an architect only. The genius of my social engineering can wait to be revealed.

The car is outside. I have my speech ready, my handkerchief is clean. My escort is waiting.

Dinner. St Paul's beautifully redesigned by me. A statue of me. A statue of Sir Christopher. The chandelier clinking and glittering. What a good joke I have just made to my neighbour. Cheese, twenty-five kinds. Port, liqueurs, Blue Mountain coffee. The speech, yes the speech, where are my notes? I am searching for my notes but then I feel the table rocking beneath me and the floor rising under my feet and my glass is cracking in my hand and the gold paint is falling from the interior of the dome. Gold paint everywhere. The company look like angels.

Why don't they notice? Why are they staring at me smiling, waiting for me to begin? Can't they see? 'My friends,' I say, 'my friends,' and as I say it I am calm again. Every face is turned towards me and the table is silent waiting for me to begin. In the silence I can hear my heart beating.

Catherine Powell

Gilbert Howard Associates have been given the Queen's Award for Industry. I'm not surprised. No one has done more to change the face of London. I have been with the company for six years and I'm leaving after the presentation tonight. I'm not well and I want to travel while I can. Gilbert Howard is not well either. I suppose there were signs soon after I joined, some would say there were signs before that. He began to see things. Warehouses, shipyards and churches that had been cleared away half a century ago began to appear in his drawings. Most of these places had been destroyed in the Blitz. I know because I researched them. I wasn't required to, it was curiosity. Then he began to include buildings that had been gone for so long that I had to look them up in the archive maps. He seemed to know them exactly, as though he really had walked round them as he sometimes claimed. I tried to alter his plans to save him embarrassment but he noticed and raved at me, so I stopped. We all got used to working around what wasn't there.

Then, about a year ago, as we were finishing the Broadgate development and he'd had permission to demolish most of the public buildings in Tower Hamlets, he started to draw people. His plans most resembled the drawings of Piranesi, the prison sequence. Vaults and spirals and hideous figures grinning in their chains. Of course we couldn't use them and since that time I've been doing the plans. He hates me for it.

Sometimes, when I'm working late, I take the lift up to his flat above our offices and leave my efforts outside his door. He's always awake, the light shining feebly in the small space between the door bottom and the thick carpet. We don't know what's wrong with him. A few nights ago, the door was open and I pushed it further, worrying suddenly that he might have had a fit or an attack. He was sitting at his desk, with the drawing-board to one side. How tiny he looked hunched in his chair. I tried to attract his attention, first by coughing and then by calling his name. Eventually I approached and came right behind his shoulder.

He'd been writing his speech for the dinner. The desk was covered with torn up pieces of paper, but a few pages seemed to be complete. I picked them up and read quickly. The scene was Poe's building. The sewers, crypts, the mansion on the Faubourg St. Germain, and the terrible House of Usher. In the margins were the figures I had come to recognize, knock-kneed in pantomime costume, some hanging by their fingers or toes from immense tracts of Gothic ironwork. He had titled his speech 'The Architect of Unrest.'

The most magical bestseller of the year

Love in the Time of Cholera

Gabriel Garcia Marquez

Out now in Penguin paperback

£4.99

GRANTA

Russell Hoban
The Man with the Dagger

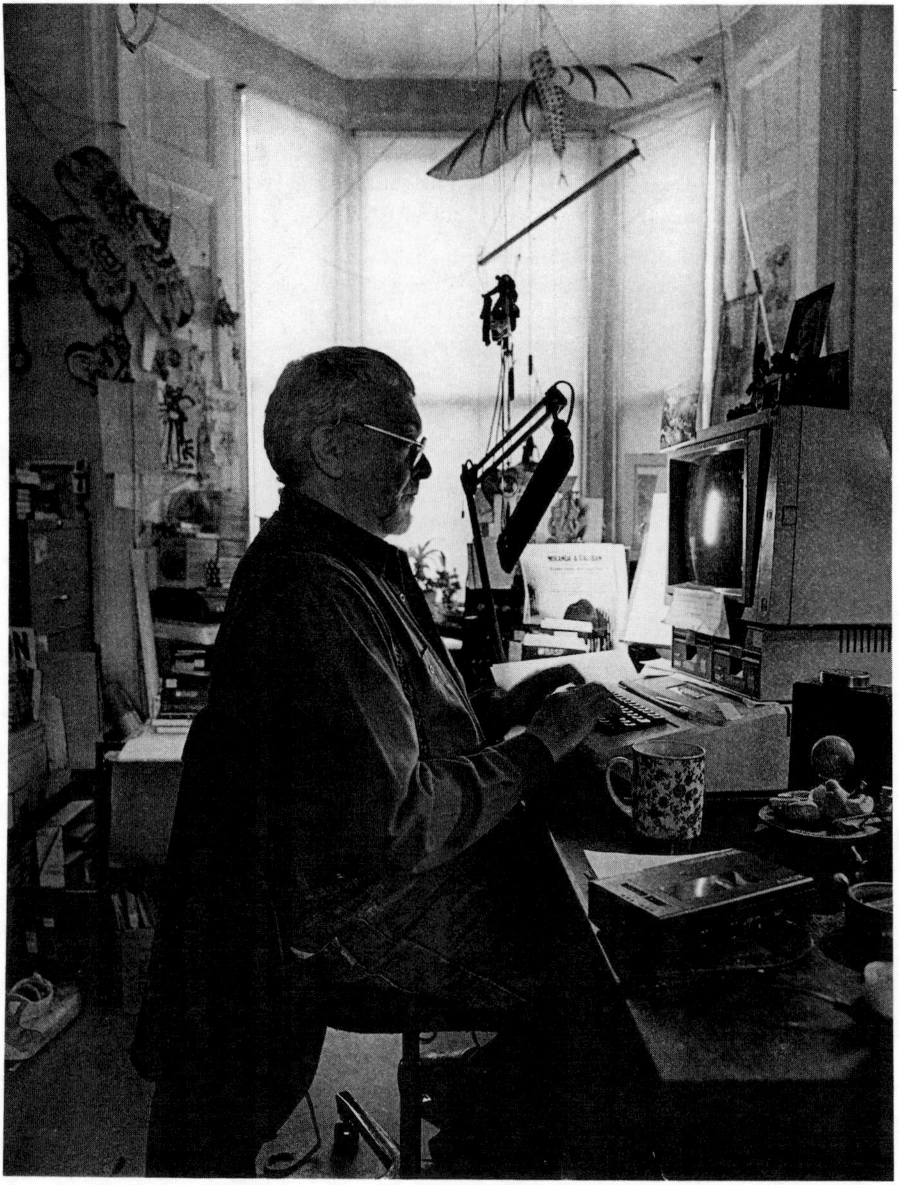

The Man With The Dagger

There is a short story by Jorge Luis Borges called 'The South'. It is a story full of sharpness, having in it a lance, a sword, the edge of a door, two knives, the strangeness of life and the familiarity of death.

The protagonist of the story is Juan Dahlmann, secretary to a municipal library in Buenos Aires in 1939. His paternal grandfather, a German immigrant, was a minister in the Evangelical Church. His maternal grandfather was 'that Francisco Flores, of the Second Line-Infantry Division, who had died on the frontier of Buenos Aires, run through with a lance by Indians from Catriel . . .' Dahlmann keeps the sword of Francisco Flores and his daguerreotype portrait and has 'at the cost of numerous small privations . . . managed to save the empty shell of a ranch in the South which had belonged to the Flores family.' He has never lived on this ranch; year after year it waits for him.

Hurrying up the library stairs one day, Dahlmann strikes his head against the edge of a freshly painted door and comes away with a bloody wound. The next morning 'the savour of all things was atrociously poignant. Fever wasted him . . .' He nearly dies of septicaemia, and after a long stay in a sanatorium he leaves the city to go to his ranch for his convalescence.

On his arrival in the South he has a meal at a general store near the railway station. Three men are drinking at another table; one of them has a Chinese look. This man provokes Dahlmann by throwing breadcrumb spitballs at him, then challenges him to a knife fight. Dahlmann knows nothing of knife-play and is unarmed but an old gaucho throws him a naked dagger which lands at his feet. 'It was as if the South had resolved that Dahlmann should accept the duel. Dahlmann bent over to pick up the dagger and felt two things. The first, that this almost instinctive act bound him to fight. The second, that the weapon, in his torpid hand, was no defence at all, but would merely serve to justify his murder.'

Dahlmann picks up the dagger and goes out into the plain to fight. 'Without hope, he was also without fear . . . He felt that if he had been able to choose, then, or to dream his death, this would

Photo: Barry Lewis

have been the death he would have chosen or dreamt.'

With the dagger Dahlmann has seized the critical moment that defines . . . what? The right time to die? No use to attempt an analysis of Borges's intention—by the time Dahlmann picks up the dagger he is a fiction of his own making.

Now for as long as there will be print on paper, even longer—for as long as there will be one rememberer to pass this story on to another, even longer, even when all the rememberers are dead, Dahlmann, with his being vibrating between the strangeness of life and the familiarity of death, will live in this moment of unknown definition that he has seized. I wanted to talk to him.

The White Street

I thought the story would be the most likely place to look for Dahlmann, so I went there. I found it in a quiet street where the trees made little black shadows in a dazzling whiteness; it was an old rose-coloured house with iron grille windows, a brass knocker and an arched door. Beside the door was a brass plaque; engraved on it in copperplate script: THE SOUTH.

I knocked, and after a time I heard slow footsteps within and the thud of bolts being drawn back. The door opened slowly and in a very narrow aperture there appeared a vertical fraction of an old woman's face at the top of a blackness of clothing. Her one visible eye was black and difficult to meet.

'Good afternoon,' I said (my watch had stopped but the street was white with heat and light and the sun seemed almost directly overhead). 'Is Señor Dahlmann at home?'

'There's no one here,' she said. 'We're closed.' The aperture and her face became narrower and disappeared with a click. There was the sound of bolts thudding home; her footsteps receded. Behind me the white street shimmered in the heat; far away a dog barked. I didn't want to turn around and see that white street again; I felt myself to be a prism through which the white light would reveal its full spectrum of terror.

I stood facing the centuries-darkened door until I felt myself flickering into black-and-white, then I turned back to the street. It too was flickering in black-and-white like an old film in which nothing had yet happened.

There was a boy flickering in front of me. His head was bent so that his straw sombrero concealed his face, his hands were behind his back. I didn't notice his feet.

'Where's Dahlmann?' I said.

'New in town?'

'Yes.'

'Do they have discretion where you come from?'

'Some do.'

'But not you.'

'I'm a writer, I need to know things.'

'What you need is not to be in too much of a hurry. I'll take you to the hotel.'

His manner was that of one who has seen everything. 'I bet the stories you could tell would make a hell of a book,' I said, 'if only you knew how to get them down on paper.'

He shrugged. 'Not everything needs to be written down.'

We walked without speaking past many churches and past many squares with fountains. Everything continued black-and-white, the streets gradually becoming populous with voices and footsteps and people. Eventually there appeared, not in the most expensive part of town, a small hotel with its name in unlit neon tubing: HOTEL DEATH. On its glass doors were the emblems of American Express, Diners Club and Visa. Opposite was a square with a fountain; on the far side of the square was a church.

'I'll see you later,' said the boy, and wasn't there any more.

Hotel Death

'What can I do for you?' said the skeleton at the desk. He was wearing a garish print shirt outside his trousers, he had a bottle of whisky and a glass and he was smoking an inexpensive cigar. The black-and-white was holding steady. A slowly turning fan in the ceiling stirred the grey shadows and the drifting dust-motes in the lobby.

'Have you got a Señor Dahlmann registered here?' I said.

He blew out a big cloud of inexpensive-smelling smoke. It came out of his mouth in the usual way. 'No.'

'You haven't looked.'

'I don't need to.' He poured himself a whisky and lifted his glass. 'Here's looking at you.'

I looked into the hollows where his eyes would have been; the shadows were not unfriendly. The whisky didn't run out of the back of his jaw, it just disappeared. He noticed my staring.

'It didn't bother you that I can talk without a tongue but you draw the line at drinking without a throat, is that it?'

'Not at all,' I lied.

'You want to check in?'

'No.'

'You look pretty old. Why not do it now and beat the rush? We got TV in every room and if you get lonesome I can send somebody around.'

'Skeleton whores?'

'Don't knock it till you've tried it.'

'Later,' I said. 'I've still got things to do.'

'Like what?'

'Like finding Dahlmann.'

'Are you sure you want to?'

'That's what I came here for.'

'Are you sure?'

'Look, let's not turn this into a philosophical exercise. I'll see you later.'

'You know it.'

I went outside and stood by the doors and stared at the flickering black-and-white of the church and the square and the fountain and the dusty street through which passed mules and ox-carts and dark people with sandalled feet and white cotton clothing. There was a smell of faeces and rotting fruit; there was the tolling of a bell and the buzzing of flies. From an upstairs window came the sound of a guitar.

There was a little whiff of lemony fragrance. 'Hi,' said a soft voice next to me. I turned and saw a really stunning skeleton with just the faintest touch of grey on her cheek-bones; I recognized it as blusher. No eye shadow, her eyes were nothing but shadows.

She was wearing a black poncho, a shiny black Rudolph Valentino hat with a flat top and a broad brim, and black boots. She was shapely in a way that made flesh seem vulgar.

'Why the blusher?' I said.

'I've seen things. Why are you looking for Dahlmann?'

'I think he may have something to tell me.'

'Perhaps I too have something to tell you.'

Together we walked off into the sunlight that would have made a blackness before my eyes if we had been in colour.

Noir's Room

I thought she would rattle but she didn't. What happened was that after the first few moments she stopped being a skeleton for me and simply became who she was, clean and elegant and more naked than I should have thought possible. With her lemony fragrance and that improbable blush on her cheek-bones she was utterly girlish in my arms while there echoed in my mind an ancient scream of desolation and all sweetness gone, gone, gone with her clean white feet running and her black poncho flapping down endless corridors of neverness.

'What's your name?' I said.

'Noir.'

'How much do I owe you, Noir?'

'Nothing, I'm not working now.'

'Why aren't you working now?'

'Sometimes I make love for money and sometimes I do it for me. This one was for me.'

'How come?'

'You ever do it with a skeleton before?'

'No.'

'I wanted your skeleton cherry,' she said, and kissed me. The room was a subtle composition of grey and black shadows with lines of brilliant white between the slats of the blinds. Through the front window came the sounds of a street market. On a table there were white lemons in a basket, there was a bottle of gin. I could feel colour impending but I held on to the black-and-white. Across the patio someone with a guitar was playing and singing a tango. The shadowy guitar and the quiet husky male voice made the gin seem miraculous.

'What do the words mean?' I asked her.

She listened for a moment, then she whispered in my ear:

'Such a little, such a little, such a little
difference, my heart—
such a little difference between the one
and the other.'

'Is it really such a little difference?' I said.

'Listen,' she said with her mouth still close to my ear, 'I'll sing you a verse of my own:

'You were with me, with me, with me, my heart—
you were naked in my arms, to you
I gave my naked self, my onliness.
Was it less than you've had from others?'

I kissed her delicate ivory face. Her mouth was sweet.

'Don't go looking for Dahlmann,' she said. 'What can he tell you that I can't?'

'I don't know. I don't even know what I'm going to ask him.' I got out of bed and put my clothes on. I didn't look back at her as I opened the door and went out.

'It could have been good,' she said.

Sidekick

Again I was hearing the buzzing of flies in a street that smelled of faeces and rotting fruit. Here also there were a square and a fountain and a church; the market stalls clustered under awnings along the near side of the square. The flickering seemed a little less steady than before.

There was a skeleton boy with his hat over his eyes, he was sitting on the ground leaning against the house I'd just come out of. He pushed the hat back and looked up at me as if expecting something.

'What is it?' I said.

'Don't you recognize me?'

'No.'

'I'm the kid that took you to the hotel.'

'Funny, I never noticed you were so bony. This place is full of regular people; why am I always talking to skeletons?'

'Maybe you speak our language.'

'Why is that? Am I dead?'

'What a question! You don't ask questions like that around here, it isn't that kind of a place, there's nothing that simple.'

'All right, then, I'll ask you something else: what's your interest in me? Why did you take me to that hotel and why have you been waiting for me here?'

'What's the matter with you? Don't you go to the movies? I'm the clever little street kid who helps you out; I'm your sidekick, I'm the only one on your side.'

'What's your name?'

'Whitey.'

'What about Noir? Isn't she on my side?'

'Shit. Women!'

'Well, is she or isn't she?'

'She's my sister but she hasn't got much sense and she gets mixed up with all kinds of people.'

'Like me.'

'And others.'

'What others?'

'All kinds. You see that big guy in the rumpled white suit down at the end of the square?'

I looked. The man was over six and a half feet tall, weighed about 300 pounds, and appeared to be the standard sort of henchman or subordinate villain one sees in films. He had nothing of a Chinese look about him and he was not entirely unfamiliar to me but I seemed not to remember who he was. 'Who's he?' I said.

'Don't you know?'

'Why should I know?'

'Because this is that kind of place, some of us are skeletons and some are extras but anybody else with any real action in the story is somebody you know.'

'Maybe I'll know him later but I don't know him now. You say he's one of the people Noir's mixed up with?'

'I'm not sure.'

'Never mind him for now. What about Dahlmann?'

'What?'

'Do you know where he is?'

'I don't exactly know where he is but I think I know when you can find him.'

'When will that be?'

'Later. Have another look around the square.'

I had another look. There was a second big man more or less the same as the first one. Now I seemed to be remembering these men from times when they were less big and I was much younger: the first one would be . . . John? John Something. Tumteetum. De Grassi? Bonanno? 'We'll settle this after school down by the boathouse,' he'd said. I'd preferred not to. Long, long ago. Some things you walk away from and they walk after you. I'd fought Joe Higgins and I'd lost but that had never bothered me. The second one, was he Sergeant Somebody from my army days whose offer to take off his stripes and step outside I'd declined? Matson? Mason?

'. . . around the square,' said Whitey.

'What did you say?'

'Have another look around the square.'

There was a third big man in a rumpled white suit. He was from no more than fifteen years ago, this one. I'd never known his name; he had been a stranger in a bar, another of my backdowns. 'What's happening?' I said. 'Is this the day when all my cowardice falls due?'

'What can I tell you? Every day has in it all your days. The past is something that sticks to your shoes like cowshit. If Yesterday had kept his pants on Tomorrow wouldn't have a big belly. Run is a good dog but Fight is a better one.'

'O God, skeleton aphorisms.'

'When I first saw you, you were knocking at the door of THE SOUTH. Why were you knocking at that door?'

'I wanted to ask Dahlmann what happened when he picked up the knife.'

'Why?'

'It's something I've thought about for a long time.'

'Why?'

'Various reasons.'

'Maybe because there were so many knives you didn't pick up?'

'What are you, the skeleton of Sigmund Freud as a boy?'

'No, I'm your sidekick. I'm the clever little street kid who helps you and I'd like to know how many big guys in rumpled white suits we're talking about. How many are there altogether?'

'More than one would like, I suppose.'

'Then let's get out of here before more of them turn up. One thing . . .'

'What?'

'What you're doing now, keep it going as long as you can until you're ready for the other.'

'You mean keep the black-and . . .'

'Discretion.'

'And the other?'

'Is what you think it is.'

It was night. Flickering steadily, I moved the slats of the blind apart and looked down into a deserted black-and-white square with a ruined fountain. 'I'm tired of running,' I said.

'I love it when you talk discreet,' said Whitey.

Night Run

We were in the deserted square. The street lamps offered only a feeble and hopeless glimmer that seemed continually to be swallowed up in obscurity. Dim lights punctuated the darkness at odd intervals. Whitey and I stood listening to footsteps that never receded into the distance quite as they should have done.

'Let's get ourselves a car,' he said. We crossed to the far side of the square and he slipped along silently trying doors until an infirm pick-up truck opened for us. We climbed in, Whitey was busy with his hands under the dashboard, there were sparks, the motor started with a roar and we were off.

'Turn on the headlamps for Christ's sake,' I said.

'It's better that you don't see too much, you'll lose your nerve.' Rattling and roaring, we disappeared into the obscurity that had swallowed up the feeble glimmer of the street lamps.

John Kobassa & Co

There was a van blocking the road. In the beams of its headlamps I saw Noir struggling in the grip of one of the big men in rumpled white suits. Whitey braked hard and we jolted to a stop in a cloud of dust. The other two big men were there as well.

'I knew this was going to happen,' I said.

'What did you expect?' said Whitey. 'Cucumber sandwiches?'

'I guess not. But really . . .'

'What?'

'What can they do to her? She's already a skeleton.'

'What a gringo you are.'

'What do you mean by that?'

'Honour is nothing to you, eh? Do you want to watch all three of them having my sister here in front of you? Is that the sort of thing you like?'

'No, I shouldn't like that at all.'

'"No, I shouldn't like that at all,"' he mocked. 'What are you going to do about it? Have you got balls or are you a miserable capon?'

'Aren't you going to help? She's your sister.'

'I'll do sidekick things, like stand on the bonnet and hit them with the starting handle if they get close enough.'

I got out of the truck. Now I remembered them clearly: John Kobassa; Sergeant Moxon; Nameless Stranger.

'You remember us, do you?' said John. He was the one holding Noir.

'Don't worry about me,' Noir said. 'There's nothing they can do to me that hasn't been done before.'

'They're not going to do anything to you,' I said. 'It's me they want. Let her go,' I said to John. 'Here I am.'

'It's about time,' said John.

'Hello, chicken,' said Sergeant Moxon. 'I've been waiting for you for forty-three years.'

'I'm here now. How come all of you are so much bigger than I remember and nobody's old except me?'

'That's how it goes when you put things off too long,' said Nameless Stranger. 'Now if you're ready, we'll do what we didn't do that other time.'

So we did it. When I came to, the pick-up's headlamps were on, the three big men and the van had gone, and Noir was kissing me. I'd been very wise to keep it black-and-white; if it had been full colour they might well have finished me off altogether. As it was, I doubted that my injuries were any worse than if I'd been run over by a medium-sized car: seven or eight of my ribs were broken along with one or two limbs, my head and my dentures; also there seemed to be a fair amount of bleeding both external and internal. All in all I thought it best not to try anything too active for a while so I stayed where I was and looked at Noir out of my one working eye.

'How are you?' she said.

'Terrific,' I mumbled toothlessly. 'If I'd known how good I was going to feel afterwards I'd have looked them up sooner.' It was then that I noticed that the blusher on her cheek-bones was pink and not grey and things weren't flickering any more. 'Where's Whitey?' I said.

'Here I am.' He was climbing down from the top of the pick-up.

'Did you stand on the bonnet and hit them with the starting handle?'

'Nobody came close enough.'

'Can we find Dahlmann now?'

'You don't have to find me,' said a new voice. 'I've found you.'

'You're Dahlmann?'

'I'm Dahlmann.'

Without ever having seen a photograph of Borges that indicated his height, I'd always thought of him as a short man and I'd assumed that Dahlmann would be short as well, so I was surprised to see that he was a tall thin man of forty or so, wearing a rumpled white suit but none the less elegant and soldierly in his bearing. His face was long and narrow, with the watchful eyes and cultivated blackness of a man of action; his hair was very black and he had just such a daguerreotypical beard as Francisco Flores must have worn.

'Why were you looking for me?' he said in a perfectly flat and uninflected voice.

Had I expected friendliness? I couldn't remember. I tried to scramble to my feet but one of my legs gave way. Noir came to me and effortlessly lifted me up, then drew back and stood watching me intently. Before the unforeseen actuality of Dahlmann I tried to be as dignified as possible. I no longer wanted to speak the words that I had planned to say but I spoke them as if damned and pre-ordained to do so: 'I wanted to talk to you about what you did, I wanted to know what happened and how it was when you took the dagger in your hand and went out into the plain.' What I said sounded wet and stupid and it was a lie: I no longer wanted to know what had happened and how it had been; I just wanted to go home. I looked at Noir and she blew me a kiss.

'You mean this dagger?' he said. He threw it into the air, the blade flashed in the light of the headlamps as it went end over end and the dagger returned haft-first to his hand. With his face still blank he said, 'What do you think happened?'

'I think you were killed.'

'That's your opinion, is it?'

'Yes.'

'Would you care to back that opinion?'

'How do you mean?'

'Would you like to try me?'

Inwardly I sighed but I said nothing aloud. It was night, the darkness was full of the many and mysterious colours of black. In the light of the headlamps there seemed to be a genuine blush on Noir's painted cheek-bones; the shadowy hollows of her eyes sparkled with tenderness. It was night, it was dark, but in my mind a vast and tawny plain opened before me under the sun of the South as Whitey threw me a long knife that made a small hiss as it stuck into the ground at my feet.

GRANTA

MARKÉTA LUSKAČOVÁ
PILGRIMS IN IRELAND

Markéta Luskačová

Two weeks before I took these photographs, in 1973, I left Czechoslovakia for the first time to join my husband in Zurich. I had waited several months for the necessary papers but our reunion was painful. My husband stated clearly for the first time that he did not want us to have children. Zurich was so clean and orderly after Prague, my home, I did not want to live there with my husband.

After twelve days in which I did not once pick up my camera, a very close friend, Josef Koudelka, phoned me explaining that he was going to Ireland. He asked me to join him to photograph the annual July pilgrimage to Croagh Patrick mountain in County Mayo. For many years I had been photographing pilgrims in Slovakia. I took the night flight.

I was inexpressibly sad. I could not make sense of my life so I tried to make some sense in my photographs. The summit of the holy mountain was bitterly cold, the rain did not stop. My hands were so wet and cold that I could hardly hold my camera. The bareness of this land was beyond anything I had imagined, but in the faces of these men, in their postures, their prayers, there was something that felt very familiar to me.

All photos: Markéta Luskačová

7UP

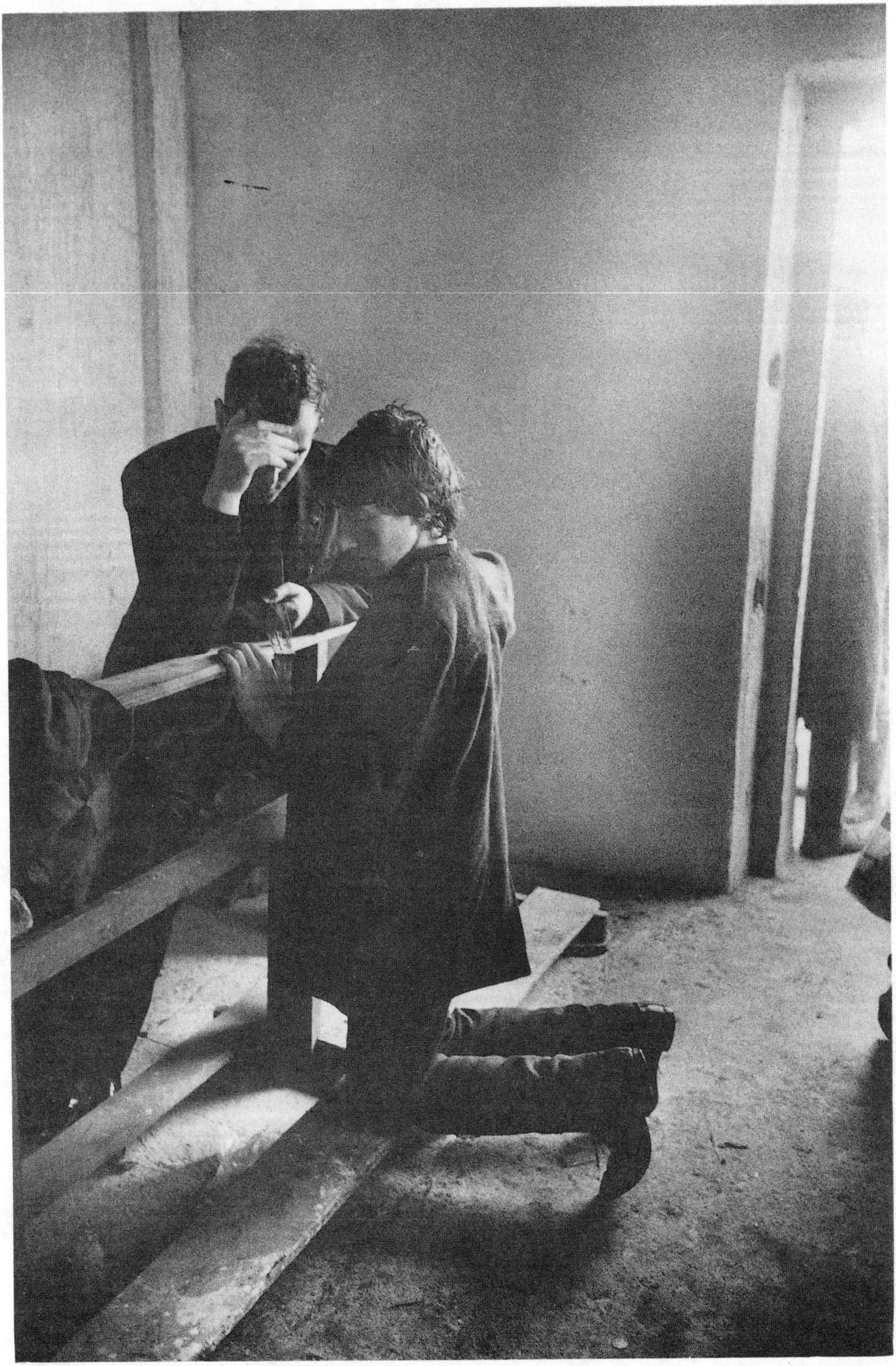

PICADOR

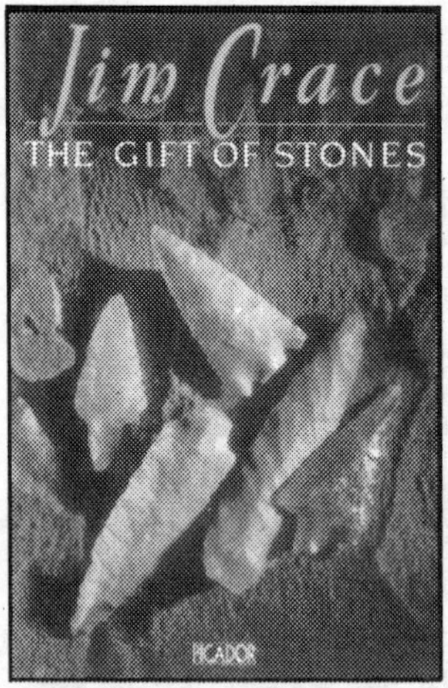

Publishing: 8 September 1989 Paperback: £3.99

THE GIFT OF STONES

'Crace has the imagination of a poet, and uses language with vivid originality' *The Telegraph*

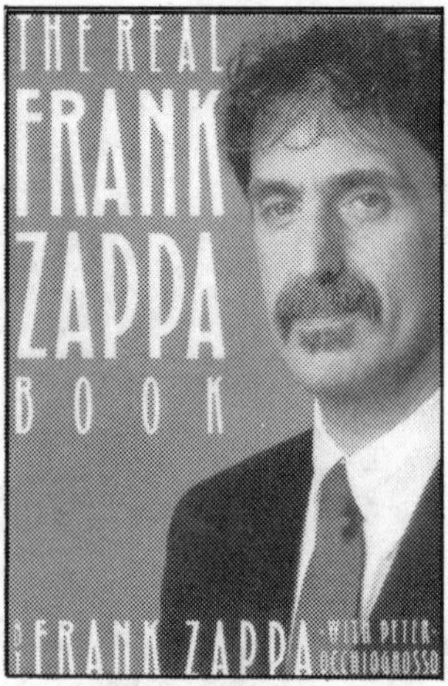

Publishing: 8 September 1989 Picador hardback: £12.95

THE REAL FRANK ZAPPA BOOK

The legendary Frank Zappa takes us on a wild, funny, outrageous trip through his life and times. First British Publication

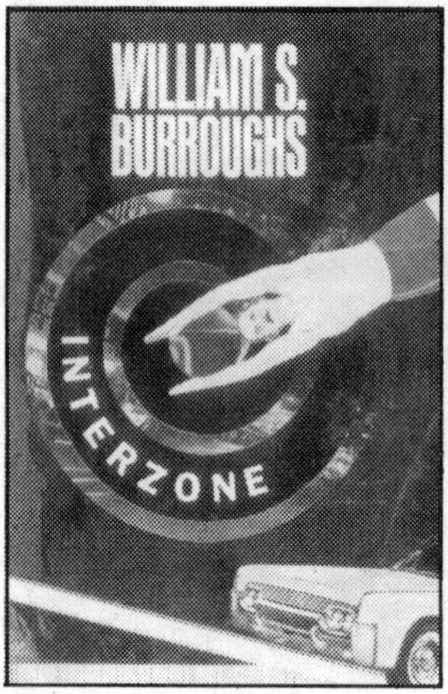

First British Publication. Available: 13 October 1989. Hardback: £11.95

INTERZONE

Writings from the crucial period leading up to the publications of *Naked Lunch* – including an extensive rediscovered section from that novel.

Available: 13 October 1989. Paperback: £3.99

EMPEROR OF THE AIR

'Some of the most emotionally satisfying and ably crafted stories I have read in years' *Newsweek*

Picador books are available at all leading booksellers including **The Pan Bookshop, 158-162 Fulham Road, SW10**

*Opening hours: Mon-Sat 10am-10pm Sun 2-9pm

GRANTA

EUGENE RICHARDS
AMERICANS

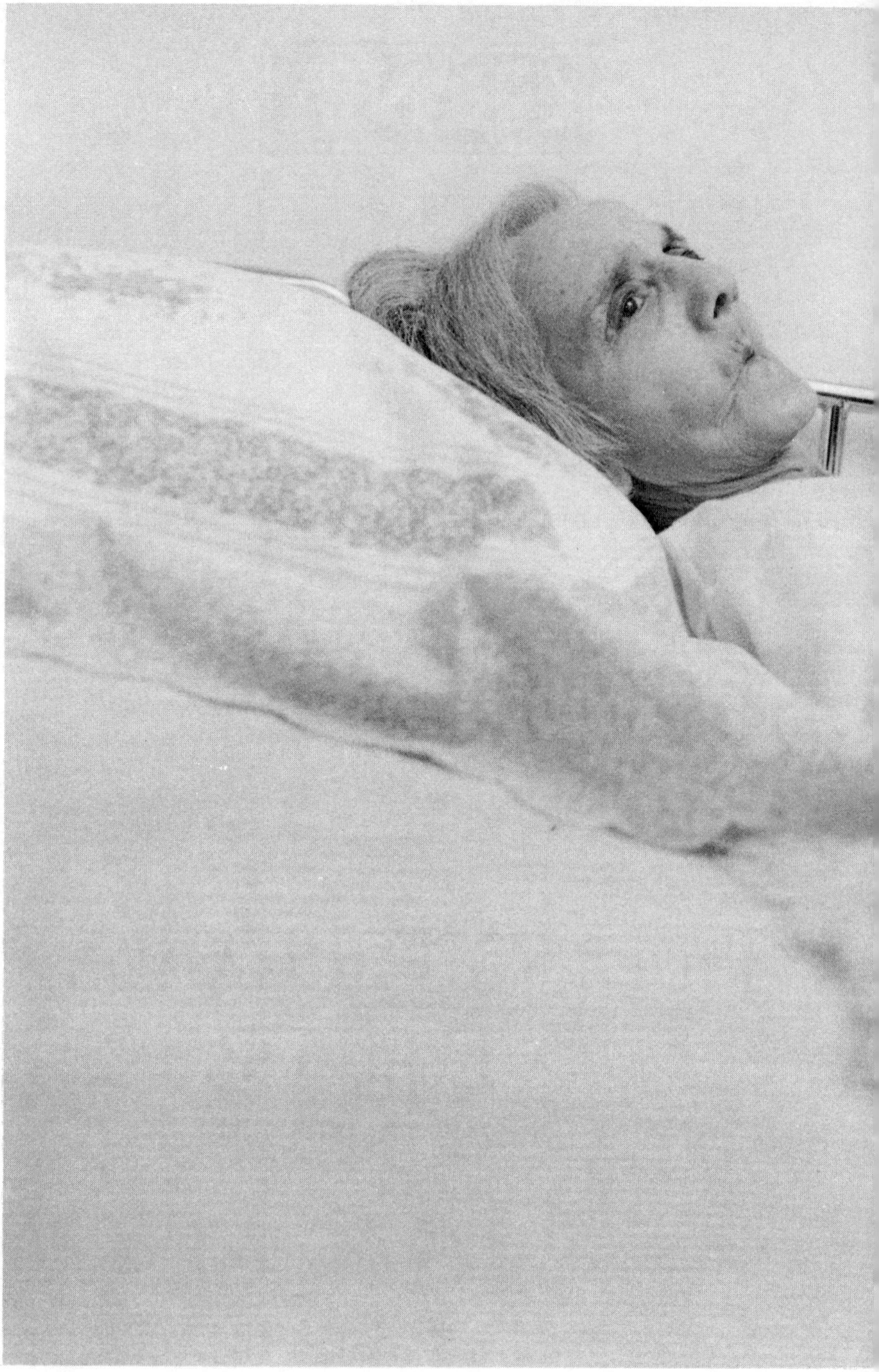

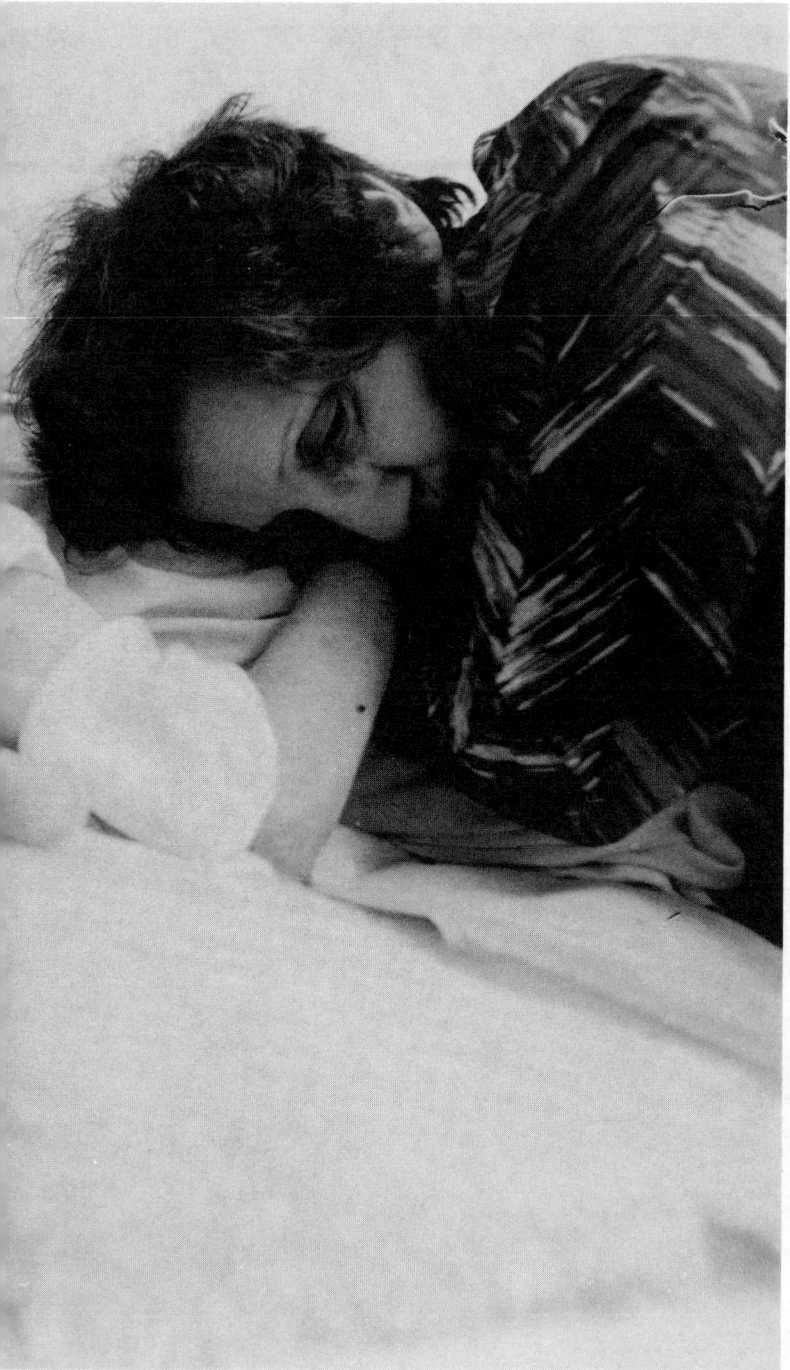

All photos: Eugene Richards (Magnum)

Two sisters, one with Alzheimer's, New York.

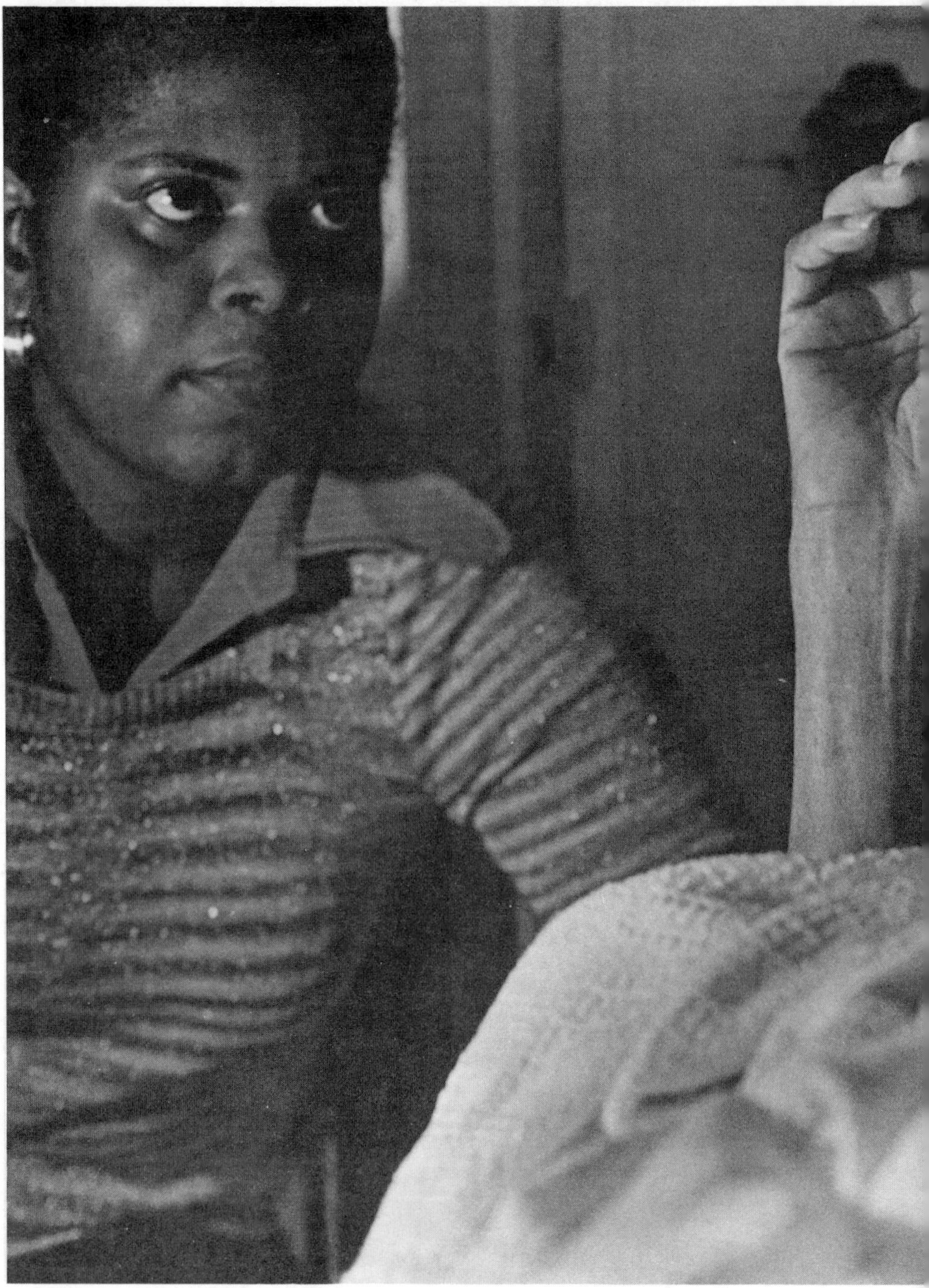

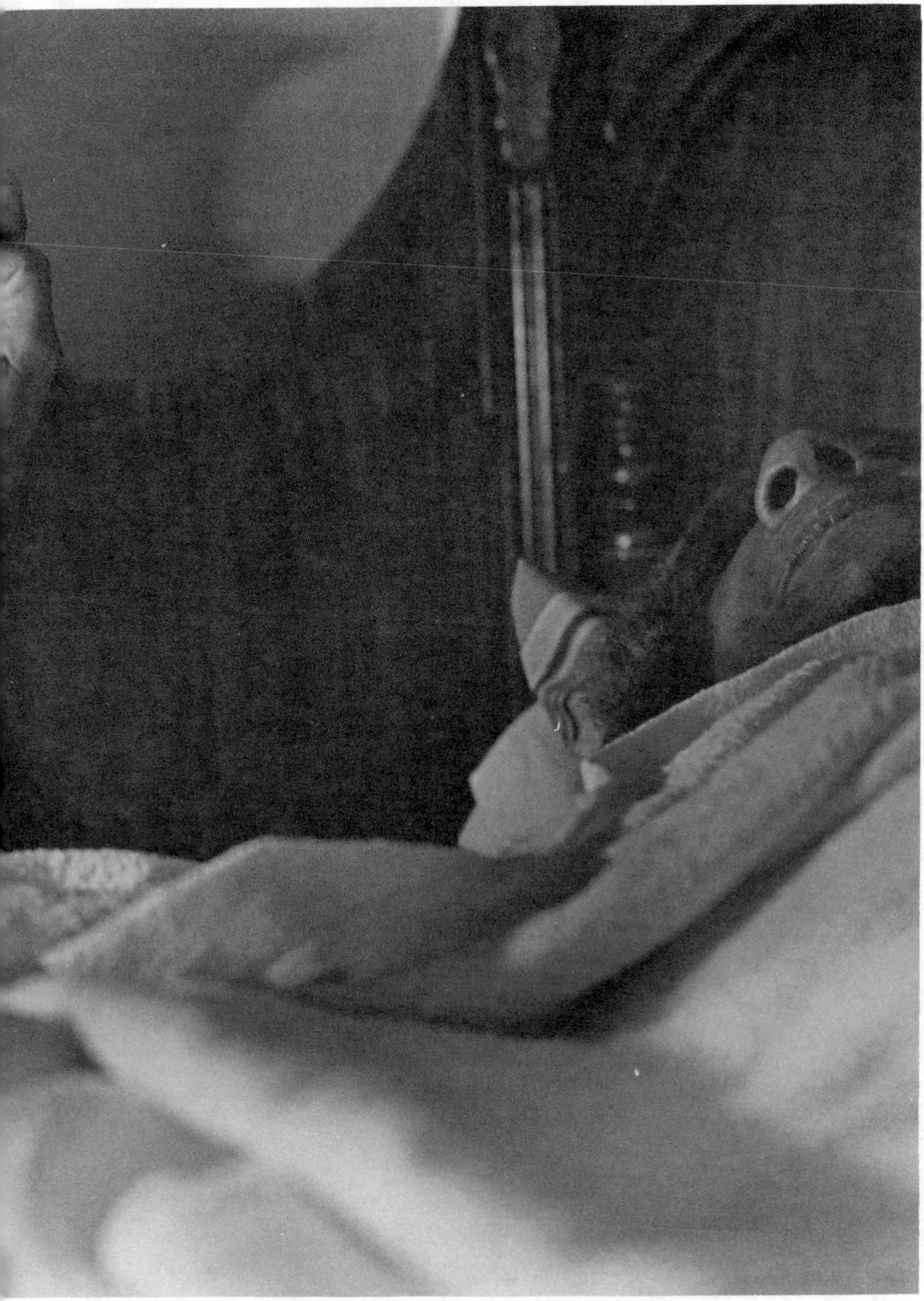

Mrs Brown's last hours, Harlem.

THE
FOR LEASE
329-6780

'Americans We', South Boston, Massachusetts.

Garbage, Earle, Arkansas.

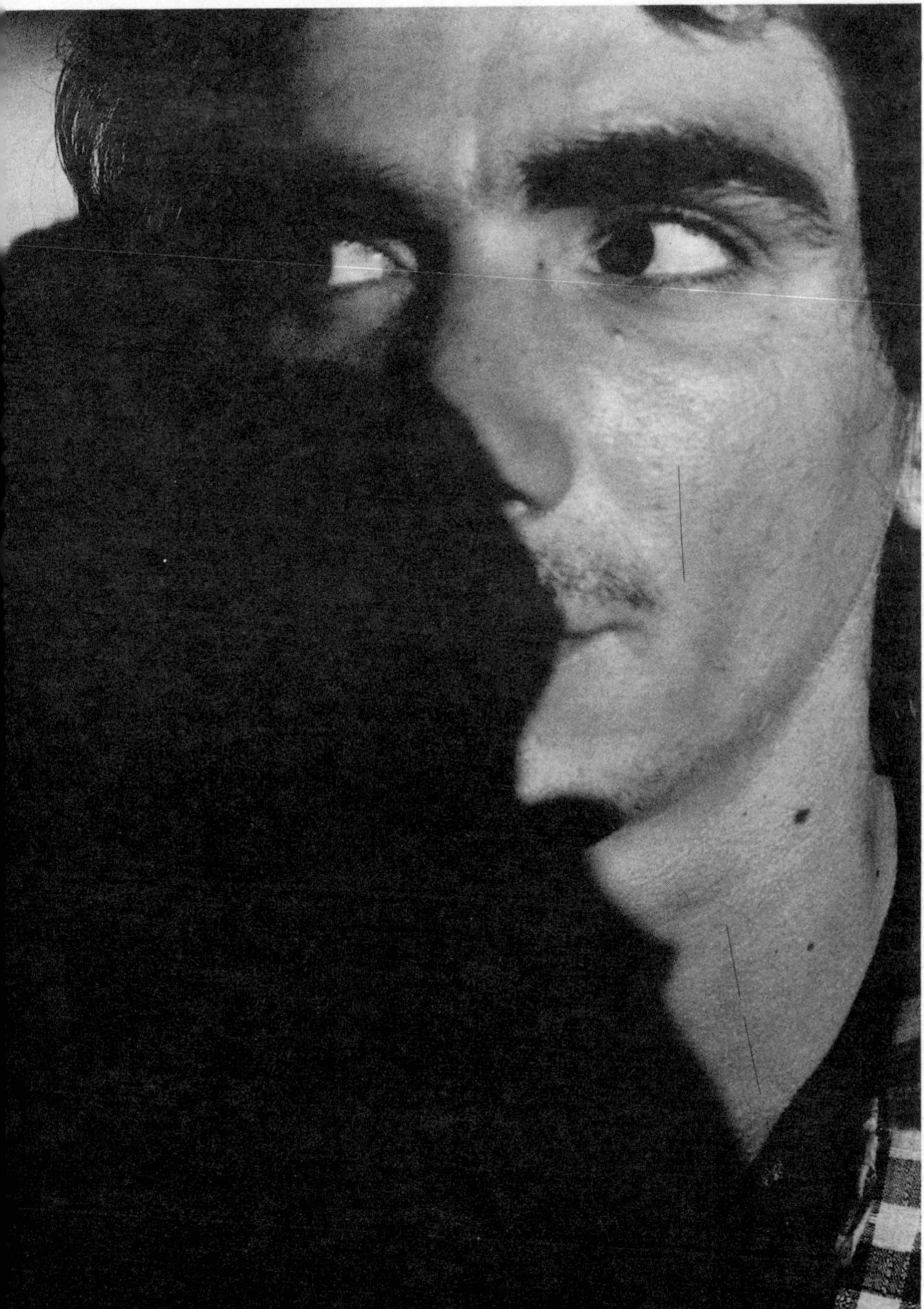

Cuban refugees, Key West.

‘Killer’, Hospital for the Criminally Insane, Ohio.

Angry boxer, Roxbury, Massachusetts.

GRANTA

JOY WILLIAMS
THE LITTLE WINTER

She was in the airport, waiting for her flight to be called, when a woman came to a phone near her chair. The woman stood there, dialling, and after a while began talking in a flat, aggrieved voice. Gloria couldn't hear everything by any means, but she did hear her say, 'If anything happens to this plane, I hope you'll be satisfied.' The woman spoke monotonously and without mercy. She was tall and dishevelled and looked the very picture of someone who recently had ceased to be cherished. Nevertheless, she was still being mollified on the other end of the phone. Gloria heard with astounding clarity the part about the plane being repeated several times. The woman then slammed down the receiver and boarded Gloria's flight, flinging herself down in a first-class seat. Gloria proceeded to the rear of the plane and sat quietly, thinking that every person is on the brink of eternity every moment, that the ways and means of leaving this world are innumerable and often inconceivable. She thought in this manner for a while, then ordered a drink.

The plane pushed through the sky and the drink made her think of the way, as a child, she had enjoyed chewing on the collars of her dresses. The first drink of the day did not always bring this to mind but frequently it did. Then she began thinking of the desert which she was leaving behind and how much she liked it. Once she had liked the sea and felt she could not live without it but now missed it almost not at all.

The plane continued. Gloria ordered another drink, no longer resigned to believing that the woman was going to blow it up. Now she began thinking of where she was going and what she was going to do. She was going to visit Jean, a friend of hers, who was having a hard time—a third divorce, after all, Jean had a lot of energy—but that was only for a day or two. Jean had a child named Gwendal. Gloria hadn't seen them for over a year, she probably wouldn't even recognize Gwendal, who would be almost ten by now. Then she would just keep moving around until it happened. She was thinking of looking for a dog to get. She'd had a number of dogs but hadn't had very good luck with them. This was the thing about pets, of course, you knew that something dreadful was going to befall them, that it was not going to end well. Two of her dogs had been hit by cars, one had been epileptic and another was diagnosed

Photo: Thomas Victor

early on as having hip dysplasia. That one she had bought from the same litter that Kafka's great-niece had bought hers from. Kafka's great-niece! Vets had never done very well by Gloria's dogs, much as doctors weren't doing very well by Gloria now. She thought frequently about doctors, though she wasn't going to see them any more. Under the circumstances, she probably shouldn't acquire a dog, but she felt she wanted one. Let the dog get stuck for a change, she thought.

At the airport, Gloria rented a car. She decided to drive until just outside Jean's town and check into a motel. Jean was a talker. A day with Jean would be enough. A day and a night would be too much. Just outside Jean's town was a monastery where the monks raised dogs. Maybe she would find her dog there tomorrow. She would go over to the monastery early in the morning and spend the rest of the day with Jean. But that was it, other than that, there wasn't much of a plan.

The day was cloudy and there was a great deal of traffic. The land falling back from the highway was green and still. It seemed to her a slightly morbid landscape, obelisks and cemeteries, thick drooping forests, the evergreens dying from the top down. Of course there was hardly any place to live these days. A winding old road ran parallel to the highway and Gloria turned off and drove along it until she came to a group of cabins. The cabins were white with little porches but the office was in a structure built to resemble a tepee. There was a dilapidated miniature golf-course and a wooden tower from the top of which you could see into three states. But the tower leaned and the handrail curving optimistically upward was splintered and warped, and only five steps from the ground a rusted chain prevented further ascension. Gloria liked places like this.

In the tepee, a woman in a house-dress stood behind a pink formica counter. A glass humming-bird coated with greasy dust hung in one window. Gloria could smell meatloaf cooking. The woman had red cheeks and white hair, and she greeted Gloria extravagantly, but as soon as Gloria paid for her cabin she became morose. She gazed at Gloria glumly as though perceiving her as one who had already walked off with the blankets, the lamp and the painting of the waterfall.

The key Gloria had been given did not work. It fitted into the lock and turned, but did not do the job of opening the door. She walked back to the office and a small dog with short legs and a fluffy tail fell in step beside her. Back in the tepee, Gloria said, 'I can't seem to make this key work.' The smell of the meatloaf was now clangorous. The woman was old, but she came around the counter fast.

The dog was standing in the middle of the turnabout in front of the cabins.

'Is that your dog?' Gloria asked.

'I've never seen it before,' the woman said. 'It sure is not,' she added. 'Go home!' she shrieked at the dog. She turned the key in the lock of Gloria's cabin and then gave the door a sharp kick with her sneaker. The door flew open. She stomped back to the office. 'Go home!' she screamed again at the dog.

Gloria made herself an iceless drink in a paper cup and called Jean.

'I can't wait to see you,' Jean said. 'How are you?'

'I'm all right,' Gloria said.

'Tell me.'

'Really,' Gloria said.

'I can't wait to see you,' Jean said. 'I've had the most god-awful time. I know it's silly.'

'How is Gwendal doing?'

'She never liked Chuckie anyway. She's Luke's, you know. But she's not a bit like Luke. You know Gwendal.'

Gloria barely remembered the child. She sipped from the paper cup and looked through the screen at the dog which was gazing over the ruined golf-course to the valley beyond.

'I don't know how I manage to pick them,' Jean was saying. She was talking about the last one.

'I'll be there by lunch tomorrow,' Gloria said.

'Not until then! Well, we'll bring some lunch over to Bill's and eat with him. You haven't met him, have you? I want you to meet him.'

Bill was Jean's first ex-husband. She had just bought a house in town where two of her old ex-husbands and her new ex-husband lived. Gloria knew she had quite a day cut out for herself tomorrow. Jean gave her directions and Gloria hung up and made herself a fresh drink in the paper cup. She stood out on the porch. Dark clouds had massed over the mountains. Traffic thundered invisibly past in the distance, beyond the trees. In the town in the valley below, there were tiny hard lights in the enlarging darkness. The light, which had changed, was disappearing, but there was still a lot of light. That's the way it was with light. If you were out in it while it was going you could still see enough for longer. When it was completely dark, Gloria said, 'Well, good night.'

She woke mid-morning with a terrible headache. She was not supposed to drink but what difference did it make, really. It didn't make any difference. She took her pills. Sometimes she thought it had been useless for her to grow older. She was thirty-five. She lay in the musty cabin. Everything seemed perfectly clear. Then it seemed equivocal again. She dressed and went to the office where she paid for another night. The woman took the money and looked at Gloria worriedly as though she were already saying goodbye to those towels and that old willow chair with the cushion.

It began to rain. The road to the monastery was gravel and wound up the side of a mountain. There were orchards, fields of young corn . . . the rain fell upon it all in a fury. Gloria drove slowly, barely able to make out the road. She imagined it snowing out there, not rain but snow, filling everything up. She imagined thinking—*it was dark now but still snowing*—a line like that, as in a story. A line like that was lovely, she thought. When she was small they had lived in a place where the little winter came first. That's what everyone called it. There was the little winter, then there were pleasant days, sometimes weeks. Then the big winter came. She felt dreamy and cold, a little disconnected from everything. She was on the monastery's grounds now and there were wooden buildings with turreted roofs and minarets. Someone had planted birches. She parked in front of a sign that said INFORMATION/GIFT SHOP and dashed from the car to the door. She was laughing and shaking the water from her hair as she entered.

The situation was that there were no dogs available, or rather that the brother whose duty was the dogs, who knew about the dogs, was away and would not return until tomorrow. She could come back tomorrow. The monk who told her this had a beard and wore a soiled apron. His interest in her questions did not seem intense. He had appeared from a back room, a room that seemed part smokehouse, part kitchen. This was the monk who smoked chickens, hams and cheese. There was always cheese in this life. The monastery had a substantial mail-order business; the monks smoked things, the nuns made cheesecakes. The monk seemed slightly impatient with Gloria and she was aware that her questions about the dogs seemed desultory. He had given up a great deal, no doubt, in order to be here. The gift shop was crowded with half-priced icons and dog beds. In a corner there was a glass case filled with the nuns' cheesecakes. Gloria looked in there, at the white boxes, stacked.

'The Deluxe is a standard favourite,' the monk said. 'The Kahlua is encased in a chocolate cookie-crumb crust, the rich liqueur from sunny Mexico blending naturally with the nuns' original recipe.' The monk droned on as though at matins. 'The Chocolate is a must for chocolate-fanciers. The Chocolate Amaretto is considered by the nuns to be their *pièce de résistance*.'

Gloria bought the Chocolate Amaretto and left. How gloomy, she thought. The experience had seemed vaguely familiar as though she had surrendered passively to it in the past. She supposed it was a belief in appearances. She put the cheesecake in the car and walked around the grounds. It was raining less heavily now but even so her hair was plastered to her skull. She passed the chapel and then turned back and went inside. She picked up a candlestick and jammed it into her coat pocket. This place made her mad. Then she took the candlestick out and set it on the floor. Outside, she wandered around, hearing nothing but the highway which was humming like something in her head. She finally found the kennels and opened the door and went in. This is the way she thought it would be, nothing closed to her at all. There were four dogs, all young ones, maybe three months old, German Shepherds. She watched them for a while. It would be easy to take one, she thought. She could just do it.

She drove back down the mountain into town, where she pulled into a shopping centre that had a liquor store. She bought gin and some wine for Jean, then drove down to Jean's house in the valley. She felt tired. There was something pounding behind her eyes. Jean's house was a dirty peach colour with a bush in front. Everything was pounding, the house, even the grass. Then the pounding stopped.

'Oh my god,' Jean exclaimed. 'You've brought the *pièce de résistance*!' Apparently everyone was familiar with the nuns' cheesecakes. They didn't know about the dogs except that there were dogs up there, they knew that. Jean and Gloria hugged each other. 'You look good,' Jean said. 'They got it all, thank God, right? The things that happen . . . there aren't even names for half of what happens, I swear. You know my second husband, Andy, the one who died? He went in and he never came out again and he just submitted to it, but no one could ever figure out what it was. It was something complicated and obscure and the only thing they knew was that he was dying from it. It might have been some insect that bit him. But the worst thing—well, not the worst thing, but the thing I remember because it had to do with me, which is bad of me, I suppose, but that's just human nature. The worst thing was what happened just before he died. He was very fussy. Everything had to be just so.'

'This is Andy,' Gloria said.

'Andy,' Jean agreed. 'He had an excellent vocabulary and was very precise. How I got involved with him I'll never know. But he was my husband and I was devastated. I *lived* at the hospital, week after week. He liked me to read to him. I was there that afternoon and I had adjusted the shade and plumped the pillows and I was reading to him. And there he was, quietly slipping away right then, I guess, looking back on it. I was reading and I got to this part about someone being the master of a highly circumscribed universe and he opened his eyes and said, "Circumscribed." "What, darling?" I said. And he said, "Circumscribed, not circumcised . . . you said circumcised." And I said, "I'm sure I didn't, darling," and he gave me this long look and then he gave a big sigh and died. Isn't that awful?'

Gloria giggled, then shook her head.

Jean's eyes darted around the room, which was in high

disorder. Peeling wallpaper, cracked linoleum. Cardboard boxes everywhere. Shards of glass had been swept into one corner and a broken croquet mallet propped one window open. 'So what do you think of this place?' Jean said.

'It's some place,' Gloria said.

'Everyone says I shouldn't have. It needs some work, I know, but I found this wonderful man, or he found me. He came up to the door and looked at all this and I said, "Can you help me? Do you do work like this?"

'And he nodded and said, "I puttah." Isn't that wonderful! "I puttah . . ."'

Gloria looked at the sagging floor and the windows loose in their frames. The mantel was blackened by smoke and grooved with cigarette burns. It was clear that the previous occupants had led lives of grinding boredom here and that they had not led them with composure. He'd better start puttahing soon, Gloria thought. 'Don't marry him,' she said, and laughed.

'Oh, I know you think I marry everybody,' Jean said, 'but I don't. There have only been four. The last one, and I mean the last, was the worst. What a rodent Chuckie was. No, he's more like a big predator, a crow or a weasel or something. Cruel, lazy, deceitful.' Jean shuddered. 'The best thing about him was his hair.' Jean was frequently undone by hair. 'He has great hair. He wears it in a sort of fifties full flat-top.'

Gloria felt hollow and happy. Nothing mattered much.

'Love is a chimera,' Jean said earnestly.

Gloria laughed.

'I'm pronouncing that right, aren't I?' Jean said, laughing.

'You actually bought this place?' Gloria said.

'Oh, it's crazy,' Jean said, 'but Gwendal and I needed a home. I've heard that *faux* is the new trend. I'm going to do it all *faux* when I get organized. Do you want to see the upstairs? Gwendal's room is upstairs. Hers is the neatest.'

They went up the stairs to a room where a fat girl sat on a bed writing in a book.

'I'm doing my autobiography,' Gwendal said, 'but I think I'm going to change my approach.' She turned to Gloria. 'Would you like to be my biographer?'

Jean said, 'Say hello to Gloria. You remember Gloria.'

Gloria gave the girl a hug. Gwendal smelled good and had small grey eyes. The room wasn't clean at all, but there was very little in it. Gloria supposed it was the neatest. Conversation lagged.

'Let's go out and sit on the lawn,' Jean suggested.

'I don't want to,' Gwendal said.

The two women went downstairs. Gloria needed to use the bathroom but Jean said she had to go outside as the plumbing wasn't all it should be. There was a steep brushy bank behind the house and Gloria crouched there. The day was clear and warm now. At the bottom of the bank, a flat stream moved laboriously around vine-covered trees. The mud glistened in the sun. Blackberries grew in the brush. This place had a lot of candour, Gloria thought.

Jean had laid a blanket on the grass and was sitting there, eating a wedge of cheesecake from a plastic plate. Gloria decided on a drink over cake.

'We'll go to Bill's house for lunch,' Jean said. 'Then we'll go to Fred's house for a swim.' Fred was an old husband too. Gwendal's father was the only one who wasn't around. He lived in Las Vegas. Andy wasn't around either, of course.

Gwendal came out of the house into the sloppy yard. She stopped in the middle of a rhubarb patch, exclaiming silently and waving her arms.

Jean sighed. 'It's hard being a single mother.'

'You haven't been single for long,' Gloria said.

Jean laughed loudly at this. 'Poor Gwendal,' she said, 'I love her dearly.'

'A lovely child,' Gloria murmured.

'I just wish she wouldn't make up so much stuff sometimes.'

'She's young,' Gloria said, swallowing her drink. Really, she hardly knew what she was saying. 'What *is* she doing?' she asked Jean.

Gwendal leaped quietly around in the rhubarb.

'Whatever it is, it needs to be translated,' Jean said. 'Gwendal needs a good translator.'

'She's pretending something or other,' Gloria offered, thinking she would very much like another drink.

'I'm going to put on a fresh dress for visiting Bill,' Jean said. 'Do you want to put on a fresh dress?'

Gloria shook her head. She was watching Gwendal. When Jean went into the house, the girl trotted over to the blanket. 'Why don't you kidnap me?' she said.

'Why don't you kidnap *me*?' Gloria said, laughing. What an odd kid, she thought. 'I don't want to kidnap you,' she said.

'I'd like to see your house,' Gwendal said.

'I don't have a house. I lived in an apartment.'

'Apartments aren't interesting,' Gwendal said. 'Dump it. We could get a van. The kind with the ladder that goes up the back. We could get a wheel-cover that says MESS WITH THE BEST, LOSE LIKE THE REST.'

There was something truly terrifying about girls on the verge of puberty, Gloria thought. She laughed.

'You drink too much,' Gwendal said. 'You're always drinking something.'

This hurt Gloria's feelings. 'I'm dying,' she said. 'I have a brain tumour. I can do what I want.'

'If you're dying you can do anything you want?' Gwendal said. 'I didn't know that. That's a new one. So there are compensations.'

Gloria couldn't believe she'd told Gwendal she was dying. 'You're fat,' she said glumly.

Gwendal ignored this. She wasn't all that fat. Somewhat fat, perhaps, but not grotesquely so.

'Oh, to hell with it,' Gloria said. 'You want me to stop drinking, I'll stop drinking.'

'It doesn't matter to me,' Gwendal said.

Gloria's mouth trembled. I'm drunk, she thought.

'Some simple pleasures are just a bit too simple, you know,' Gwendal said.

Gloria felt that she had been handling her upcoming death pretty well. Now she wasn't sure, in fact, she felt awful. What was she doing spending what might be one of her last days sitting on a scratchy blanket in a weedy yard while a fat child insulted her? Her problem was that she had never figured out where it was exactly she wanted to go to die. Some people knew and planned accordingly. The desert, say, or Nantucket. Or a good hotel somewhere. But she hadn't figured it out. En route was the closest she'd come.

Gwendal said, 'Listen, I have an idea. We could do it the other way around. Instead of you being my biographer, I'll be yours. *Gloria by Gwendal*.' She wrote in the air with her finger. She did not have a particularly flourishing hand, Gloria noted. 'Your life as told to Gwendal Crawley. I'll write it all down. At least that's something. We can always spice it up.'

'I haven't had a very interesting life.' Gloria said modestly. But it was true, she thought. When her parents had named her, they must have been happy. They must have thought something was going to happen now.

'I'm sure you must be having some interesting reflections though,' Gwendal said. 'And if you're really dying, I bet you'll feel like doing everything once.' She was wringing her hands in delight.

Jean walked towards them from the house.

'C'mon,' Gwendal hissed. 'Let me go with you. You didn't come all this way just to stay here, did you?'

'Gloria and I are going to visit Bill,' Jean said. 'Let's all go,' she said to Gwendal.

'I don't want to,' Gwendal said.

'If I don't see you again, goodbye,' Gloria said to Gwendal. The kid stared at her.

Jean was driving, turning this way and that, passing the houses of those she had once loved.

'That's Chuckie's house,' Jean said. 'The one with the hair.' They drove slowly by, looking at Chuckie's house. 'Charming on the outside but sleazy inside, just like Chuckie. He broke my heart, literally broke my heart. Well, his foot is going to slide in due time as they say and I want to be around for that. That's why I've decided to stay.' She said a moment later, 'It's not really.'

They passed Fred's house. Everybody had a house.

'Fred has a pond,' Jean said. 'We can go for a swim there later. I always use Fred's pond. He used to own a whole quarry, can you imagine? This was before our time with him, Gwendal's and mine, but the kids were always getting in there and drowning. He put up big signs and barbed wire and everything but they still got in. It got to be too much trouble, so he sold it.'

'Too much trouble!' Gloria said.

Death seemed preposterous. Totally unacceptable. Those silly kids, Gloria thought. She was elated and knew that she would feel tired soon and uneasy, but maybe it wouldn't happen this time. The day was bright, clean after the rain. Leaves lay on the streets, green and fresh.

'Those were Fred's words, the too much trouble. Can't I pick them? I can really pick them.' Jean shook her head.

They drove to Bill's house. Next to it was a pasture with horses in it. 'Those aren't Bill's horses, but they're pretty, aren't they?' Jean said. 'You're going to love Bill. He's gotten a little strange but he always was a little strange. We are who we are, aren't we? He carves ducks.'

Bill was obviously not expecting them. He was a big man with long hair wearing boxer shorts and smoking a cigar. He looked at Jean warily.

'This used to be the love of my life,' Jean said. To Bill, she said, 'This is Gloria, my dearest friend.'

Gloria felt she should demur, but smiled instead. Her situation didn't make her any more honest, she had found.

'Beautiful messengers, bad news,' Bill said.

'We just thought we'd stop by,' Jean said.

'Let me put on my pants,' he said.

The two women sat in the living-room, surrounded by wooden ducks. The ducks, exquisite and oppressive, nested on every surface. Buffleheads, canvas-back, scaup, blue-winged teal. Gloria picked one up. It looked heavy but was light. Shoveller, mallard, merganser. The names kept coming to her.

'I forgot the lunch so we'll just stay a minute,' Jean whispered. 'I was *mad* about this man. Don't you ever wonder where it all goes?'

Bill returned, wearing trousers and a checked shirt. He had put his cigar somewhere.

'I *love* these ducks,' Jean said. 'You're getting so good.'

'You want a duck,' Bill said.

'Oh yes!' Jean said.

'I wasn't offering you one. I just figured that you did.' He winked at Gloria.

'Oh you,' Jean said.

'Take one, take one,' Bill sighed.

Jean picked up the nearest duck and put it in her lap.

'That's a harlequin,' Bill said.

'It's bizarre, I love it.' Jean gripped the duck tightly.

'You want a duck?' Bill said to Gloria.

'No,' Gloria said.

'Oh, take one!' Jean said excitedly.

'Decoys have always been particularly abhorrent to me,' Gloria said, 'since they are objects designed to lure a living thing to its destruction with the false promise of safety, companionship and rest.'

They both looked at her, startled.

'Oh wow, Gloria,' Jean said.

'These aren't decoys,' Bill said mildly. 'People don't use them for decoys any more, they use them for decoration. There are hardly any more ducks to hunt. Ducks are on their way out. They're in a free fall.'

'Diminishing habitat,' Jean said.

'There you go,' Bill said.

Black duck, pintail, widgeon. The names kept moving towards Gloria, then past.

'I'm more interested in creating dramas now,' Bill said. 'I'm getting away from the static stuff. I want to make dramatic moments. They have to be a little less than life-sized, but otherwise it's all there . . . the whole situation.' He stood up. 'Just a second,' he said.

Once he was out of the room, Jean turned to her. 'Gloria?' she said.

Bill returned carrying a large object covered by a sheet. He set it down on the floor and took off the sheet.

'I like it so far,' Jean said after a moment.

'Interpret away,' Bill said.

'Well,' Jean said, 'I don't think you should make it too busy.'

'I said interpret, not criticize,' Bill said.

'I just think the temptation would be to make something like that too busy. The temptation would be to put stuff in all those little spaces.'

Bill appeared unmoved by this possible judgement, but he replaced the sheet.

In the car, Jean said, 'Wasn't that *awful*? He should stick to ducks.'

According to Bill, the situation the object represented seemed to be the acceptance of inexorable fate, this acceptance containing within it, however, a heroic gesture of defiance. This was the situation, ideally always the situation, and it had been transformed, more or less abstractly, by Bill, into wood.

'He liked you.'

'Jean, why would he like me?'

'He was flirting with you, I think. Wouldn't it be something if you two got together and we were all here in this one place?'

'Oh my God,' Gloria said, putting her hands over her face. Jean glanced at her absent-mindedly. 'I should be getting back,' Gloria said. 'I'm a little tired.'

'But you just got here, and we have to take a swim at Fred's. The pond is wonderful, you'll love the pond. Actually, listen, do you want to go over to my parents' for lunch? Or it should be dinner, I guess. They have this big television. My mother can make us something nice for dinner.'

'Your parents live around here too?' Gloria asked.

Jean looked frightened for a moment. 'It's crazy, isn't it? They're so sweet. You'd love my parents. Oh, I wish you'd talk,' she exclaimed. 'You're my friend. I wish you'd open up some.'

They drove past Chuckie's house again. 'Whose car is that now?' Jean wondered.

'I remember trying to feed my mother a spoonful of dust once,' Gloria said.

'Why!' Jean said. 'Tell!'

'I was little, maybe four. She told me that I had grown in her stomach because she'd eaten some dust.'

'No!' Jean said. 'The things they tell you when they know you don't know.'

'I wanted there to be another baby, someone else, a brother or a sister. So I had my little teaspoon. "Eat this," I said. "It's not a bit dirty. Don't be afraid."'

'How out of control!' Jean cried.

'She looked at it and said she'd been talking about a different kind of dust, the sort of dust there was on flowers.'

'She was just getting in deeper and deeper, wasn't she?' Jean said. She waited for Gloria to say more but the story seemed to be over. 'That's a nice little story,' Jean said.

It was dark when she got back to the cabins. There were no lights on anywhere. She remembered being happy off and on that day, and then looking at things and finding it all unkind. It had gotten harder for her to talk, and harder to listen to, but she was alone now and she felt a little better. Still, she didn't feel right. She knew she would never be steady. It would never seem all of a piece for her. It would come and go until it stopped.

She pushed open the door and turned on the lamp beside the bed. There were three sockets in the lamp but only one bulb. There had been more bulbs in the lamp last night. She also thought there had been more furniture in the room, another chair. Reading would have been difficult, if she had wanted to read, but she was tired of reading, tired of books. After they had told her the first time and even after they had told her the other times in different ways, she had wanted to read, she didn't want to just stand around gaping at everything, but she couldn't pick the habit up again, it wasn't the same.

The screen behind the lamp was a mottled bluish green, a coppery, oceanic colour. She thought of herself as a child with the spoonful of dust, but it was just a memory of her telling it now. She stood close to the screen, to its raw, metallic smell.

In the middle of the night she woke, soaked with sweat. Someone was just outside, she thought. Then this feeling vanished. She gathered up her things and put everything in the car. She did this all hurriedly, and then drove quickly to Jean's house. She parked out front and turned the lights off. After a few moments, Gwendal appeared. She was wearing an ugly dress and carrying a suitcase. There were creases down one side of her face as though she'd been sleeping hard before she woke. 'Where to first?' Gwendal said.

What they did first was to drive to the monastery and steal a dog. Gloria suspected that fatality made her more or less invisible and this seemed to be the case. She drove directly to the kennel, went in and walked out with a dog. She put him in the back seat and they drove off.

'We'll avoid the highway,' Gloria said. 'We'll stick to the back roads.'

'Fine with me,' Gwendal said.

Neither of them said anything for miles, then Gwendal asked, 'Would you say he had drop dead good looks?'

'He's a dog,' Gloria said. Gwendal was really mixed up. She was worse than her mother, Gloria thought.

They pulled into a diner and had breakfast. Then they went to a store and bought notebooks, pencils, dog food and gin. They bought sun-glasses. It was full day now. They kept driving until dusk. They were quite a distance from Jean's house. Gloria felt sorry for Jean. She liked to have everyone around her, even funny little Gwendal, and now she didn't.

Gwendal had been sleeping. Suddenly she woke up. 'Do you want to hear my dream?' she asked.

'Absolutely,' Gloria said.

'Someone, it wasn't you, told me not to touch this funny-looking animal, it wasn't him,' Gwendal said, gesturing towards the dog. 'Every time I'd pat it, it would bite off a piece of my arm or a piece of my chest. I just had to keep going, "It's cute," and keep petting it.'

'Oh.' Gloria said. She had no idea what to say.

'Tell me one of your dreams,' Gwendal said, yawning.

'I haven't been dreaming lately,' Gloria said.

'That's not good,' Gwendal said. 'That shows a lack of imagination. Readiness, it shows a lack of readiness maybe. Well, I can put the dreams in later. Don't worry about it.' She chose a pencil and opened her notebook. 'OK,' she said. 'Married?'

'No.'

'Any children?'

'No.'

'Allergies?'

Gloria looked at her.

'Do you want to start at the beginning or do you want to work backwards from the Big Surprise?' Gwendal asked.

They were on the outskirts of a town, stopped at a traffic light. Gloria looked straight ahead. Beginnings. She couldn't remember any beginnings.

'Hey,' someone said. 'Hey!'

She looked to her left at a dented yellow car full of young men. One of them threw a can of beer at her. It bounced off the door and they sped off, howling.

'Everyone knows if someone yells "hey" you don't look at them,' Gwendal said.

'Let's stop for the night,' Gloria said.

'How are you feeling?' Gwendal asked . . . not all that solicitously, Gloria thought.

They pulled into the first motel they saw. Gloria fed the dog and had a drink while Gwendal bounced on the bed. He seemed a most equable dog. He drank from the toilet bowl and gnawed peaceably on the bed-rail. Gloria and Gwendal ate pancakes in a brightly lit restaurant and strolled around a swimming-pool which had a filthy rubber cover rolled across it. Back in the room, Gloria lay down on one bed while Gwendal sat on the other.

'Do you want me to paint your nails or do your hair?' Gwendal asked.

'No,' Gloria said. She was recalling a bad thought she'd had once, a very bad thought. It had caused no damage, however, as far as she knew.

'I wouldn't know how to do your hair actually,' Gwendal said.

With a little training this kid could be a mortician, Gloria thought.

That night Gloria dreamed. She dreamed she was going to the funeral of some woman who had been indifferent to her. There was no need for her to be there. She was standing with a group of people. She felt like a criminal, undetected, but she felt chosen too, to be here when she shouldn't be. Then she was lying across the opening of a cement pipe. When she woke, she was filled with relief, knowing she would forget the dream immediately. It was morning again. Gwendal was outside by the unpleasant pool, writing in her notebook.

'*This was happiness then*,' she said to Gloria, scribbling away.

'Where's the dog?' Gloria asked. 'Isn't he with you?'

'I don't know,' Gwendal said. 'I let him out and he took off for parts unknown.'

'What do you mean!' Gloria said. She ran back to the room, went to the car, ran across the cement parking-lot and around the motel. Gloria didn't have any name to call the dog with. It had just disappeared without having ever been hers. She got Gwendal in the car and they drove down the roads around the motel. She squinted, frightened, at black heaps along the shoulder and in the littered grass, but it was tyres, rags, tyres. Cars sped by them. Along the median strip, dead trees were planted at fifty-foot intervals. The dog wasn't anywhere that she could find. Gloria glared at Gwendal.

'It was an accident,' Gwendal said.

'You have your own ideas about how this should be, don't you?'

'He was a distraction in many ways,' Gwendal said.

Gloria's head hurt. Back in the desert, just before she had made this trip, she had had her little winter. Her heart had pounded like a fist on a door. But it was false, all false, for she had survived it.

Gwendal had the hateful notebook on her lap. It had a splatter black cover with the word 'COMPOSITION' on it. 'Now we can get started,' she said. 'Today's the day. Favourite colour?' she asked. 'Favourite show tune?' A childish blue barette was stuck haphazardly in her hair, exposing part of a large, pale ear.

Gloria wasn't going to talk to her.

After a while, Gwendal said, '*They were unaware that the fugitive was in their midst*.' She wrote it down. Gwendal scribbled in the book all day long and asked Gloria to buy her another one. She sometimes referred to Gloria's imminent condition as the Great Adventure.

Gloria was distracted. Hours went by and she was driving, though she could barely recall what they passed. 'I'm going to pull in early tonight,' she said.

The motel they stopped at late that afternoon was much like the one before. It was called the Motel Lark. Gloria lay on one bed and Gwendal sat on the other. Gloria missed having a dog. A dog wouldn't let the stranger in, she thought, knowing she was being sentimental. Whereas Gwendal would in a minute.

'We should be able to talk,' Gwendal said.

'Why should we be able to talk?' Gloria said. 'There's no reason we should be able to talk.'

'You're not open is your problem. You don't want to share. It's hard to imagine what's real all by yourself, you know.'

'It is not!' Gloria said hotly. They were bickering like an old married couple.

'This isn't working out,' Gloria said. 'This is crazy. We should call your mother.'

'I'll give you a few more days, but it's true,' Gwendal said. 'I thought this would be a more mystical experience. I thought you'd tell me something. You don't even know about make-up. I bet you don't even know how to check the oil in that car. I've never seen you check the oil.'

'I know how to check the oil,' Gloria said.

'How about an electrical problem? Would you know how to fix an electrical problem?'

'No!' Gloria yelled.

Gwendal was quiet. She stared at her fat knees.

'I'm going to take a bath,' Gloria said.

She went into the bathroom and shut the door. The tile was turquoise and the stopper to the tub hung on a chain. This was the Motel Lark, she thought. She dropped the rubber stopper in the drain and ran the water. A few tiles were missing and the wall showed a grey, failed adhesive. She wanted to say something but even that wasn't it. She didn't want to say anything. She wanted to realize something she couldn't say. She heard a voice, it must have been Gwendal's, in the bedroom. Gloria lay down in the tub. The water wasn't as warm as she expected. *Your silence is no deterrent to me*, Gloria, the voice said. She reached for the hot water faucet but it ran in cold. If she let it run, it might get warm, she thought. That's what they say. Or again, that might be it.

GRANTA

LEONARD MICHAELS
JOURNAL

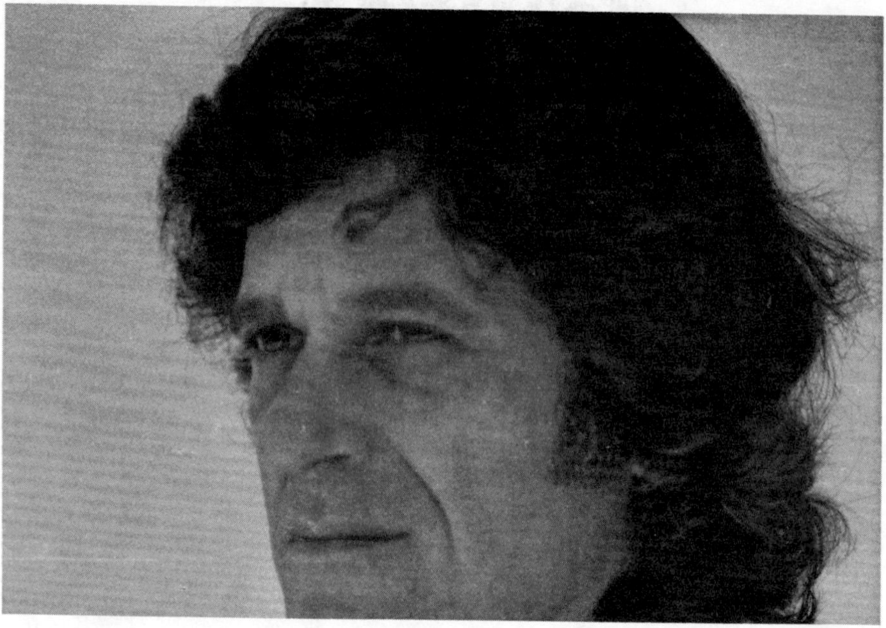

I'm so furious at Sonny I almost hate her.

I told Sonny I love her. She said, 'I'm a sucker for love.'

Sonny reads in the paper about a child who was sexually assaulted and murdered. She says quietly, as if to herself, 'What are we going to do about sex?'

We made love all afternoon.

Sonny said, 'Was it good?'

I said, 'Never in my life . . .'

She said, 'I should be compensated.'

We made love all afternoon. Sonny said, 'Was it good?'

I said, 'Never in my life . . .' The irrelevance of words, the happiness of being free of all such clothing. Articulateness is a kind of embarrassment. I lay on my back. Dumb. Savouring dumbness. My mother said she found my father on the bedroom floor, staring up at her with a dumb little smile on his face, as if it weren't bad being dead. He'd gone like himself, a sweet gentleman, not wanting her to feel distressed.

Lunch with Beard following letters and phone calls. He wrote saying he'd heard there was 'bad blood' between us. We'd met only two or three times. There was hardly anything between us. I wrote back, impelled by guilt, though I could imagine nothing to feel guilty about. Then came the phone calls. We tried and failed to make a date for lunch. He didn't want to come to Berkeley. I didn't want to go to San Francisco. He said if he came to Berkeley, I'd pay for lunch. If I came to San Francisco, he'd pay. Again guilt. Which did he prefer? I couldn't tell. I said I'd go to him. It was difficult to find a place to park, and then I had to walk five blocks to his apartment house. I feared the punishment would never end. He answered the door with a letter in his hand. Irrationally, I supposed it was for me. On our way to lunch, he said it was a letter of condolence to the wife of a friend, a famous writer, who had just died. He said it was easy for him to write the letter, having had to write so many of them lately. He flipped it into a mailbox. We ate in a local restaurant. He left the table several times to say hello to women at other tables and at the bar. Walking back to his apartment, he told me about a time when a friend died and he didn't write a letter of condolence to the wife. He didn't like her, he said. Her husband, his good friend, had also been a famous writer. She'd been sexually unfaithful to him with his friends. She taunted him with it, made him feel despised, lonely, wretched. Finally he died. Soon afterwards she phoned Beard and asked why he hadn't written her a letter. It was the middle of the night. She was drunk. He said she raved about the many letters of condolence she had received. Everybody of importance in the literary world had written her, so why not Beard? I thought it was a good story and asked if I could have it. He looked puzzled. Apparently, he hadn't thought the story was anything special, but now he wondered and was reluctant to say I could have it. Again guilt. I'd enjoyed the story too much and I'd understood it differently from what he intended. I'd seen the woman raving drunkenly into the phone at Beard. I supposed he had fucked her, but that wasn't interesting. I was fascinated by her agony. At his apartment we had a drink. Then, as we stood in the narrow hallway to his door, saying goodbye, assuring each other there was no bad blood, he farted. The tight space instantly became noxiously suffocating. Very eager to get out, I said for perhaps the third time, 'There is no bad blood.' He shrugged, as though it hadn't really mattered, and said, 'A puff of smoke.'

I phoned Boris. He's sick. He gets tired quickly, can't think, can't work. I asked if he'd like to take a walk in the sun. He cries, 'It's a nice day out there. I know it, believe me.'

Afterwards, afterwards, it is more desolating than when a good movie ends or you finish a marvellous book. We should say 'going', not 'coming'. Anyhow, the man should say, 'Oh God, I'm going, I'm going.'

Boris, like a philosopher, thinks how he thinks.

Stewart, the dancer, says, 'You can't dance and think.'

'Think' and 'thank' grow in the same semantic field.

Whenever Hamlet stops thinking, he kills someone.

The pain you inflict merely trying to get through the day. Pavese talks about it. I'm sure he had a woman in mind. If Pavese does his work, he kills her. If Pavese reads a newspaper . . . If Pavese makes an appointment to see an old friend . . . Finally he killed himself.

Sartre says to kill another is to kill yourself. He spent hours in coffee shops and bars. He liked to carry money in his pocket, lots of money. He compared it to his glasses and cigarette lighter. So many companions. He'd never have killed himself. You must first know what it is to be alone.

I hear sirens at night—fire, burglary, murder, rape. Despite its idea of itself, Berkeley is America.

She says, 'Why don't you let me do it? Are you afraid you might like it?'

'You don't love me.'

'I can't live without you.'

'It's not the same thing.'

An evening at Evelyn's:

'Did you know X is Jewish?'

'You were in Morocco last year? Me, too!'

'You're an Aquarius—that's incredible.'

'You went to Malibu High? I don't believe what I'm hearing.'

'I'm allergic to shellfish.'

She and her friends live mainly for boring surprises. Why did I enjoy myself?

After her experience in Italy with Italian men, she became a lesbian.

There are many forms of murder, but the victim's reality is always the same. No explanation undoes the significance of what happened, including the explanation that he brought it on himself or somehow participated in it. They used to define rape as being 'Against her will and without her consent'. Today some argue even with her consent.

Tracy doesn't like oral sex because she'd once been forced to do it at gunpoint in the parking-lot outside Brennan's where the guy picked her up. I wish she hadn't told me. I hear the freight trains. I see people coming out of the bar, laughing, drunk, calling to one another as they go to their cars. Tracy crouches in misery and fear, the gun at her head. How good it would feel, if I had the gun at his head, to pull the trigger. Of course I wouldn't. It would be politically incorrect, as is anything really personal.

Jimmy visits me with his feelings. He says he fell in love with a married woman. She had a little affair with Jimmy, then stopped and told her husband. He keeps her home now, won't let her use the phone. Jimmy is depressed. He can't not talk about it even with his girl-friends. He's afraid he's going to lose all of them, but he's really in pain. He has to talk about it. If the woman stays with her husband, it means she is deeply controlled by guilt. Jimmy says, if she can't walk away from her husband, nothing in her life will ever make her happy. Everything will be qualified by guilt. She will always find reasons not to feel happy. Happiness, he says, can be a reason for guilt, a reason to feel unhappy. He says last night he fucked one of his girl-friends who is very sympathetic to his depressed state. He was surprised that he could take great pleasure in fucking her. It was like being in love. He was surprised, pleased, grateful to her. I said maybe he needs a psychotherapist. He said, 'Man, don't you hear what I'm saying? I'm in touch with my feelings. I never had an education, you know what I mean?'

David tells me about the woman he is living with. He calls her Stop-and-Go because she's up very early and moving, or else she collapses into hours of marijuana. It's like everything with her. There are no degrees. There is truth or lies, good or bad, stop or go. She criticizes David constantly. He wants to break up with her, but can't figure out how. He needs an occasion. Wants her to do it. He plans to provoke her into doing it by hanging a certain picture she doesn't like in a place she finds disturbing. He says the picture will upset her. She'll see that he is saying the house is his. She'll go. Then he begins to brood. He says, after a fight, she always becomes affectionate. He finds her adorable then. He says she dislikes his father for his Jewish traits and also dislikes David for his. Then he says she doesn't even know what they are.

LEVEL 42
The Definitive Biography
MICHAEL COWTON
Published 12th October £12.95
Published to celebrate their 10th anniversary.

I'M STILL HERE
EARTHA KITT
Published 14th September £12.95
Scintillating, honest, revealing autobiography.

DUSTY
LUCY O'BRIEN
Published 28th September £12.95
First biography, written with the co-operation of Dusty Springfield.

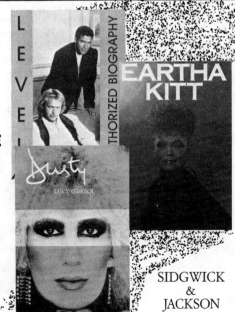

SIDGWICK & JACKSON

THE QUINCUNX

The Inheritance of John Huffam

Charles Palliser

'. . . a striking publishing debut.' *The Observer*

This ambitious and hugely readable novel has already been compared with authors as diverse as Charles Dickens and Umberto Eco.

It tells the story of one man's search for identity. A search which drives him through a maze of assignations, clues and conspiracies to the impoverished streets of late Regency London. As family secrets are uncovered John's search turns into an epic quest for wealth and vengeance.

£14.95 hbk   800 pages   September 1989

CANONGATE PUBLISHING

GRANTA

Jay McInerney

Jimmy

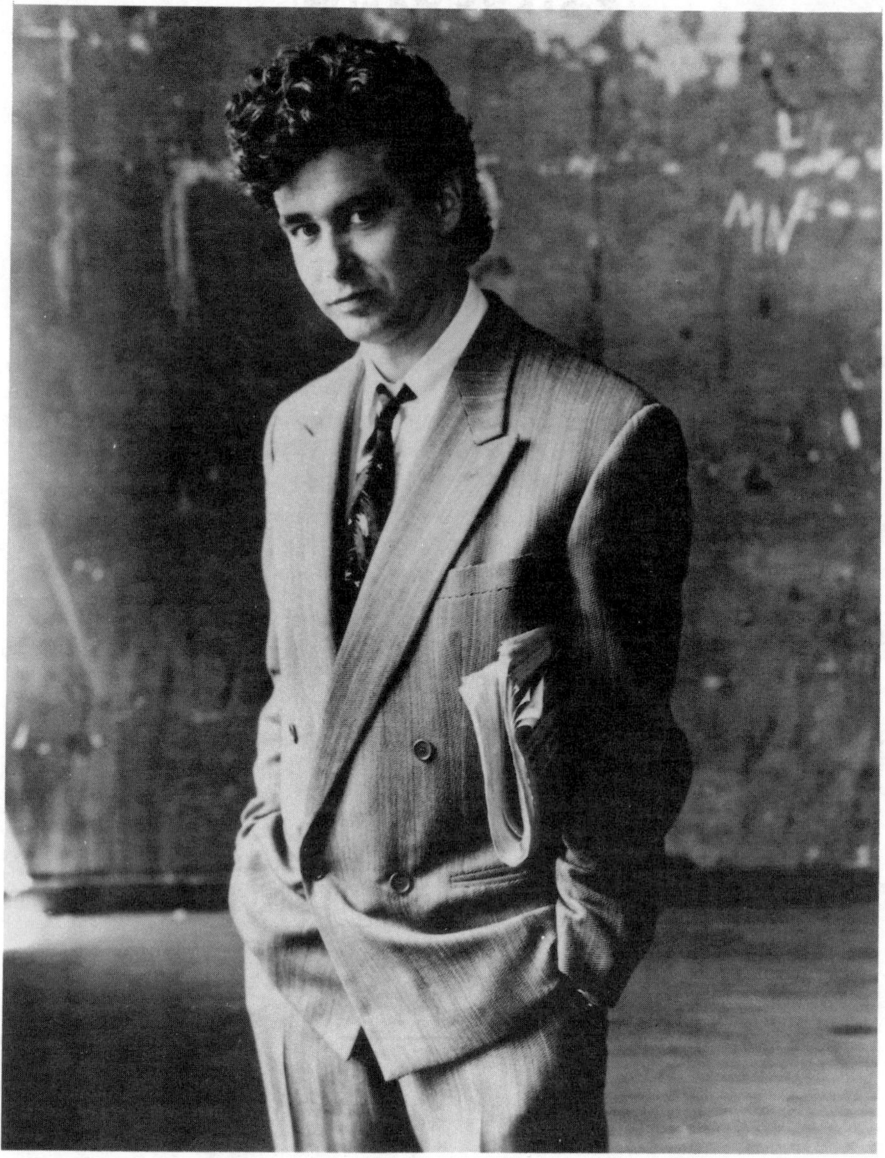

The route from the train station was lined with white colonial houses, in the style indigenous to suburban Connecticut. Jared had grown up in a place like this. Laura always wanted to move up here, he thought. She'd finally got her wish.

The cab driver kept looking up into the rear-view mirror. Jared had come to expect that look, but it still pleased him.

'Hey—excuse me, but aren't you that actor?'

Jared nodded, his manner that of the shy and weary martyr to an admiring public.

'Yeah, I thought that was you. Don't tell me. What's your name?'

Jared told him.

'Right, that's it. All *right*. You were in that movie.'

'Been in a few,' Jared noted.

'How about that!' he exploded. 'This is great! I woke up this morning, I had a feeling something was gonna happen today. You know what I mean?'

'I had the same feeling,' Jared said.

'So, you checking into the Valley?' the driver asked.

Jared pondered the question for a moment. Then he said, 'Me? I'm not checking in. I'm visiting someone.'

'Hey, no offence. Lots of famous people come through here. In fact, this place is kind of famous for that. Of course, they come here so they can, you know, have their privacy. No publicity.'

'I'm just visiting.'

'OK, OK. I'm just saying, you'd be amazed at the famous people here.' He ran through a list of celebrities. 'Listen, do you think you could sign your autograph for my kid?'

The cab pulled up a long, tree-lined driveway to a cluster of buildings which might have been the estate of a prosperous gentleman farmer, or the campus of a small New England prep school—a Georgian mansion surrounded by white clapboard satellites on many acres of blue-green lawn. It was hard to believe this was just an hour from New York.

God, I'm wiped out, Jared thought, looking out over the mower-striped lawn, which reminded him that he had to try and call Jimmy back in New York. He hoped Jimmy was in town.

For Jared, there was a Jimmy in every town. In London he was

Photo: Annie Liebowitz

called Clyde and in Los Angeles his name would be Trent and in Dallas it was Jud. They were the people who could get you what you wanted if you needed to be discreet; they were always glad to see you and could tell you where the parties were. Jimmy would have the *new* unlisted numbers of friends you hadn't talked to in months, the people who belonged to the desirable fraternity.

Signing his autograph on the back of a taxi receipt, Jared heard his name called out. Laura was waving from the door of one of the houses. A large black woman stood beside her. Jared strode across the lawn, Laura and her companion coming out to meet him. She threw her arms around him and squeezed as hard as she was able. She was thinner than ever, he thought. He saw that the creases across her forehead had deepened. It had been four months since their last meeting.

She was still beautiful, even in her distress, a tall and elegant if lately too angular brunette. Her eyes fastened on to his, tugging at him, asking for answers to all her questions.

'This is Doreen,' Laura said, drawing back to indicate the woman beside her. 'Doreen's my special.'

'Your what?'

'That's what they call them. She's like my nurse. She stays with me.'

Jared shook hands with Doreen.

'All the time?'

'Not all the time. She's with me from seven to three. Then from three to eleven another special comes on. Then there's the night shift.'

'Someone sleeps with you?'

'She sits in the chair beside the bed.'

'This is all so you won't . . .' Jared halted.

Laura nodded, made a slicing motion across one of her wrists.

'You're still . . .'

She shrugged. 'They think I'm still suicidal. I don't know.' She looked at the ground.

'Sorry,' she said. 'I know it's expensive here.' Though her voice had been animated for a moment with the excitement of seeing him, she spoke almost tonelessly now, in the barely audible monotone he had come to know over the phone during the past month.

'Forget it,' Jared said, happy to appear noble. He felt he should lighten the mood. 'You know, Doreen,' he continued, in a John Wayne drawl, 'ever since I was a kid I've always thought I was kind of special. But it must be nice to know you're *a* special.'

It was pretty weak, but she responded with a large smile.

'You want to see my room?' Laura asked.

'Sure,' he said. 'Great.'

The three of them walked across the lawn, Doreen at Laura's elbow. Before they reached the house, Jared abruptly pulled from his jacket a small, gift-wrapped package and presented it to Laura. 'I'm afraid I'll have to open that,' Doreen said, confiscating it. Then she smiled a little sheepishly and returned the box to Laura. 'Sorry, it's just the rules. But I suppose just this once . . .'

'Thanks,' Jared said, looking her in the eyes.

'I sure liked that movie of yours.'

Laura stopped walking, bringing them to an awkward halt. 'Take it,' she said, holding out the box to Doreen. 'Go ahead, take it. Rules are rules.' Doreen dutifully reclaimed the package.

'This is my tiny part of the world,' Laura said to Jared. 'It's not much. It's the funny farm. But it's all I've got right now. You have the rest of America. So please try not to charm everyone here. Please don't win everyone's heart right off the goddamned bat, OK?'

Laura had filled her room with photographs, including several of Jared, and stuffed animals. It was a corner room with two windows overlooking the woods and a stream. A hospital bed with metal railings provided the institutional note.

Sitting on the bed beside Jared, Laura opened her gift, a bottle of Chanel perfume.

'It's Number Nineteen,' she said.

'Your fave.'

'I hate Number Nineteen. It's Number Five I like.'

'Are you sure?'

'Of course I'm sure. I can't stand Number Nineteen.' She threw the bottle across the room. Doreen retrieved it from the carpet.

'I'd swear it was Nineteen you liked,' Jared said.

'One of your other girls,' Laura said.

Jared had given her Chanel for years; he couldn't believe he would forget the number. But there had been several Chanel purchases since he'd last seen Laura.

'Wait a minute, for Christ's sake. Remember a week ago when I told you I was flying to London for an audition and we discussed how I should call Tony and Brenda and Ian and Carol and I gave you my schedule. Remember? And then I called you two nights later and you said, What are you doing in London? After we'd talked about it for half an hour?'

'OK, I'm sorry, my short-term memory's not so hot. The doctors said it was a symptom.'

'So maybe you forgot what kind of perfume you like.'

'Jared, you're unbelievable. You could probably talk your way off death row and steal the warden's wife on your way out.'

'It wouldn't work on you,' Jared said.

'Unfortunately it would,' she said. 'Sometimes I still want you back.'

'Don't be crazy.'

'This is Wharton House,' Laura said, stopping in front of the largest house in the complex. 'The substance abuse facility.'

Jared nodded.

'You'd really like some of the people in there. Writers, actors, professors. There's this one guy I really want you to meet—James. Amazing guy. He's made a fortune on Wall Street.'

'Why would I want to meet a goddamned stockbroker?' Jared asked, tugging at Laura's arm in the hope of accelerating their tour of the grounds.

'I don't know—I just thought of you the minute I met him. He's got these eyes, like yours. Anyway, he's in for cocaine, used to deal to all the stars and still ran his own investment firm. He's had an incredible life, lived with beautiful women, Miss Brazil, and that model that's on the cover of *Cosmo* all the time.'

'You hate people like that.'

'And eventually he went to Colombia and bought quantity himself, so he gets busted and put in jail in Cartagena and within two weeks he has mercenaries blow up the jail and smuggle him out of the country. I think you'd like him.'

'If I told you about this guy you'd say he sounded like an ass-hole.'

'He's charming,' she said, 'and besides, I admire his courage for coming here. That takes even more guts than breaking out of jail.'

'Sounds like love.'

'No,' she said. 'Except insofar as he reminds me of you.'

'That's one of the things I've missed about you,' Jared said. 'The way you can use "insofar as" in conversation. Or "ergo." We don't get that out in L.A. much. Anyway, I've never been in jail in Cartagena.'

'Time for lunch,' said Doreen.

On the way to the big house they were joined by some of Laura's housemates. A sixty-year-old professor of Philosophy at Yale, Eric was not visibly depressed or sedated.

'Has Laura told you she's our best basket-maker?' Eric asked.

'I'm an arts and crafts hero,' Laura said. 'I'm thinking of opening up a crafts boutique after I get out of here. Call it the Basket Case.'

After they'd moved through the cafeteria-style food line Laura introduced Jared around the table.

'Just arrive today?' asked Tony, a young man with a scimitar-shaped scar across his throat.

Jared nodded, his mouth full of tough, cold veal.

'Where are you, Wharton House?'

'I'm just visiting,' Jared said.

'He's my husband,' Laura explained.

'Oh, I see.'

Jared wondered if the man was perhaps making a point of pretending not to know who he was.

The talk around the table was of food and drugs. Connie, a middle-aged blonde, cheerfully informed the group that she had tried to kill herself with valium—thirty of the five milligrams—the yellows. But she had thrown up, and anyway, everyone told her it wouldn't have done the trick.

'Thirty blues might have done it, but not the yellows,' Jared suggested, eliciting general agreement. 'Thirty seconals would do nicely. But for real sledge-hammer results, dilaudids are your best bet. Thirty of those would kill you and your two best friends plus all their household pets.' He got a laugh. 'Three thousand in the water supply would take out a medium-sized city.' Then in Ronald Reagan's voice: 'The hell with nuclear weapons, you commies, we got the neuron bomb.'

Everyone laughed except Laura, and Jared avoided looking at her.

Jackson, a Unitarian minister, explained how he had closed his garage door, climbed into his Oldsmobile, inserted a tape in the cassette-player and turned on the ignition. When the tape turned over for the second play and he found himself conscious as well as nauseous, he gave up and went back into the house.

'It was a new car, a 1988,' he said. 'The new emission-control systems are so good you can't even kill yourself anymore.'

'What was the tape?' Laura asked.

'Pachelbel,' answered Jackson.

'Good choice,' Laura said.

Laura had always approached the world with an eye to irrelevant details, thought Jared. It was like her to be interested in the musical accompaniment to the suicide attempt. He was surprised she didn't ask what colour the car was. But after two years of separation he was still unable to divorce her. She exerted a pull. Which reminded him.

'Gotta make a quick call,' he told the company. 'Keep the veal patties cold for me, guys.'

Jared was directed to a phone booth and called Jimmy in New York. He listened through ten rings, then another ten. It was strange, he thought, that Jimmy didn't have a machine. But maybe he had moved—Jared hadn't seen or talked to him in six months. He saw Jimmy all the time when he lived in New York.

'What was the phone call?' Laura asked, as they were walking back to her house with Doreen.

This, he remembered, was one of the things he hated about Laura—suspicion.

He said he was calling his agent.

'Just try and give me these few hours, will you please, Jared. You'll be back in the world soon.'

'I'm here. It was only a phone call.'

She took his hand as they walked. 'I'm sorry James wasn't at lunch,' she said. 'I really wanted you guys to meet.'

'Who?'

'James. The ex-drug dealer guy.'

'Next time.'

'Will you come back soon?'

'Real soon. I gotta be in L.A. tomorrow night but maybe I can come back next week.' She turned away, and he added: 'I have an audition.'

They sat on lawn chairs in front of the house. 'Your hand is trembling,' Jared said.

'It's the lithium,' she responded. 'Your hand's trembling too.'

'Jet lag,' he said, waving his hand.

'Is it really? Or booze and blow?'

'I'm working too hard to abuse myself,' he said.

'You always fidget when you tell a lie.'

'You're the one with the problems,' he said. 'I'm functioning quite well out there, thanks.'

Doreen sat behind them, staring off into the trees. After a familiar, sullen silence he asked about her therapy and eventually, as the sun dropped in the sky and the suburban lawn came to resemble other suburban lawns, they talked about family and friends. Laura asked about one of his friends he'd forgotten entirely.

Jared was distracted, already thinking ahead to the city.

Laura asked him something about when he would visit her again, but Jared's attention was drawn to a man who was approaching them across the lawn. He was tall, with a young man's figure and an old man's motion. He greeted Laura warmly.

Jared stood up. He felt dizzy.

'Jimmy?'

'This is James,' Laura said. 'I've been telling you about him.' She looked hard at Jared. 'You know each other?'

'It's possible,' the man said wearily. 'You could fill a book with what I've seen and don't remember.'

It wasn't Jimmy. Suddenly Jared wondered if he could pick Jimmy out of a police line-up. Jared was breathing too fast.

'Are you all right?' Laura asked.

'I'm fine,' said Jared. 'But I've got to go now.' He pressed Laura's hand. 'I'll call you tonight.'

As he walked past the beautiful houses and down the sweeping driveway, Jared told himself that he would preserve an impression of this man, Laura's friend, so that if they ran into each other many years from now on the streets of a foreign capital, he would be able to say, 'Yes, I remember you.'

WEIDENFELD & DENT
New this Autumn

STORM OVER FOUR
A personal account of Channel Four's stormy first years
Jeremy Isaacs
£14.95 Weidenfeld

JUSTICE NOT VENGEANCE
The long-awaited story of his life-long fight to bring Nazi war criminals to justice
Simon Wiesenthal
£16.95 Weidenfeld

THE BRIDESHEAD GENERATION
Evelyn Waugh and his friends
Humphrey Carpenter
£17.95 Weidenfeld

ROBERT GRAVES:
The years with Laura 1926-40
A sequel to *Robert Graves: The Assault Heroic 1895-1928*
Richard Perceval Graves
January 1990 £19.95 Weidenfeld

TO NOTO
London to Sicily in a Ford
Duncan Fallowell
£13.95 Dent

GRANTA

JOHN UPDIKE
THE LENS FACTORY

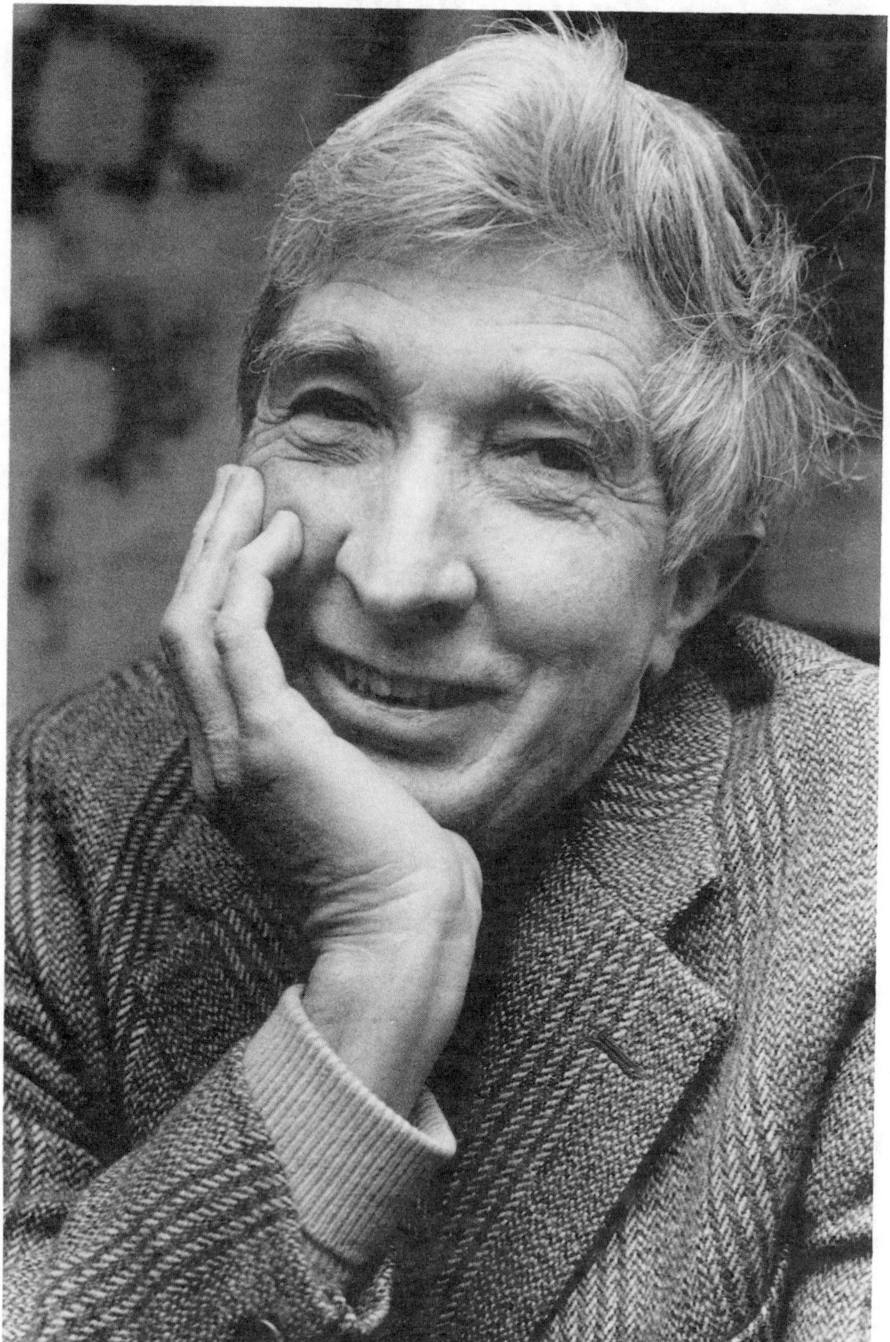

David Kern, in these three days, had felt himself become pulplike—shapeless, lost and swallowed somehow, and helplessly open to impression, as though he had no eyelids. Everything seemed abysmal or towering: the brick factory wall, springing right off the sidewalk, as he entered in the morning; its many wide-stretched floors, flickeringly lit, stuffed with the noise and tremor of the machines; even the space of dirt and weeds behind the factory, where the other workers ate and played quoits for the half-hour allowed, felt huge to him, and he huge and swollen with momentary relief, as he crossed the diagonal line of shadow into the sunshine where Eddie already sat on a bench made of a plank and cement blocks. He felt swollen with relief at these minutes of intermittence from tending his machine, but not completely, the inflation was imperfect, there was a pocket of limp dread within him that he must carry back to the job and even into sleep and out the other side. It made him feel lopsided, this sense of being plucked at by nervousness and dread.

'How goes it?' Eddie asked him, as David presumed to sit beside him. Eddie had been here several years, since dropping out of high school, and David supposed the older boy must have many friends at the factory. But the bench was empty, and Eddie's friendly interest in him seemed unfeigned. When David reported to work three days ago—a Monday, and this was only Wednesday—Eddie had been assigned by the foreman of that part of the floor to show him how to mount the caps of sun-glass lenses on the pivots, how to stack them on the cart when their twenty minutes in 'the mud'—the liquid abrasive in its long trough—was over, and how to keep track of their numbers on the wire overhead. The work seemed simple, yet it was a terrible race to keep the machine from getting ahead; and then the inspector came around once every morning and afternoon with his chalk, marking dozens of lenses ruined, through some error of David's. The timing had to be exact—too little, they weren't polished, and too much, they were 'cooked'.

'I guess better,' David said, unfolding his paper bag and taking out the sandwich of Lebanon baloney his mother had made. She had tucked in an apple, which made him want to cry, somehow—its *naïveté*, its embarrassing redness, its country smell. The apple

Photo: Allan Titmuss

seemed something he could never get back to, from this abyss he felt he was in, here behind the factory.

Eddie was smoking a Pall Mall and eating a ten-cent TastyKake, with caramel icing and lemon-yellow insides. He was faintly yellow himself, as if the flickering factory lights had given him their own kind of tan. Smoke and crumbs were mixed in his mouth as he talked. 'The thing is to get the rhythm,' he said. 'The machine has a rhythm and after two weeks here it'll be second nature to you, you won't even have to think what you're doing.'

The Lebanon baloney had flecks of spice in it, and these flecks burned in David's stomach, touching the sensitive soreness that was always there now. 'What do you think about instead?' he asked the other boy.

Eddie laughed, disclosing small uneven teeth. 'Dirty stuff,' he said cheerfully.

David felt invited to ask what dirty stuff but instead rolled his face away, staring upward into the weed tree, trees of heaven his mother called them, that had grown surprisingly tall here, in the shadow of the factory. Its leaves were parallel, like rapid crayon strokes, dark down closer but golden up high where the sunshine struck. David's mind squeezed up there as if out of a deep well, high into the tree where he would never have climbed when he was a child, being shy of heights and this kind of tree being too brittle, too jungle-quick in its growth, to climb anyway. The tree's presence here—a touch of nature, like the apple—seemed a blessing, though. While he was staring off into space, feeling his childhood hovering just above him, like something from which he had just this minute fallen, Eddie's hand had come to rest on his thigh. It was a light, yellow hand, a bit undernourished like everything else about Eddie. Even his mind, David imagined, was curled in there like a shrivelled walnut, blackened.

'You're a good kid, Davey,' Eddie told him. 'You'll get the hang of things.'

Nobody called David 'Davey'. Irritable in his sensitive sad state, he twitched his thigh away from Eddie's consoling hand. He longed to express the horror of life that this job had opened to him, but didn't know quite how without insulting Eddie, whose life it was. 'Yeah, but then so what?' he did say. 'How do you stand it, day after day, all summer and all? I mean, you don't have any summer.'

The other boy blinked, little pink lids and colourless short lashes. 'You get as much summer as most people,' he argued. 'There's weekends, and lots of light hours after four.'

Something in the concentrated set of Eddie's thin lips, and the watery way his dull blue eyes stayed on David's face, suggested that the boy was determined not to be insulted. David despaired of expressing the completeness of the eclipse the factory's massive bulk had imposed on him. He took in breath but there was nothing to say, it was all too big. His comforter saw this and continued for him, 'This ain't going to be your life, Davey. You'll do it for the summer and be going back to school. It ain't going to be my life, neither. I'm thinking of joining one of the services, the Navy probably. All kinds of action in the Navy. This city is dead. There's nothing in this city for anybody who wants to be a little different.'

It was strange, the way the older boy's voice so softly and insistently went on, embroidering, saying this and that, as if searching for something.

'I don't want to be different, exactly,' David told him. 'I just want room to breathe. When I'm standing there beside the trough of sloshing mud and everything timed to the split-second, with all the noise, it's like I can't breathe.'

Eddie lit another cigarette without taking his eyes off of David's face. 'You'll breathe,' the other boy strangely said. 'You'll take lots of breaths before you're done, Davey boy.' Puffs of smoke tumbled from his mouth, and he shook his red pack of Pall Malls so one cigarette jumped up for David to take. Eddie had this nimbleness, this sly slippery trickiness, clinging to him like a yellowish film. 'You know what "blow" means?' he asked.

David pretended not to have heard him. He quickly put his paper bag down and stood up and said, 'Think we can get a game of quoits in?' His heart was racing. The entire vacant space here, behind the factory, cut diagonally in two by shadow, felt gathered and focused behind him with a certain pressure, as if the small of his back were blocking the tip of a funnel.

There were two pairs of quoit stakes, and both were taken right now, by quartets of men in grey pants and khaki shirts or bib overalls stained and smeared but nowhere near as dirty as David's own dungarees, filthy with dried mud especially around the fly, where he leaned against the trough to change the caps. The clinks of the quoits mixed with eager laughter and yells from the men, and he saw there would not be any free stakes for ten more minutes at least. He sat down again on the bench, in the neutral presence of the weed tree, and looked in his paper bag to see if his mother had put in a cookie.

Eddie hadn't moved, just sat and smoked. There was a lemon-coloured crumb on the edge of his lip, where he couldn't feel it. He asked, 'What do you want to be in life, Davey?'

'Oh . . .' He couldn't think, through his pounding blood. 'Something stupid. Something where you sit at a desk in New York.'

'New York's a great town. Not like this town, dead. There's a helluva lot to do in New York.'

'How often've you been there?'

It was a tactless cruel question, it turned out. Eddie's pale colour reddened a little. 'Once or twice. Penn Station, I couldn't believe it, so beautiful. And the Empire State Building right up the street. And Times Square, all that action. You ever been up that way, Davey?'

He didn't want to hurt Eddie's feelings by saying how often. 'A couple times. My parents took me. I have an aunt lives there.'

'Yeah, and what kind of places they take you to? Yankee Stadium? Polo Grounds? Madison Square Garden?'

'I don't know, museums,' David said.

'That a fact? Museums? Your folks must be pretty stuck-up to go to museums.'

'No, it's just where my aunt likes to take us. They're free or pretty near, I guess.'

Eddie jumped on it. 'The best things in life are free,' he said. 'Isn't that what they say? The best things in life are free.' There was a suggestion of a tune, the second time, that made his voice croak and reach high pathetically. 'You know what they mean by that, don't you?'

'No. By what?'

'By the best things in life are free.' Eddie's hand reappeared on the knee of David's filthy-orange dungarees, but with a smoking cigarette between two of the fingers, which made it less dangerous. 'You know what they mean by the best things, don't you?'

'Air,' David offered. 'Sunshine.' There was now a pressure making his ears ring, and he kept his head bowed, his eyes on his crusty fly, to relieve the pressure.

Eddie laughed in his ear, lightly, with the friendly dried-up delicacy he had, like that of a little old man. 'Naa. They don't mean that. You got to let me show you sometime what they mean.'

'OK,' David said, to say something, to get out of this. He wasn't ready for this. The green door back into the factory, at the low corner of the building as it loomed in its numbing largeness, beyond a blue scattering of cinders to keep the weeds down, seemed reachable only through a tunnel in the transparent air, a tunnel back to the safety of the metal stairs, the flickering bright lights of his floor, his long dirty patient machine waiting for him to bring it to life once more.

'Davey.'

The voice came from far away, from outside the imagined tunnel.

'Was you every blowed?'

This time when David stood, he accidentally knocked the cigarette from Eddie's hand. 'Sorry,' he said. The other boy looked up only mildly surprised and hurt. David discarded Eddie's pale face like a wrapper, forever. The quoits were being clinked into a stack by four men who were finished with their game, but to David's great relief there wasn't time to play, and he wouldn't be here tomorrow.

GRANTA

10 YEARS

GRANTA 1: *NEW AMERICAN WRITING* — William Gass, Joyce Carol Oates, Leonard Michaels, Stanley Elkin and Susan Sontag.

GRANTA 2: George Steiner, *THE PORTAGE TO SAN CRISTOBAL OF A. H.* — Plus: Walter Abish and Robert Coover.

GRANTA 3: *THE END OF THE ENGLISH NOVEL* — Salman Rushdie, Angela Carter, Alan Sillitoe and Emma Tennant.

GRANTA 4: *BEYOND THE CRISIS* — Guy Davenport, David Caute, Per Gedin, Martin Amis and Raymond Carver.

GRANTA 5: *THE MODERN COMMON WIND* — Don Bloch, Jorge Ibarguengoitia, Russell Hoban, Susan Sontag and Jonathan Schell.

GRANTA 6: *A LITERATURE FOR POLITICS* — Peter Weiss, Milan Kundera, Nadine Gordimer, Gregor von Rezzori and Boaz Evron.

GRANTA 7: *BEST OF YOUNG BRITISH NOVELISTS* — Martin Amis, William Boyd, Maggie Gee, Kazuo Ishiguro, Adam Mars-Jones, Salman Rushdie, Julian Barnes and Graham Swift.

GRANTA 8: *DIRTY REALISM* — Richard Ford, Jayne Anne Phillips, Raymond Carver, Tobias Wolff and Bobbie Anne Mason.

GRANTA 9: John Berger, *BORIS* — Plus: Russell Hoban, Mario Vargas Llosa, Patrick Marnham and Gabriel García Márquez.

GRANTA 10: *TRAVEL WRITING* — Jonathan Raban, James Fenton, Colin Thubron, Martha Gellhorn, Bruce Chatwin, Norman Lewis, Saul Bellow, Jan Morris and Paul Theroux.

GRANTA 11: Milan Kundera, *GREETINGS FROM PRAGUE* — Plus: Ian McEwan, Salman Rushdie and Mario Vargas Llosa.

GRANTA 12: Stanley Booth, *THE TRUE ADVENTURES OF THE ROLLING STONES* — Plus: Günter Grass, Breyten Breytenbach, Raymond Carver and *The Guardian* and Sarah Tisdall.

GRANTA 13: *AFTER THE REVOLUTION* — Milan Kundera, Josef Škvorecký, Orville Schell, Martin Amis, and Anita Brookner.

GRANTA 14: *AUTOBIOGRAPHY* — Don McCullin, Beryl Bainbridge, Eddie Limonov, Todd McEwen and Jaroslav Seifert.

All back issues are now in print and available at £5.00 each (including postage) from: Granta, Dept BIS28, 44a Hobson Street, Cambridge, CBl lNL

GRANTA

Peregrine Hodson
Thursday Night in Tokyo

There was a traditional love-song playing. The man collecting tickets recognized Tony and flashed a big smile, embellished with gold teeth. The room was smaller than I'd expected, with a low ceiling. A dim spotlight glowed over a tiny, semi-circular platform which projected several feet into the first few rows of the audience. Only the front half of the room had any seating; the rest was filled with men standing in groups or alone, smoking cigarettes and talking excitedly. Those sitting closer to the stage were gazing at the curtains behind the spotlights. Some of the men in the front row were leaning against the stage itself.

I followed Tony as we made our way to the far side of the room. There were no seats available, so we positioned ourselves against a wall. It was crowded; more than a hundred men pressed into the cramped space. Tokyo rents are expensive. I made a quick calculation: half a million yen for a couple of hours' basement space, three or four times an evening. It was a respectable return per square foot—probably a lot better than the return on the floor space at the office where I worked.

In front of us two men, who looked like construction workers, were talking in Korean. The music disappeared into the babble of the audience's conversation. The spotlight grew brighter, there was a movement behind the curtain, and a dwarf with a painted clown's face stepped into the circle of light.

'Welcome, honoured customers and friends.' He bowed deeply. 'It is my pleasure to introduce the evening's entertainment. I hope the girls who dance for you will be to your satisfaction. We have Mariko-chan with us again: we confidently expect she will meet with the approval of those of our regular customers who, over the past few weeks, have asked repeatedly to see her. Unfortunately, Mariko-chan was on holiday with her family in Osaka . . .'

'Why didn't you tell me?' someone called out from the audience. 'I was there last Wednesday!'

'But we are delighted she is with us again. Then we have something a little exotic, America girl Suzi-chan.'

The dwarf began to move to one side of the stage. His walk was clumsy and disjointed. His shoes were uneven; one was much larger than the other and looked like a surgical boot. He stopped in mid-

Photo: Barry Lewis

stride and, for an instant or two, the spotlight lost him and wandered uncertainly over the empty corner of the stage.

A Japanese song, a slow, old-fashioned and slightly wistful melody, pre-prosperity music from the fifties, emerged from the amplifier by our heads and the dwarf hobbled out of the spotlight. The bright circle of light remained. There was a movement in the folds of the curtains, then another, and with a jerk the sparkling material began to open before our eyes.

A woman in a brightly coloured kimono stepped into the light and advanced towards the front of the stage. The light penetrated the white cosmetic that covered her face, revealing the set of her eyes and the contours of her cheeks, and the shape of her mouth under the vermilion of her painted lips. The music receded.

'Dear patrons,' the dwarf's voice intoned from the shadows, 'it is my honour and pleasure to present our very special friend Mariko-chan!'

There was polite applause, and someone in the audience called out, 'Good to see you again, Mariko-chan.' The woman in the brightly coloured kimono bowed. The brilliance of the spotlight was unrelenting: as it showed a woman in an imitation of geisha finery, it uncovered a face of worn beauty and corruption.

She began to dance. The central spotlight dimmed and other lights, set out to the front of the stage, glowed into life, no brighter than paper lanterns; a play of light and shadow in the art of illusion. I listened to the words of the song: a woman singing about a man who was far away. It was a simple story but finely calculated to pluck the heart-strings of every man in the room. Thirty or forty years ago the song would have had a particular poignancy, when the last of the men were coming home from the war and the bombed towns and cities were drawing in the labour force from the surrounding countryside to help in the rebuilding of Japan.

A girl in a mountain village was waiting for her lover to return from far away. Mariko-chan's movements were cramped with grief and desire. It was midsummer in the village. Mariko-chan was on her knees. The upper part of her kimono was loose and as she lowered her fan from her face the silk material slipped from her shoulder. With a gesture of self-conscious modesty, Mariko-chan rearranged her kimono, casually revealing as much as she concealed. Her breasts were small, but even in the softened light it was possible to see they were not the breasts of a young woman.

The girl in the village was lying awake at night, thinking of her lover; Mariko-chan was half kneeling, half reclining in the middle of the platform, supporting her body with her right hand while her left hand moved under the folds of her kimono. One of the Koreans whispered to his companion and they both laughed. The girl was describing the gentleness of her lover. Mariko-chan moved her legs slightly, deepening the shadow that was just visible under the border of her kimono, in between the whiteness of her knees.

Some of the men in the front row were leaning against the stage, their faces no more than a few inches from Mariko-chan's feet, which were neatly enclosed in white cotton *tabi* socks. Mariko-chan did not register their presence; instead she turned her head, very slowly, to the left and to the right. Then, like a time-lapse film of a flower in the final stages of disintegration, she unravelled the last length of the obi at her waist and lay back. For a while she remained still, almost rigid.

The rhythm of the music changed. I couldn't tell whether it was another song altogether, or a different part of the same one.

A young man in the front row was gazing reverently between Mariko-chan's knees towards a dark triangle which was surely more shadow than revelation. Beside him a man took off his spectacles, wiped the lenses with his tie, adjusted them carefully to the bridge of his nose and leaned forwards again. Mariko-chan rolled on to her back, reached her right hand under her right thigh and gradually raised it until her knee touched her shoulder. The left half of her body hardly moved.

A man wearing a baseball hat in the second row leaned his head to one shoulder, like a prospective customer in a used car showroom looking into the engine of a car. With a quick, showgirl flick of her legs, Mariko-chan offered her body to another section of the audience, and the man in the baseball hat cocked his head to the other shoulder.

Once the audience had had an opportunity to examine her, Mariko-chan adopted a more formal kneeling position. She was still wearing her kimono loose and untied. She reached into the left-hand sleeve and drew out a dark silk wallet from which she took half a dozen or so rubber contraceptives.

The dwarf, who was still standing in the semi-darkness at the edge of the stage, made another announcement. 'Unfortunately, due to the recent legislation, it is no longer possible for Mariko-chan to get to know her playfellows as closely as she would like. However, any member of the audience who is—how shall I say?—curious to know Mariko-chan better is most welcome.'

Mariko-chan made a formal bow, with the delicacy of a maid welcoming a customer to a traditional tea-house. The man in the baseball hat lifted his index finger. Mariko-chan flashed an arch expression and said something which I could not hear. Several other men close to the stage raised their index fingers.

Mariko-chan stood up and bowed to each customer before she rolled a contraceptive on to his upraised finger. After distributing three or four contraceptives, Mariko-chan knelt down at the edge of the stage, spread her knees and leaned back on one hand, while with the other she guided the rubber-clad index finger of a man in the front row into her body. For a minute or so she balanced on the balls of her feet, supporting herself with her hands, and watched the uncertain probing of the man between her legs. 'Careful, sir!' she gripped the man's wrist. There was an edge to her voice. 'I'm not a man, you know.' She drew his hand away from her body, and took a tissue from the silk wallet which she folded round the contraceptive before removing it. Then she bowed, smiled and moved on.

It was the turn of the man in the baseball hat. Once again, Mariko-chan guided his finger into her. The man bent forward, and Mariko-chan adjusted herself to accommodate his curiosity. The man did not look at her face, but Mariko-chan kept a constant eye on him and just when it seemed as if his attentions might become too familiar, she drew back her hips with a swift, agile motion, leaving him bending forwards, staring at the tip of his finger wrapped in a glistening condom.

As the laughter subsided, another customer, emboldened by the party atmosphere, raised his hand, this time with two fingers inserted into the contraceptive. '*Damme!*' Mariko-chan pretended to smack the man's wrist. 'Certainly not. You've only paid for one finger, not two. Don't be unfair.'

For the last inspection Mariko-chan chose a young man in the front row who was watching her with an almost religious intensity. He was less confident than the others, and as she rolled the condom on to his finger he bowed so deeply and so frequently that she had difficulty putting it on. Once again she opened her thighs and drew his hand towards her. As she did so, the young man looked at her face and smiled apologetically. She nodded encouragement. He frowned with concentration, like a small boy. After a minute or so, Mariko-chan nodded again and the young man, bowing, withdrew his finger. Mariko-chan whisked another tissue from the wallet and deftly plucked the contraceptive from his finger. Then she bowed to him, smiled and rearranged her kimono.

Mariko-chan slipped her arms through the sleeves of her kimono and began to collect the discarded tissues into a neat pile, but some of the men in the front row were calling for more. 'Come on, Mariko-chan, give us another look. Let's see what you've got, don't be shy.'

Mariko-chan gave a mock frown. 'Girls are supposed to be modest. Haven't you seen enough?'

'No! Not yet! Show us everything!'

Mariko-chan pouted, walked to the front of the stage and lifted her leg over a particularly noisy customer, completely covering his head and shoulders with the hem of her kimono. There was a momentary pause, a muffled cry of '*Wah! Kusai!*'— and a burst of delighted laughter from the audience at the man's exclamation of disgust. I noticed a smile widening on Mariko-chan's face as she stepped back and drew her kimono about her.

'There now,' the dwarf interrupted, 'I hope Mariko-chan has satisfied your curiosity, sir. But if you're still wondering, don't worry, there are two acts to come!' Mariko-chan placed the last of the tissues in a small square of red silk, which she tied loosely together to make a *furoshiki*. Then with the bundle in one hand and her obi in the other she gave a hurried, informal bow. 'Thank you, Mariko-chan,' said the dwarf, his voice rising, 'everyone please, a round of applause for Mariko-chan!' The spotlight returned and settled on her unsteadily. A few in the audience were still clapping as Mariko-chan began to make another bow and the curtains closed unceremoniously in front of her.

GRANTA

10 YEARS

GRANTA 15: James Fenton, *THE FALL OF SAIGON* — Plus: Nadine Gordimer, George Steiner and Günter Grass.

GRANTA 16: *SCIENCE* — Oliver Sacks, Italo Calvino, Stephen Jay Gould, Primo Levi, William Broad and Germaine Greer.

GRANTA 17: Graham Greene, *WHILE WAITING FOR A WAR* — Plus: Patrick Marnham, Milan Kundera and John Updike.

GRANTA 18: James Fenton, *THE SNAP REVOLUTION* — Plus: Primo Levi, John Berger, Seamus Deane and David Hare.

GRANTA 19: *MORE DIRT* — Richard Ford, Ellen Gilchrist, Louise Erdrich, Jayne Anne Phillips and Richard Rayner.

GRANTA 20: *IN TROUBLE AGAIN* — Redmond O'Hanlon, Salman Rushdie, Martha Gellhorn, Amitav Ghosh, Timothy Garton Ash and Orville Schell.

GRANTA 21: *THE STORY-TELLER* — Bruce Chatwin, Ryszard Kapuściński, John Berger, Isabel Allende and Raymond Carver.

GRANTA 22: Hanif Kureishi, *WITH YOUR TONGUE DOWN MY THROAT* — Plus: Nadine Gordimer, Doris Lessing, Carlos Fuentes, James Fenton and 'An Escape from Kampala'.

GRANTA 23: *HOME* — Bill Bryson, Anton Shammas, Jeanette Winterson, Nicholas Shakespeare and T. Coraghessan Boyle.

GRANTA 24: INSIDE INTELLIGENCE — Anthony Cavendish; Plus: Philip Roth, Peter Carey, Tobias Wolff and E.L. Doctorow.

GRANTA 25: Martin Amis, *THE MURDEREE* — Plus: Ian Jack in Gibraltar, Angela Carter, Raymond Carver and Don DeLillo.

GRANTA 26: *TRAVEL* — Ryszard Kapuściński, Jeremy Harding, John Ryle, Colin Thubron, Bruce Chatwin, Norman Lewis, Ian Buruma and Hans Magnus Enzensberger.

GRANTA 27: *DEATH* — John Gregory Dunne, Edmund White, Mary McCarthy, Adam Mars-Jones, Louise Erdrich, Michael Ignatieff and John Treherne.

All back issues are now in print and available at £5.00 each (including postage) from: Granta, Dept BIS28, 44a Hobson Street, Cambridge, CBl lNL

GRANTA

Mario Vargas Llosa Mouth

I lost my left ear from a bite. I think it was in a fight with another human. Through the thin slit that remains I can hear the sounds of the world. I can see too, but with difficulty and things look somewhat twisted. That bluish protruberance, the one to the left of my mouth, is an eye although I realize that at a glance it doesn't look like one. The fact that it's there, taking in shapes and colours, is a prodigy of medical science. I should have been condemned to perpetual darkness owing to the fumes from the great fire—I can't remember if it was a bomb or an attack—survivors were left blind and bald. I was lucky to lose only one eye; the other was saved by the ophthamologists after sixteen operations. It is without an eyelid and it waters continuously, but it enables me to watch television, and, above all, to detect the appearance of the enemy.

The glass cube I am in is my house. I can see through its walls but nobody can see me from outside: convenient and secure. Such terrible traps can be set these days. My walls are bullet-proof, germ-proof, radiation-proof and sound-proof. They are permanently scented with the smell of armpits and musk which to me—only to me, I know—gives great delight.

My sense of smell is very developed. It is through my nose that I experience my greatest pleasure and my greatest pain. Should I call it a nose, this gigantic, membraneous organ that registers so many smells, even the most subtle? I refer to the greyish lump with the white scabs: it starts at the level of my mouth and drops, getting bigger, down to my neck, which is fat like a bull's. It's fat not because of a goitre or an Adam's apple but because it has been enlarged by acromegaly. It's my nose. I know it's neither beautiful nor useful, and its excessive sensitivity becomes an indescribable torment when there's a rat rotting in the neighbourhood or when foul-smelling material is passing down the drains that run through my house. Even so I venerate it. I sometimes think that my nose is the seat of my soul.

I don't have any arms or legs: only four stumps. They have healed properly and they are tough, therefore, I can get around on the ground and quite easily—even with speed if necessary. My enemies have never managed to catch up with me. I cannot remember how I lost my hands and feet.

My sexual organs are intact. I can make love provided that the

Photo: Neil Libbert

young boy or the female acting as my *partenaire* lets me position myself so that my boils don't chafe: if they burst, stinking pus gushes out, and I suffer excruciating pain. I like fornicating, and, in a certain sense, I would say I'm a voluptuary. It doesn't always work out and there are instances of humiliating premature ejaculation. But at other times I have prolonged and repeated orgasms that make me feel as if I am airborne and radiant like the archangel Gabriel. The disgust I inspire in my lovers changes into attraction and even into delirium, once they've overcome—almost always with the help of drink or drugs—their intitial reluctance and have agreed to entwine themselves with me on a bed. Women come to love me; the boys become addicted to my ugliness. In the depths of the soul, beauty is always fascinated by the beast, as so many fables and mythologies remind us, and it's rare not to find a streak of the perverse in the heart of a handsome young boy. None of them ever regrets being my lover. They learn that everything is and can be erogenous; that, when linked with love, the lowest functions of the body, including those of the bowels, are spiritualized and ennobled. They dance the dance of the gerunds—belching, urinating, defecating—and this descent into slime—to which we are all tempted but rarely succumb—remains with them afterwards like a melancholy memory.

My greatest pride is my mouth. It is not wide open because I am howling in desperation. I keep it that way to show off my sharp, white teeth. Aren't they enviable? There are only two or three teeth missing. The others are strong and carnivorous. They can grind stones. But they prefer to devour the nipples and buttocks of calves, to sink themselves into the breasts and thighs of hens and capons or the gullets of little birds. Eating meat is a prerogative of the gods.

I am not an unfortunate wretch and I do not wish to be pitied. I am as I am and that's enough. Knowing that others are worse off is of course a great consolation. It is possible that God exists, but is that fact, at this stage in history, with all that has happened, of any importance? Perhaps the world could be better. Perhaps. But what's the point of asking? I have survived and, appearances to the contrary, I form part of the human race.

Look at me closely, my love. Recognize me, recognize yourself.

Translated from the Spanish by Diana Thorold.

GRANTA

Colin Thubron

Mistakes

In twenty or thirty years' time, perhaps, a monument will be raised to the martyrs of Tiananmen Square, innocent harbingers of a more liberal age. They will be reclassified, of course—transfigured from 'counter-revolutionaries' to 'people's heroes'—and the political talk will be of their persecutors' 'mistakes', as if the death of thousands were a slip of the hand.

The jargon is blinding. These sacrificial dead were not political clichés, but impatient and susceptible students and workers, some heroically brave, others naïve—youths trapped in the home of their atrophied grandparents. No label really fits them. No label really fits anyone.

Some twenty years ago, in Beijing, a Chinese student bludgeoned to death an elderly porter during the Cultural Revolution because the old man was reading a Westernized novel. Decades later this murderer stood before me in a zoo-park with his daughter's hand in his. He was quiet-spoken, neatly dressed. He and his gang had come upon the porter one evening in the street, he said. 'It was a mistake. People said hit him, so you hit him . . .'

I stared at him. Looking back on those years, he seemed not to comprehend the person he had been. Now that society was regulated again and authority telling him how to think and feel, he saw only a nightmare self, a sleep-walker from whom all constraints had been lifted. He did not understand. Nor did I. He said bleakly: 'We thought the porter was a revisionist.'

'Counter-revolutionary', 'hooligan'—the vocabulary was meaningless to me. Such labels, I remember thinking, were a distortion of the old Confucian hunt for definition. Classify something (or somebody) correctly and you would know how to act.

But to classify is to dehumanize. It is easier to execute a 'revisionist' than to batter an old man to death.

The murderer's feet shuffled unhappily. His daughter was feeding sweets to the animals. 'We were just the tools of the others,' he said.

Classification is the business of authority. And in China the vesting of conscience in authority is timeless, cleansed by the sanctity of the emperor, the Son of Heaven. And what is an individual in the face of the imperial or Marxist Son of Heaven?

'In China we don't ask *Why?* like you do in the West,' a woman

Photo: Barry Lewis

once told me. '*Why?* is not a Chinese question.'

In Tiananmen Square the army did not need the amphetamine injections reported in the British press. Its soldiers mostly came from a peasant world of harsh expedience. They simply did what they were ordered to do. The army, in the end, is the arch-collective: a paradigm (some say) of China itself.

During the Cultural Revolution a Chinese church warden, educated in mission school, witnessed Red Guards smash his church's organ and its violin. The old man wondered aloud to me why no monitor inside these people had called a halt. Where was individual conscience? 'How could anyone break a violin?'

Because, I suppose, it had been re-labelled: a Westernized, counter-revolutionary violin. But I did not understand any better than he. Culturally, we were both Christian. When he talked about God, he meant the personalized Christ, not communism's heaven-on-earth or the remote deity of Confucius.

Only after months of travelling in China's bitter interior did an unhappy realization dawn. It was not a conscious revelation: simply a thinning away of what I had once accepted. In the poverty of the hinterland, it was not cruelty which needed explanation, but compassion.

Once I disembarked at a rural train station in an area forbidden to me. The peasants were dressed, literally, in rags. They stared at me in disbelief. In this town, a poor year would bring starvation, and most people lived with malnutrition. Girls might be sold off as child-brides or drowned at birth. In such places the anomaly, the miracle, is pity.

Outside another railway station, in the nation's heart, I watched a parade of convicted criminals being humiliated before a silent crowd. There were fifteen of them—fourteen men and a woman—but the crowd numbered thousands. The punishment of the few would educate the many, the individual would serve the mass. That is what the individual is there for. The prisoners' arms were bound behind them with coarse rope. On either side, a policeman thrust down their heads. These images of ritual degradation are now familiar from television: the offering up of individual pain for mass example.

The woman almost fainted in the arms of her guards. The man beside me said: 'She's just a thief.'

She was sentenced to twenty years hard labour.

'There are too many of us,' a Chinese once told me. 'We say, "The people is a mountain, the people is a sea."'

And only after I returned to England did this brief and ugly understanding wane: the mercantile reckoning that when something is over-produced and in poor condition its value declines. Then, back in England, cruelty again demanded explanation, as if it were peculiar to China or Stalin and not somewhere in the neighbouring street, or in myself.

In Tiananmen Square, eye-witnesses report that a soldier shot six kneeling and supplicating girl students, one by one.

The Chinese sage Mencius said that compassion is common to all men.

Notes on Contributors

John Simpson is Foreign Affairs Editor for the BBC. **Salman Rushdie**'s writing was first published in *Granta* in 1980, the third issue of the magazine, 'The End of the English Novel.' **Ian Jack** won the British Press Reporter of the Year Award for his coverage of the Gibraltar killings (*Granta* 25). He is working on a book about India and Britain for Jonathan Cape. **Ryszard Kapuściński**'s next book, *The Soccer War*, will be published by Granta Books in January. **Nadine Gordimer**'s most recent novel is *Something Out There*. She lives in Johannesburg. For the last six years **David Goldblatt** has been photographing buildings in South Africa. He lives in Johannesburg. **Richard Rayner**, a former *Granta* editor, is the author of *Los Angeles without a Map*. **George Steiner**'s 'Desert Island Discs' was published in *Granta* 15. *Real Presences* was published last spring. **Walter Abish**'s *How German is it?*—published as a work-in-progress in *Granta* 2—won the American PEN/Faulkner Award. **Guy Davenport**'s 'Fifty-seven Views of Fujiyama' appeared in *Granta* 4. **William Boyd** is completing a novel that will be published next spring. His 'Alpes Maritimes' appeared in *Granta* 15, 'Autobiography'. *Sexing the Cherry*, **Jeanette Winterson**'s fourth novel, is published in September. **Russell Hoban** has recently completed the libretto for a chamber opera entitled *Some Episodes in the History of Miranda and Caliban*. **Markéta Luskačová**'s photographs are included in the Barbican exhibition, 'Through the Looking Glass', which ends in October. **Eugene Richards**'s emergency-ward photographs appeared in *Granta* 27, 'Death'. **Joy Williams** teaches at the University of Arizona. 'Escapes', the title story of the collection that Atlantic Monthly Press publishes in January, was first published in *Granta* 19, 'More Dirt'. **Leonard Michaels** is Professor of English at the University of California at Berkeley. Part of **Jay McInerney**'s *Bright Lights, Big City* was published in *Granta* as a work-in-progress. **John Updike** lives in Massachusetts. His memoir *Self-Consciousness* was published last spring. **Peregrine Hodson** is writing a book about Japan where he lived for five years, working as an investment banker and studying swordsmanship. **Mario Vargas Llosa** is a presidential candidate in the forthcoming Peruvian elections. **Colin Thubron**'s book on China, *Behind the Wall*, won the Thomas Cook award for travel writing.

NOTE: Information about ordering back issues of *Granta* is on pages 270 and 278. All back issues are now in print. A *Granta* Index is available for £4.99 from Granta, 44a Hobson Street, Cambridge CB1 1NL.